RESEARCH METHODS IN
SPORT

University Centre at
Blackburn
College

Telephone: 01254 292165

Please return this book on or before the last date shown

RESEARCH METHODS IN
SPORT

MARK F. SMITH

2ND EDITION

SAGE | Learning Matters

Learning Matters
An imprint of SAGE Publications Ltd
1 Oliver's Yard
55 City Road
London EC1Y 1SP

SAGE Publications Inc.
2455 Teller Road
Thousand Oaks, California 91320

SAGE Publications India Pvt Ltd
B 1/I 1 Mohan Cooperative Industrial Area
Mathura Road
New Delhi 110 044

SAGE Publications Asia-Pacific Pte Ltd
3 Church Street
#10-04 Samsung Hub
Singapore 049483

Editor: Jai Seaman
Assistant Editor: Alysha Owen
Production Controller: Chris Marke
Project Management: Swales and Willis Ltd,
Exeter, Devon
Marketing Manager: Alison Borg
Cover Design: Wendy Scott
Typeset by: C&M Digitals (P) Ltd, Chennai, India
Printed in the UK

First published 2010
Reprinted 2012 (twice), 2014, and 2015

Library of Congress Control Number: 2017943256

British Library Cataloguing in Publication Data

A catalogue record for this book is available from the British Library

ISBN: 978-1-5264-2350-4
ISBN: 978-1-5264-2351-1 (pbk)

At SAGE we take sustainability seriously. Most of our products are printed in the UK using FSC papers and boards. When we print overseas we ensure sustainable papers are used as measured by the PREPS grading system. We undertake an annual audit to monitor our sustainability.

Contents

About the author

Dr Mark F. Smith is both the Director of Education within the College of Social Science and Principal Lecturer within the School of Sport and Exercise Science at the University of Lincoln. Having obtained his PhD in Sport Science at the University of Kent, he began teaching in Higher Education in 2001 and is a Senior Fellow of the Higher Education Academy. As an active researcher and practitioner, he is responsible for providing strategic leadership in the enhancement of student learning opportunities as well as supporting teaching innovation.

Pedagogical guide

The second edition of *Research Methods in Sport* is packed full of key features that offer you essential tools and tips to undertaking research within real-world sport. Throughout the book you will be exposed to:

- *key points* that help summarise themes and topics within each chapter. Bite-sized pockets of information, definitions and guidance ensure you capture the important elements in a quick and accessible way;

- *reflection points* that make you stop and pause for a moment. Taking time to reflect on the content and applying it to your own research allows you to use the material covered within the book directly within your own research project;

- *learning activities* that extend beyond the pages and enable you to draw upon wider research and your own experiences to develop further an understanding of research methods in practice;

- *research focuses* that allow you to delve into published studies linked to each research approach. The full references provided can act as a vital starting point to explore research within a wide range of areas;

- *student case studies* that reflect real student research projects. An exploration of their approaches and findings enables you to identify the type and nature of student research, hopefully generating ideas for your own studies;

- *further readings* that allow you to explore further beyond the chapters. With up-to-date references they can begin to extend your understanding of research methods.

1

The context of sport research

By linking your understanding of sport in practice to sport-related research examples, this chapter is designed to help you:

- explain the nature of sport research and describe the characteristics of a scientific approach;
- outline the building blocks of research and establish which approach would link to particular sport-related research questions;
- identify the importance of a research strategy to the overall research framework.

Introduction

Research is the gateway to new discoveries – discoveries such as new technology to improve the speed of a cyclist around a track, novel training programmes to enhance swim start performance or creative initiatives that evaluate children's enjoyment in sport. Research provides us all with the chance to learn more and acquire new knowledge to help ourselves and others.

This opening chapter of *Research Methods in Sport* will provide a brief, but important, starting point to help examine the very nature of research within a sporting context. It will introduce the concept of research and provide an important review of the underpinning philosophy to scientific inquiry. By examining a range of sport-related research questions the chapter will uncover the role that the philosophy of science plays in shaping the framework in which we view our sporting research and how such understanding may lead us to the selection of our research strategy.

By further reviewing this research framework, a clear link will be made between the very nature of our sporting problems – that is, the questions we wish to answer – and the ways in which we can begin to answer them. Highlighting the need to select the right design and method in the quest to solve our problems, this chapter is considered essential reading before you embark on other chapters.

It is not the intention of this chapter to outline the research process in detail or explain how to write your research project. Rather this opening chapter will provide you with an all-important starting point that will help you to understand research methods and their value and then, if you progress to undertaking your own research project, assist you in selecting the most appropriate research strategy. To outline a discourse on the debate about the structure of science or the nature of knowledge is outside the scope of this book; however, where appropriate, you will be made aware of how such debates may impact on your own research activities. It is acknowledged that in simplifying models and examples used to outline approaches to scientific inquiry, terminology may not be aligned with those from a natural and social science background and, therefore, for more in-depth and thorough accounts the reader is directed to the text by Grix (2002).

The nature of sport research

Sport, as an area of study, is unique. In how many other disciplines would you cover as many different subjects as you do in sport? Ranging from the natural sciences such as physiology, chemistry, mathematics and physics to the social sciences such as social psychology, philosophy, pedagogy and coaching, politics, economics and sociology, the study of sport requires a tremendous appreciation of so many different things. By adding to this ergonomics, technology, research methods and all the practical elements involved in studying sport, a wonderfully diverse picture can begin to be painted that highlights the interconnected nature of sport.

With the continual growth of sport from both a participatory and academic study point of view, there is little doubt that, to be able to appreciate the complex web of connections researching in sport offers, a plethora of information that informs understanding and builds knowledge must be sought. Whether examining the way the human body responds to physical work in order to develop new strategies to improve athletic performance, evaluating the role sport plays in bringing communities together or describing how sport has given many people hope and belief following times of personal suffering, it can be liberating for all involved.

This thirst for understanding about sport and its impact on our lives has led to a significant advancement in our knowledge over the last 100 years. From both a natural and social science perspective, the pursuit of knowledge through sport-related research has led to our current level of understanding acted out in the lectures we attend, practical sessions we perform in, journals and textbooks we read and internet pages we scan through.

Reflection point 1.1

Scientific discoveries allied to sport began in early civilisations through the practices and writings of ancient Greek physicians, such as Herodicus (fifth century BC). With early discoveries relating to physical training and nutrition influencing inquiry through research practice, the emergence of educated scholars keen to develop new knowledge in the area of sport flourished over the course of the next two millennia.

The pursuit of sporting excellence has led to the emergence of important developments through research to assist athletes and exercisers in their own sporting activities. If we journey back over the last decade or so alone, we can begin to identify, for example, how the appliance of science to sport has enhanced athletes' capabilities to perform. Take the following, for example:

- training methods, such as hypoxic training, to enhance physiological capacity;

- pre-event acclimatisation strategies to ensure the athlete's capability to perform in a range of environment conditions;

- techniques such as ice-bath submersion to aid post-event recovery;

- differentiated coaching practice that maximises athlete development and optimises performance;

- technological developments in bicycle design and swimsuit composition to reduce drag and allow the athlete to travel faster;

- psychological skills training packages (i.e. visualisation and imagery) that can be implemented to prepare athletes for competition;

- training aids, such as heart rate monitors, ergometry systems and performance profiles, to support advanced preparation for competition;

- nutritional strategies that offer the exerciser pre-, during and post-exercise fuel supplements to support training and event performance.

Whatever the area of interest, the process of looking back through time and identifying key research milestones presents an opportunity to celebrate the significant impact research has played in the advancement of sport. By doing this it is clear to see that changes in the way sport has been perceived in society and its value to all those that participate have occurred not through chance or luck, but through systematic investigation to discover new knowledge and push the boundaries of what we know.

The importance of research to the area of sport, therefore, is fundamental not just to the advancement of our discipline, but also to our own personal and professional development. Sport provides us with a sense of freedom and release, not bound by the day-to-day hectic lives we now live. We lose ourselves in sport, embracing the rollercoaster of emotions that sport always delivers us. What draws us back to sport time and time again is the need for that fix. Being able to develop and change, improve and compete, offers us the motive to want to continue. Undertaking research as a student should provide us with the same exhilaration, leading us on the same emotional journey, allowing us to develop, change and improve knowledge for the greater good.

Why is research in sport of value?

We are constantly bombarded with research all the time, whether through books, newspapers, television programmes, advertising boards or university lecturers. The discovery of many new things can occur through research and their findings can help make sense of the world. We have all at some point undertaken research, trying to solve problems by working through them in a logical step-by-step fashion. It is often the case, however, that we do not actually recognise the process of finding a solution as research and often take this approach for granted. It is only when we stand back and examine our approach or it is located in a different context that we begin to identify what research involves and the value it can bring.

It is not uncommon to use the term 'research' very loosely. Those new to research often perceive that all tasks involve some kind of research, and to some extent this may be true. Many view the mere *gathering* of facts or information as research. Simply reading a few book chapters, a couple of web pages and a vaguely relevant journal article may lead some to draw the conclusion that research has taken place and something new was discovered. An alternative conclusion drawn by many is that the practical pursuit of collecting data constitutes research. Asking people about the success of a newly opened sports centre, recording heart rate response during a hockey match or observing a coaching session and noting down negative behaviour may be considered research. This process of collecting data, carried out in a systematic and accurate way, can certainly be viewed as an important part of research, although it does not in itself constitute research.

Research allows for the undertaking of information-finding activities: establishing facts and reaching new conclusions. Undertaken in a controlled, critical manner, research allows questions to be asked and then attempts are made to solve them in a systematic scientific way. Research is about thinking strategically and logically, not haphazardly or irrationally. Research requires planning and organisation, constant reflection and assessment. Creativity and innovation will lead to novel and original approaches, whilst the ability to draw accurate conclusions will show an awareness and attention to detail.

 **Key point 1.1**

Research has been defined as:

diligent and systematic inquiry or investigation into a subject in order to discover facts or principles.

(Blaxter et al., 2010, p5)

the formal, systematic application of scholarship, disciplined inquiry, and most often the scientific method to the study of problems.

(Fraenkal et al., 2011, p7)

systematic inquiry that is characterised by sets of principles, guidelines for procedures and which is subject to evaluation in terms of criteria such as validity, reliability and representativeness.

(Hitchcock and Hughes, 2003, p5)

When the term research is used, then, the assumption is made that a systematic process has been undertaken that allows for the development and testing of a question in order to arrive at a new conclusion. Reflecting on experience alone and arriving at some conclusions may not therefore be sufficient to be called research. Instead, research aims to combine experience and reason to create a method of rational inquiry. It is when experience is combined with logical reasoning that the foundation of scientific inquiry is born.

 Key point 1.2

Characteristics of research include:

- a controlled, critical approach conducted in a systematic way;
- information-finding that establishes facts and generates new conclusions that are open to public scrutiny and criticism;
- the combination of experience and logical reasoning to generate new facts and principles.

The scientific inquiry of knowledge

Science in its most basic definition is a way of investigating nature and discovering reliable knowledge about it. The scientific approach to discovering new knowledge is distinct from other ways in that it seeks to generate reliable knowledge that is justifiably true. According to advocates of the scientific method of inquiry, other methods of acquiring knowledge, such as personal experience, intuition or authority, may provide what is believed to be true but it may not be justified or reliable. In our own sporting pursuits, we acquire new knowledge through our own sensory experiences, agreement with our team mates, from experts' opinion on television sport shows or by logically reasoning things through.

Although each will provide us with a sense of new knowledge, can we really be confident that the knowledge acquired in this way is complete and accurate? How do we know that the football pundits are right, or our own sensory experiences are complete? Can our own logical reasoning be based on false premises from the start and therefore produce unreliable knowledge? Relying on knowledge that is untrue or unjustified may lead to inappropriate actions. It is therefore thought that, by undertaking the scientific method of inquiry, a higher degree of certainty can be gained about knowledge that can be deemed both reliable and justifiably true.

The building blocks of sport research

Our perception of reality, that is, how we view the world, influences how knowledge is characterised and ultimately legitimised through our research endeavours. The view a researcher holds will have an impact on how research is planned, conducted and evaluated. Therefore, for junior researchers wishing to undertake a research project in sport, awareness of the predominant models provides a foundation for effective practice.

Take the two examples of a sports physiotherapist and a mountain explorer. Some researchers operate in the same way sports physiotherapists would. Therapists are in possession of detailed knowledge of the anatomy and physiology of the body, knowing where to find a problem if one occurs. They know what to look for based on facts, where to look for it and what to expect once they find the problem. Like sports physiotherapists, these researchers would work in a linear, step-by-step logical fashion.

In contrast, some researchers more closely resemble mountain explorers, trying to map uncharted territory with little or no prior knowledge of the landscape. They have the skills to explore but might not know what they were looking for or what to expect if they found something. Whereas the main aim of the sports physiotherapist would be based on discovery, analysis and prediction, the explorer's main task would be based on exploration, discovery and description.

 **Key point 1.3**

The steps in scientific research are as follows (adapted from Cohen et al., 2017):

  Step 1: Identify a problem, have a hunch, or develop a question.

  Step 2: Formulate a tentative solution or hypothesis associated with the question or problem.

  Step 3: Conduct practical or theoretical testing of solutions or hypotheses.

  Step 4: Eliminate or adjust unsuccessful solutions to evolve or support theory.

These two approaches begin to explain the varying positions researchers take when attempting to discover new knowledge. Different views of social reality in the pursuit of true and reliable knowledge have been discussed and debated for millennia. These philosophical positions sit right at the very centre of any research that is undertaken, because how reality is viewed dictates the approach taken to answer the research question. It is these philosophical approaches to research that should form the very building blocks of effective research practice.

Paradigms of research

Philosophy, quite simply, is an individual's or group's belief about something. In the case of research, it concerns the belief of what knowledge is and how it is acquired. How reality is viewed by researchers shapes their approach to research – in other words, the rules by which they work and the strategies that fit within the rules and beliefs they subscribe to. Because of the diverse nature of sport and the wide range of natural and social science disciplines encountered when sport is studied, it is no surprise that researchers will view reality differently and, depending on the philosophical position they hold, the pursuit of new knowledge through research will take different forms. In other words, the fundamental building blocks of their research will be different.

One way of understanding each philosophical position is to view them as different sets of sunglasses. Each set has different-coloured lenses and therefore, when you wear them, you see the same thing, just in a different way. In essence, when research is conducted, the researcher's philosophical position (that is, the type of sunglasses worn) will govern the way the researcher views reality. Awareness of the different views enables the researcher to:

- establish a personal philosophical approach to research;

- understand the philosophical approach of others and recognise the types of arguments being made;

- assess each position's influence on a research question and understand its wider social impact.

The philosophy of how social reality is viewed is known as *ontology*. This is the starting point of all research. For the natural scientist, and those undertaking research in the areas of sport physiology, biomechanics or exercise biochemistry, for example, social reality would be viewed from an *objectivist* perspective. Objectivists believe that all social phenomena exist independently of any social influence. Researchers from this ontological position look at 'social facts' for reliable and justifiable truth.

For social scientists, researching in areas relating to social psychology, sociology of sport or historical aspects of exercise, for example, reality would be viewed from a *constructivist* position. They would assert that social phenomena are not independent of social influence; rather they are in a constant state of revision and are socially constructed. Such researchers search for 'social meaning', being aware that reality is in a state of flux and revision.

It is clear to see, therefore, that each of these two competing ontological standpoints will impact differently on how researchers conduct their research. Such world view, or ontology, has an impact on how we go about discovering knowledge. The act of formulating a research question and then undertaking a process to discover an answer is very tightly bound within an ontological view of reality. Although the student researcher may not be aware, how research is undertaken is governed by a set of fundamental principles about how reality is viewed. For effective student researchers, linking the question with a philosophical position will enable more constructive debates to emerge, recognising others' points of view, and defending their own position. Table 1.1 provides clear definitions that show the differences between these key terms.

Table 1.1   The branch of science can be summarised into three key hierarchical principles: ontological, epistemological and methodological

Branch of science	Natural science (e.g. physiology and biomechanics)	Social science (e.g. sociology)
Ontological view	**Objectivism**	**Constructivism**
Belief	That all social phenomena (behaviour that influences or is influenced by others) and their meanings have an existence that is independent of social actors (the way in which others' actions and reactions modify behaviour) (Grix, 2002; Bryman, 2015)	That all social phenomena and their meanings are continually being accomplished by social actors, implying the social phenomena are in a constant state of revision and flux (Grix, 2002; Bryman, 2015)
Epistemological view	**Positivism**	**Interpretivism**
Belief	Holds the position that everything is ultimately measurable and applies the methods of the natural sciences to study social reality	Selecting strategies that respect the differences between people and the objects of the natural sciences and therefore requires a grasp of the subjective meaning of social action
Methodological view	**Quantitative**	**Qualitative**
Belief	A deductive position that emphasises quantification in collection and analysis of data through the process of precise numerical measurement	An inductive position that emphasises an understanding of human behaviour through methods such as interviews, observations, focus groups, surveys and/or case studies

If ontology is concerned with how we view the world, *epistemology* is a further branch of philosophy that is concerned with the theory of knowledge. Put simply, epistemology focuses on the knowledge-gathering process and the underpinning assumptions that govern methods of inquiry. As this book concerns the use of research design and methods in sport research, and recognising that our ontological and epistemological views will have an impact on our research approach, we can start to see how knowing the building blocks of research can impact on our design and associated research methods.

 Learning activity 1.1

If students wanted to conduct a research project based around the topic of coaching behaviour and player performance they could:

1. collect some numerical data on coach-to-player ratio and identify whether a low ratio was associated with performance success (i.e. number of games won);

2. plot the coach's movement patterns in metres during training games and try to identify whether they influence player movement patterns;

3. observe and record particular phrases the coach uses when talking to the players to assess the impact on players' attitudes towards training and performance;

4. assess the coach's non-verbal behaviour and link observations to how the players' behaviour alters throughout the session.

Examples 1 and 2 focus on establishing 'social facts', that is, quantification through measurement of numerical data. Examples 3 and 4 concern 'social meanings', and focus on obtaining subjectivity of response. Based on these approaches, students will have to decide on their philosophical standpoint – *objectivism* or *constructivism* – and then the corresponding epistemology (i.e. *positivism* or *interpretivism*) and then the methodological position (i.e. *quantitative* or *qualitative*). It is important to remember as a researcher that one is no better than the other; rather, each standpoint will lead to a more suitable way of acquiring the knowledge, selecting the approach and drawing more meaningful conclusions.

Methodological approaches to sport research

The two broad methodological approaches to research are *quantitative* and *qualitative*. Such approaches are typically used according to whether numerical data are collected or not. Although this is certainly one aspect, there are many other differences that distinguish quantitative from qualitative research approaches. In quantitative research, hypotheses and research questions tend to be based on theories that the researcher seeks to test. Take, for example, the theory that if we are over-aroused as a performer we under-perform in sport. In this approach the question is derived from the theory and the objective is to test it. In qualitative research, the researcher may generate a theory following observations or examine an existing theory from different perspectives (i.e. using different-coloured lenses). This being the case, each methodology will have its own unique strengths and weaknesses that will impact on the researcher's ability to answer the research question (Tables 1.2 and 1.3).

Table 1.2 Strengths and weaknesses of the quantitative research approach (extracts from Johnson and Onwuegbuzie, 2004)

Strengths
• Testing and validating already constructed theories about how (and to a lesser degree, why) phenomena occur
• Testing hypotheses that are constructed before the data are collected. Can generalise research findings when the data are based on random samples of sufficient size
• Can generalise a research finding when it has been replicated on many different populations and groups
• Useful for obtaining data that allow quantitative predictions to be made
• The researcher may construct a situation that eliminates the confounding influence of many variables, allowing one to assess more credibly *cause-and-effect* relationships (i.e. experiment)

(Continued)

Table 1.2   (Continued)

• Data collection using quantitative data collection methods is relatively quick (e.g. self-completion questionnaire)
• Provides precise, quantitative, numerical data
• Data analysis is relatively less time consuming (using statistical software)
• The research results are relatively independent of the researcher (e.g. statistical significance)
• It may have higher credibility with many people
• It is useful for studying large numbers of people

Weaknesses
• The researcher's categories that are used may not reflect others' understandings
• The researcher's theories that are used may not reflect others' understandings
• The researcher may miss out on phenomena occurring because of the focus on theory or hypothesis *testing* rather than on theory or hypothesis *generation* (called the *confirmation bias*)
• Knowledge produced may be too abstract and general for direct application to specific local situations, contexts and individuals

Table 1.3   Strengths and weaknesses of the qualitative research approach (extracts from Johnson and Onwuegbuzie, 2004)

Strengths
• The data are based on the participants' own categories of meaning
• It is useful for studying a limited number of cases in depth
• It is useful for describing complex phenomena
• Provides individual case information
• Can conduct cross-case comparisons and analysis
• Provides understanding and description of people's personal experiences of phenomena (i.e. the insider's viewpoint)
• Can describe, in rich detail, phenomena as they are situated and embedded in local contexts
• The researcher identifies contextual and setting factors as they relate to the phenomenon of interest
• The researcher can study dynamic processes (i.e. documenting sequential patterns and change)
• Can determine how participants interpret constructs (e.g. self-esteem, IQ)

- Data are usually collected in naturalistic settings in qualitative research

- Qualitative approaches are responsive to local situations, conditions and stakeholders' needs

- Qualitative researchers are responsive to changes that occur during the conduct of a study (especially during extended fieldwork) and may shift the focus of their studies as a result

- Qualitative data in the words and categories of participants lend themselves to exploring how and why phenomena occur

- One can use an important case to demonstrate vividly a phenomenon to the readers of a report

Weaknesses

- Knowledge produced may not generalise to other people or other settings (i.e. findings may be unique to the relatively few people included in the research study)

- It is difficult to make quantitative predictions

- It is more difficult to test hypotheses and theories

- It may have lower credibility with some people

- It generally takes more time to collect the data when compared to quantitative research

- Data analysis is often time consuming

- The results are more easily influenced by the researcher's personal biases and idiosyncrasies

Theory building versus theory testing

It is through the combination of experience and logical reasoning played out in the natural world that the researcher is provided with an opportunity to conduct research in a diligent and systematic manner. Based on the nature of the question, there are three forms of reasoning: *inductive*, *deductive* or a combination of the two.

 Reflection point 1.2

According to Hitchcock and Hughes (2003), a theory concerns the development of a systematic construction of knowledge employing the use of concepts, systems, models, structures, beliefs and ideas in order to make statements about particular actions, events or activities. Built upon one or more hypotheses, and upon evidence, a theory contains logical reasoning and connections between the hypothesis and evidence. Created after observation and testing, theories are designed to explain or predict phenomena. Research attempts to develop (inductive) or test/confirm (deductive) a theory in the quest for new knowledge.

(Continued)

(Continued)

From an inductive perspective, a study by Cunningham and associates (2012) examined the decision-making and decision-communication within elite rugby league officials. Four core themes emerged from semi-structured interviews with three elite rugby union referees with international experience focusing on successful/acceptable decision-making, contextual judgements, strategies deployed to filter information, and communication skills needed to perform effectively: (1) corporate theatre; (2) pre-game preparation and post-game analysis; (3) refereeing philosophy and approach; and (4) within-game psychological skills. Through careful analysis of previous evidence, combined with new emergent findings, the authors generated new hypotheses that can be tested under a number of conditions (deductive perspective). Practical application of their findings pointed towards the evaluation of communication skill training, conflict management, resolution management, role play decision-making training, the use of journals or diaries to aid reflection and self-awareness to facilitate decision-making and communication strategies whilst officiating.

Consider a researcher who over the last 5 years has attended Wimbledon fortnight. In every match she observed she noticed that both players always ate bananas at some point during the match. She had observed over 100 matches and, based on logical reasoning, concluded that all tennis players at Wimbledon eat bananas. Based on this premise, she inductively constructed a theory that stated all tennis players at other championship competitions also eat bananas during their matches. To test this theory, she decided to attend the US Open and watch as many tennis matches as possible. Over the course of the first week her theory seemed to be true, until she watched a men's quarter-final. At no point did either player eat a banana. With this being the case, her theory could not be confirmed and she had to make adjustments to accommodate her observations. As illustrated in Figure 1.1, the application of induction and deduction research, either in combination or isolation, provides the researcher with a logical framework to develop and then test theories, concepts and/or ideas.

Inductive approach to research

Theory building begins by using *inductive reasoning*. Inductive research concerns generating theories or ideas from research, that is, attempting to make some kind of generalisable inference from observations. So the sport researcher may make a number of observations about crowd behaviour at a number of rugby games, and then start to generate a theory about the way the crowd interact under different match situations. Such theories attempt to make sense of the observations and are produced afterwards (*post factum* or after the facts).

Let's assume a number of observations are made on elite runners' maximum oxygen consumption (Vo_{2max}) values and it was observed that all those measured had high aerobic capacities (> 70 ml.kg. min^{-1}). From a theory-building approach it can therefore be concluded that '*all* elite runners have a high aerobic capacity' (*the new theory*). In this inductive process, specific observations move to more general statements and theories.

From this position, in order for the researcher to make generalisations and formulate theories, inductive reasoning must confirm a number of conditions. Firstly, a number of observations must be made to ensure confidence that the generalisable statement applies to all. Obviously this very much depends on the nature of the observations made. You don't need to observe too often that dropping

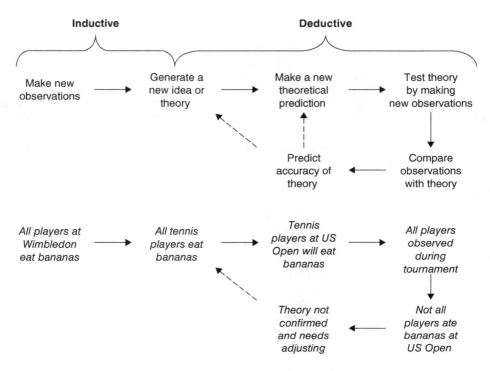

Figure 1.1   A basic model of the scientific inquiry of knowledge that incorporates both inductive and deductive approaches to research.

a barbell on your foot results in pain. However, you would not want to jump to the rash conclusion about the aerobic capacities of *all* elite runners having only observed a handful.

Secondly, observations need to be repeated under a large range of conditions. The choice of conditions, however, can be difficult and the question of how many different conditions are needed to make an inductive generalisation can be hard to determine. Because of these factors, generalisations made through induction can lead to conclusions, but only to a degree of certainty governed by the observations made.

Research focus 1.1

Swann and colleagues (2017) investigated the psychological state underlying excellence in sporting performance in 26 athletes. The overarching intentions were to develop an integrated theoretical model (inductive approach) that described the development of flow and clutch states that typify optimal psychological performance during competition. The authors outline that such states are *encompassed by the term optimal experience, which is often used to describe positive states of consciousness that provide strong positive feelings associated with happiness and self-fulfilling experiences that result from*

(Continued)

13

(Continued)

exerting effort. The aim was to capture recent, detailed insights into the psychological states experienced by athletes during excellent performance, in terms of how such states are experienced, how they occur and which skills are used to manage or prolong them.

Participants competing in world-class elite (e.g. Olympians; Commonwealth Games) through to recreational events (e.g. running marathons) were interviewed soon after (~ 4 days) they had competed in an event they deemed of exceptional performance. Based on a pre-defined interview guide, the researchers undertook a semi-structured open-ended approach allowing freedom for athletes to elaborate and extend their responses. In addition, athletes not involved in the event-focused data capture were interviewed about their experiences more generally. This enabled the researchers to develop and refine emergent themes that would inform their theoretical model.

Within this study sample the authors reported a range of distinct states, each occurring in separate contexts and processes. Their findings suggested that the facilitation of flow occurrence requires focus on confidence-enhancing strategies in exploratory contexts and open goals should be set. The use of 'positive distractions' and dissociative strategies to help maintain flow and 'stay out of their own way' (i.e. avoid the critical thoughts that can disrupt flow states) should be maximised. For clutch states to occur the focus should be on strategies that enhance perceived control in contexts involving importance and 'fixed' goals should be set. Associative strategies – the segmentation of tasks into smaller chunks so they are more manageable – should also be used to maintain these states.

Deductive approach to research

Theory testing begins by using *deductive reasoning*. This approach starts with a theory that guides the researcher into making observations that attempt to test the worth of a theory. By applying the theory built from inductive reasoning, outlined above, the worth of the theory can be tested. The theory developed through inductive research stated that all elite runners have a high aerobic capacity ($Vo_{2max} > 70$ ml.kg.min^{-1}). Supposing a new elite runner appeared on the scene: based on the theory she should also have a high aerobic capacity.

So, using deductive logic, all elite runners have a high Vo_{2max} and therefore the new runner must also have a high Vo_{2max}. This theory should be challenged, however, as this may not actually be true. A question of confidence begins to arise about the theory. How confident is the researcher that the theory will always be true? The researcher may wish to ask how the theory was derived and how many times it has been tested. The theory that all elite runners have high aerobic capacities ($Vo_{2max} > 70$ ml.kg.min^{-1}) will only hold true until an elite runner is found to have a Vo_{2max} value lower than 70 ml.kg.min^{-1}. When this is discovered the theory will then have to be refined and a new one developed. This will then hold true until such a time that this is disproved and refined again.

 Research focus 1.2

Wellington et al. (2017) conducted a study to investigate the impact of caffeine on repeat high-intensity running performance in rugby league players. Using an experimental approach (double-blind, placebo-controlled, cross-over design), they compared two trials that involved completing repeat high-intensity efforts after either caffeine ingestion (300-mg dose) or a placebo (vitamin H supplement). Undertaken with 11 semi-professional players, each trial involved three sets of 20-metre sprints interspersed with bouts of tackling.

The results revealed that the total time to complete the caffeine trial was 1% (28.46 seconds) faster when compared to the placebo condition (28.77 seconds). The authors conducted that it is very likely that the caffeine had a beneficial impact on performance (99% likely to have been beneficial).

In summary, Wellington and associates noted that, although these improvements were small, they were likely meaningful given that the difference between winning and losing at elite level is often determined by very small differences in physical performance during crucial stages of play.

When theories are tested, reliable knowledge is sought so that the theory can either be retained as true or refuted as false. By assessing more and more elite runners, the researcher attempts to disprove the theory. It is this very act of trying to disprove or *falsify* that strengthens the theory. The more times the researcher tries to falsify it and can't, the stronger the theory becomes.

When attempting to test a theory, the researcher must begin by developing statements that are to be tested. These statements are called *hypotheses* and, when used in an attempt to retain or refute a theory, this is commonly referred to as the *hypothetico-deductive method*. It is this approach that is synonymous with the *scientific method* of research.

By applying deductive or inductive methods or a combination of both, research therefore subscribes to the notion that questions that are generated lead to the development of clear objectives which are achieved through a carefully planned and executed *research strategy*. This allows for meaning to be reached from the collected facts, which form a reasoned argument to support the conclusions. Knowledge is then expanded and advanced, giving rise to further research problems.

 Reflection point 1.3

- How is the world viewed? And what can be researched? *Ontology*

- What do we know about what can be studied? *Epistemology*

- How are we going to acquire what is out there? *Methodology*

- What plan will be used to acquire what is out there? *Research design*

- What techniques/tools can be used to collect and analyse what is out there? *Research methods*

The different types of research

Research starts off by asking fundamental questions bound within a particular problem or area of interest. It is through these questions that the research strategy begins to emerge. Selecting the right strategy will help us find the right answer. In the most basic of ways, as described in Table 1.4, the

Table 1.4   *Research can be categorised into four broad types: exploratory, descriptive, analytical or explanatory and predictive*

Type of research	Description	Type of questions that may be asked
Exploratory	Attempts to establish patterns, ideas or hypotheses through the gathering of preliminary information rather than testing or confirming a theory (can lead to explanatory research to provide deeper understanding)	• What is known about the new sport of bossaball (a mix of football, volleyball and gymnastics on trampolines)? • What are the emerging political developments relating to the sport-tourism link in Cumbria? • How do the perceptions of emotional climate among injured athletes impact on their personal and social interactions within a sporting team?
Descriptive	Describes phenomenon as it exists, used to obtain data on the characteristics of a particular issue	• How many football clubs nationally do not have charter standard status? • What are the feelings of older adults (> 65 years) about the introduction of local physical activity road shows? • What are the ground reaction forces on take-off for a group of high jumpers?
Analytical or explanatory	Attempts are made to analyse and explain why or how something is happening	• How can the number of first-serve errors in tennis be reduced? • Why is the introduction of self-administered training plans found on the internet seen as a threat by professional fitness trainers? • How can a more athlete-centred delivery approach increase retention rates?
Predictive	Attempts to forecast the likelihood of a similar situation occurring elsewhere through generalisation	• Will the introduction of a new coach lead to higher performance levels throughout the team? • How will the introduction of specific short-term goals impact on motivational levels in junior athletes?

research question will relate to wanting to know, for example, *what* is going on (descriptive), *why* it is happening (explanatory) or *how* it may impact on others (predictive). The questions that are asked (i.e. what, how, when, where and why?) dictate which research approach is necessary to provide a solution to the problem. Such questions will also be wrapped up in an ontological position, so identifying early within the research journey which position (objectivism or constructivism) the question links to should be an important task for any researcher. It may well be the case that some problems may be solved through a quick review of the literature, for example; however, there may be no logical answer found from the evidence and therefore research must be undertaken to generate new knowledge and understanding.

The research framework

Identifying where and how research design and methods fit into the overall research framework is an important first step in developing a research project. It is not the intention here to cover the research process or provide a step-by-step guide to developing a research project; other books in the series do this well. What is necessary at this stage, however, is to identify where the overarching research strategy, that is, the design and method, fits into the overall research journey and how the design and data collection methods impact meaningfully on the overall ability to plan, conduct and evaluate the project. Hopefully, Figure 1.2 should come as no surprise, providing a logical and systematic journey through the research process. From the inception of a tentative problem or question to the dissemination of the findings through a report or presentation, the process involves several method-related components that are at the centre of any research project. As highlighted in grey in Figure 1.2, understanding what needs to be established in each of these boxes and making the right and most appropriate decision based on the nature of the question will result in the ability to solve the problem or answer that question.

- *Identifying a research strategy that links to the problem* is an essential early part of the research process. Working thoughtfully through this stage ensures the researcher selects the most suitable research design(s) and method(s) to answer the emerging research question(s).

- *Conducting a secondary review to find a problem* is essentially a research strategy in itself, requiring the researcher to employ a design and method to research the literature comprehensively. This stage is not always necessary and can actually be a research project on its own.

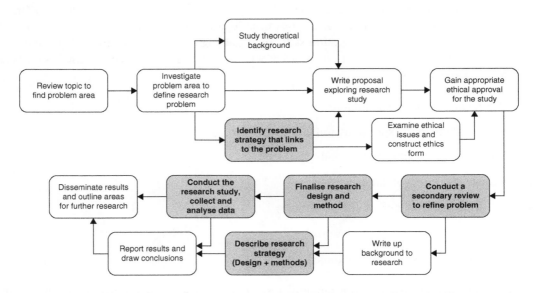

Figure 1.2   Research design and methods are integral parts of the overall research process. As highlighted in the shaded boxes, the research strategy selected will have a direct impact on the ability to draw meaningful conclusions from the data collected.

- *Finalising the research design and method* provides the researcher with the confidence that the approach is matched to the initial problem. At this stage, pilot study work can be conducted to confirm the research orientation.

- *Describing the research strategy (design + method)* demonstrates an understanding of the approach taken. Correctly describing the strategy allows others to replicate the research and demonstrates a level of comprehension and communication skill.

- *Conducting the research study, collecting and analysing the data* require a range of practical and technical skills linked to an underpinning knowledge of the selected strategy. At this stage, inappropriate implementation, evaluation and interpretation can result in invalid, unreliable and unrepresented findings.

A critical approach to research methods

The link between research strategy, that being the design and methods combined, and research question is an important one and can be achieved through a critical approach to research. Adopting a critical approach towards the selection of the research design and associated data collection methods is about accepting nothing at face value, but rather examining the strengths and weaknesses of each in relation to the research question. Each chapter throughout this book has been structured so as to aid the development of understanding of the relative merits and drawbacks associated with each approach. Further to this, each offers a range of valuable practical examples to help guide you through the selection of research approaches.

To adopt a critical approach to research methods, the researcher must be able to evaluate different sides of an argument, and to draw conclusions from logical arguments and data analysis. Critical thinking, therefore, requires background skills such as imagination and creativity, logic and reasoning, conceptual thinking, reflection and feedback. Fisher (2011) noted that the critical-thinking researcher should be able to:

- identify and evaluate assumptions;

- clarify and interpret expressions and ideas;

- judge the acceptability, and credibility, of claims;

- evaluate arguments of different kinds;

- analyse, evaluate and produce explanations;

- analyse, evaluate and make decisions;

- draw inferences and produce arguments.

By applying this approach to the range of research strategies available, the researcher must begin to consider how each provides different opportunities to acquire knowledge from the sporting world.

Chapter review

In this chapter we have considered the importance of research and placed it within a sporting context. We will all at some point undertake research in some shape or form. By developing our awareness of the building blocks of research, the philosophical positions that underpin different research approaches and the varying types of research we may encounter, we can be prepared to start our research journey. In preparation for creating our research question and then selecting the most appropriate research strategy, this chapter has provided a valuable starting point. By using a range of sport-related research examples throughout this chapter you should now be able to:

☑ explain the nature of research within the context of sport and describe the characteristics of the scientific approach;

☑ describe the building blocks of research and identify which research type would link to particular sport-related research questions;

☑ identify where a research strategy fits into the overall research framework and establish its role within the research process.

Further reading

Bryman, A (2015) *Social Research Methods*. 5th ed. Oxford: Oxford University Press.

This broad textbook provides a perfect compendium to this opening chapter. Although not sport-specific, many practical examples simplify often complex passages.

Grix, J (2002) Introducing students to the generic terminology of social research. *Politics*, 22: 175–86.

For students and tutors wishing to grasp the more complex terminology covered in this chapter, this paper demystifies often confusing terms through a step-by-step approach to social science research.

Blaxter, L, Hughes, C and Tight, M (2010) *How to Research*. Maidenhead: McGraw-Hill Education.

O'Leary, Z (2017) *The Essential Guide to Doing Your Research Project*. 3rd ed. London: SAGE Publications.

Walliman, N (2011) *Your Research Project: Designing and Planning Your Work*. London: SAGE Publications.

Each of the above books extends further the discussions put forward in this chapter, presenting a comprehensive framework on which to base further application. Each is well presented and accessible to all undergraduate levels.

2

Selecting an appropriate research strategy

By linking your understanding of sport in practice to sport-related research examples, this chapter is designed to help you:

- explain the importance of research strategy selection;
- describe and define the terms *research design* and *research methods*, exploring the range that can be accessed by the researcher;
- link these key concepts together in a logical and justified manner.

Introduction

Whether playing a round of golf, identifying the roles members of a team play when under pressure or making a decisive race-winning breakaway, selecting the right strategy will ensure that time and time again the correct preparation will lead to the selection of the most suitable approach and the desired outcome. The *research strategy* therefore is the logical set of principles that inform the researcher in the process of planning, managing and implementing a single or collection of research methods based on one or more research designs.

In Chapter 1, the two broad approaches to research were reviewed: *positivistic* from a natural science perspective and *interpretivistic* from a social science perspective. With each approach linked to a set of underpinning assumptions (i.e. paradigms) that impact on the nature of the research question, the selection of the most suitable strategy is a fundamental component to any project. Therefore, before unravelling the intricacies of research design and method, the researcher must gain a wider appreciation of the overarching strategies available. This provides a much more concrete link between the philosophical position of the research and the more pragmatic aspects of data collection and analysis.

Establishing a research strategy

A tennis player is two games away from winning the championship. With the score 4–2 in the final set of a five-set thriller, both players return to their seats to work out their individual game plans. Drawing on past experience and evaluating the opponent's strengths and weaknesses, both players work through their options in a logical and rational manner. Based on the objectives of their task, they systematically apply a logical set of principles (*research strategy*) that will shape their decisions. This will allow for a plan to be devised (*research design*). The player who is behind opts to attack the opponent's weakest shot – backhand – with deep forehand ground shots (the plan). Holding the opponent deep in the court would then allow for a surge to the net for a volley into the open court (*research methods*).

 Reflection point 2.1

In an excellent book that provides extensive advice on research planning, Blaikie (2009) makes a clear distinction between research strategy and other aspects of the research process that are often used synonymously and subsumed under the umbrella term of research methods:

- *research strategy*: a logic of inquiry (set of ground rules/principles that shape the decisions we make when selecting and implementing our research design and methods);

- *research design*: all aspects relating to the structure or plan by which data collection can occur;

- *research method*: execution of the project (incorporating the implementation of instruments, techniques and procedures used to collect data).

Being able to establish a sense of order to these terms will help in planning the research process, as outlined in Chapter 1. Before determining ethics, participant recruitment and protocol/instrument design, the framework or research strategy must be determined and developed in accordance with the nature of the research question.

So the research strategy, which can comprise one or more designs and one or more methods, is the logical manner by which the researcher shapes the data collection process. Viewing research in such a way allows the researcher to be confident that the strategy selected is best suited to answer the research question. This doesn't always mean that the findings will be what are expected, but it will provide confidence that the process and the logic of conducting the research are achieved in the most suitable way.

Recognising a research project's strategy

Each research project undertaken will have a *research strategy* built within it. It is often the case, however, that most undergraduate research projects are formed without the student knowing the strategy selected. The tendency of most is to jump start into focusing on the research methods, developing questionnaires, constructing treadmill protocols or structuring and planning interviews, for example. When identifying how to go about collecting data to answer the research question, the immediate concern often is centred on aspects of research construction and implementation, namely deciding on the design and methods and then conducting the study to collect and analyse the data (Chapter 1, Figure 1.2). Although incredibly important aspects of the research process and ones that need time and attention, the initial emphasis for the researcher should be on recognising the research strategy.

If researchers identify the research strategy early in the research process, question and debate it, and build arguments to support their choice, they can be confident that the selection and evolvement of the design and methods will be based on a logical framework that fits the research question being asked. Without such research strategy or overall research orientation, it is difficult to have a clear direction from the start and decide on which design/methods would allow for effective data collection. The act of undertaking research and devising a strategy that is ultimately governed by the research problem will provide the philosophical and practical framework that supports the research process. It is important to recognise that the strategy selected will typically fit firmly into one of the ontological positions (i.e. objectivist or constructivist), the corresponding epistemology positions (i.e. positivist or interpretivist) and the linked methodological positions (i.e. quantitative or qualitative). Understanding these positions early in the research planning will help shape an opinion on the strengths and limitations of the chosen strategy.

As outlined previously, questions we ask ourselves when deciding on our research approach relate to: (1) what does our world consist of, and what constitutes reality? (*our ontological position*); (2) what do we know about our world and how can we gain appropriate knowledge about it? (*our epistemology position*); and (3) how are we going to go about acquiring the knowledge that is in our world (*our methodological position*)? Each of these questions will lead us to make decisions that will have a direct influence on the research strategy. As outlined in Figure 2.1, ontological, epistemological and methodological positions can be broadly divided into contrasting paradigms. Each paradigm has its own logic and set of rules, governed by certain principles. Each will, to some extent, dictate the range of research designs and methods that allow for suitable data collection in order to establish knowledge in our world. Working through the figure in a logical direction (from left to right) enables researchers to approach their design and method selection in a manner that ensures a broad awareness of their selected research positions. The choice of design and method is not arbitrary, but systematically selected based on the paradigm that is governed by both the researcher's own position and the research question.

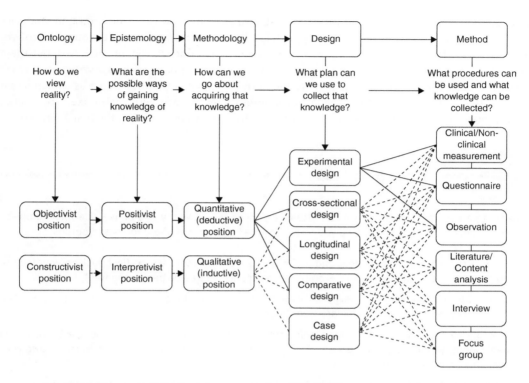

Figure 2.1   The building blocks of research provide a gateway to the design and methods we may choose in order to answer our research question.

Each chapter within this book has been carefully developed to help the researcher make the right decision based on the type of sport-related question(s) that may need answering. By working through the individual research strategies and their associated design(s) and method(s), the researcher will gain a sense of the philosophical and practice importance of each. In turn, this will aid in the implementation and interpretation of findings within the overall research process.

Problem-led versus strategy-led approaches

It is important to remember that research should always be problem-led and not strategy-led. This means that it should be the research problem that dictates the selection of a strategy, as the researcher should be searching for the most suitable approach to answer the question fully. Although it may be difficult, researchers must view all approaches evenly without bias towards their own ontological position. Such an approach will lead to new questions being asked from different perspectives and the creation of new opportunities of research that would otherwise be missed.

For the purposes of this book, research strategies have been broadly placed into seven distinct categories that incorporate ontological, epistemological and methodological positions, as well as appropriate designs and suitable methods. Figure 2.1 provides a representation of the relationship between each position, research design and research methods. Systematic literature review, experimental, correlational, survey, observational, ethnographic and case study research strategies are the most common types of research approaches the sports researcher will encounter through-out the course of studies. In some research projects more than one strategy may be used, but these tend to be larger research studies that begin with an exploratory phase, such as a systematic review or survey strategy, that may be inductive, followed by an explanatory phase, such as experimental research, that would be deductive. The last chapter of the book deals with such mixed approaches and explores ways in which researchers can approach their research to develop the best approach.

 **Key point 2.1**

Generating a new research question can often be difficult when we try and arrive at a final complete endpoint. Some simple steps may help you formulate the question with more focus and purpose:

Step 1: Create a list of board ideas and topics that are of interest to you (reflect back on your lecture notes, slides, reading materials or even the assessments where you performed well).

Step 2: Develop key words and terms linked to your ideas. Make these specific, and if necessary, use a thesaurus to expand your vocabulary (see Chapter 3).

Step 3: Use these words and terms within common literature search tools (i.e. Google Scholar) and begin identifying the types of research that have been undertaken in these areas. Narrow down your searches and refine steps 1 and 2 along the way.

Step 4: *Read!* This is now the most important part, given you have defined your topics and located research. Now you need to increase your knowledge and understanding, which will help inform your decisions.

Step 5: Start to formulate initial questions based around your themes. Use these as decision points with your supervisor. Begin to explore the types of questions to ask and what type of approach you may need to take to arrive at an answer.

The link between the research question and research strategy

The most important part of research is linking the question that has emerged to an appropriate research strategy. In reality, many research questions fit nicely into one of the seven strategies and the emerging design and methods can be easily deciphered, both by looking back at past research and through logical reasoning. As already mentioned, it is a common mistake to let the tail wag the dog – that is, the research strategy shapes the nature of the question. What is fundamental is that the dog wags the tail, so the research question dictates the selected strategy. The research question or problem the researcher develops can be answered in a number of different ways. Therefore, reviewing each approach, identifying the linked designs and methods (Figure 2.1) and considering the nature of the data the researcher wants to collect will provide the signpost to the most suitable strategy. The following sections should provide researchers with a starting point in identifying each strategy and the type of questions that can be answered. Remember that some questions can be answered using a number of different strategies that may be applied independently or mixed. The nature of the question will dictate whether one or more approaches are needed.

Systematic literature review research

The purpose of this research strategy is to identify, evaluate and interpret all available research (i.e. primary and secondary evidence) relevant to a particular research question, topic area or phenomenon of interest. The reasons for undertaking this approach may be to: (1) summarise existing evidence concerning a treatment, procedure or technology; (2) identify any gaps in the current research in order to suggest areas for further investigation; or (3) provide a framework in order to give recommendations or guidelines of best practice. Systematic literature reviews are particularly useful when there is uncertainty regarding potential benefits or harm of an intervention, such as the supposed performance-enhancing effect of ginseng, or when there are wide variations in practice, such as recommended protein intake among strength and endurance athletes. By applying the systematic literature review process to provide empirical answers to focused questions, this strategy may also help in planning new primary research (Figure 2.2).

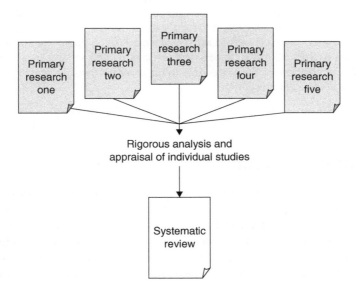

Figure 2.2   The systematic literature review strategy offers an opportunity to answer research questions by using a range of primary research evidence.

The types of questions that can be answered using this strategy may include:

- What research evidence exists that informs us of safety guidelines when prescribing exercise programmes to post-operative patients?

- What protocol designs have been applied to evaluate incremental exercise in runners and how does each impact on measurement error?

- What strategies have been documented that attempt to prevent injury prevalence in adolescent sport?

- What published research is available to generate recommendations for increasing participation in sport?

Research focus 2.1

In a study by Gupta et al. (2016), a systematic literature review was conducted to profile the objective and experienced characteristics of sleep among elite athletes. Given that no previous review had been undertaken to date, the authors aimed to (1) assess the structure, patterns and quality of sleep in elite athletes; and (2) consider the specific risk factors for sleep disturbance arising from the demands of elite sport. The authors performed electronic searches in four widely accessed databases (SPORTDiscus, PubMed, Science Direct and Google Scholar), including all cross-sectional and longitudinal studies that were published as original journal articles. A range of defined search terms (i.e. sleep, sleep quality, insomnia, elite athletes, high-performance athletes, training, travel, competition and recovery) were used that corresponded with the research question. Studies were required to meet a number of criteria, including that participants had to be at elite level, all participants were over 18 years old, there were quantitative reports of sleep outcomes and the articles were peer-reviewed and available in full text. Two reviewers independently evaluated the full text of all retrieved articles using a standard scientific paper appraisal scale. This form prompted the reviewers to record information regarding the study design, methodological features, analysis, clinical relevance, scientific merit, strengths and weaknesses of each study. The two reviewers appraised studies for their relevance to the research question and the quality of evidence. All forms were collated and data presented.

Experimental research

The purpose of this research strategy is to compare cases under controlled conditions (e.g. laboratory or fixed environments) in order to establish *causality*. Causality refers to the relationship between the cause of something and the subsequent effect. Manipulating a single phenomenon while controlling all others allows the researcher to determine what may cause such an effect. By establishing causality, the researcher is able to make generalities to support or refute a theory. Therefore, by attempting to establish cause and effect, this deductive approach sets out to test theory. The experimental research strategy fits firmly within the objectivist position and therefore conforms to the objectivity of measurement.

Typically characterised by an intervention/treatment group and a control group, this approach treats situations like a laboratory, attempting to control all confounding factors that may impact on the ability to establish causality (Figure 2.3). A range of experiment-specific research designs can be chosen and, when combined with the large range of data collection methods available within the area of sport, varying approaches can be taken to answer specific research questions to establish cause and effect.

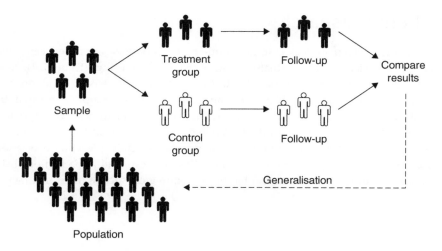

Figure 2.3 The experimental research strategy, as illustrated with a between-group pre–post-test design, establishes causality through the manipulation and control of variables.

The types of questions that can be answered using this strategy may include:

• What is the impact of a 6-week plyometric training programme of swim start performance in junior swimmers?

• Can an acute 2-week bout of imagery training improve target accuracy in expert pistol shooters?

• Does hypnosis prior to high-dive performance improve concentration and focus in elite competitors?

Research focus 2.2

In a study by Rønnestad and colleagues (2016), an experimental research strategy was selected to examine the effect of a 10-week heavy-strength intervention training programme on cycling performance indices in elite athletes. The researchers applied a between-group design, encompassing a pre- and post-assessment (within-group factor). Within a group of 20 elite cyclists, the researchers randomly assigned 12 to a heavy training programme, comprising a resistance exercise schedule carried out twice a week (20 sessions overall), whilst the remaining eight cyclists undertook their normal endurance training programmes. Testing before and after the intervention was completed as follows: (1) on the first day, the measurement of lean lower-body mass; (2) on the second day an incremental cycle test for determination of blood lactate profile followed by a maximal oxygen consumption test; (3) on the third day, maximal strength test, squat jump test and 30-second Wingate test; and (4) on the final day, a 40-minute all-out trial. The collection of numerical data for the pre- and post-testing allowed for a range of statistical assessments to be made on the data.

Correlational research

The purpose of this research strategy is to determine patterns of association between phenomena. In simple terms, this relates to the mutual relation of two or more things (Figure 2.4). Numerically orientated, this deductive approach is of value to the researcher who wishes to identify the inter-relationships between measured variables. Sometimes referred to as descriptive research, because it describes existing relationships between variables, the correlational strategy attempts to describe the degree to which one or more quantifiable variables relate. Although the degree of agreement between these can be established, a causal link cannot be made. Only a level of association can be determined using statistical techniques. Correlational research can lead to predictions being made based on the strength of the association and has been used to great success in estimating percentage of body fat.

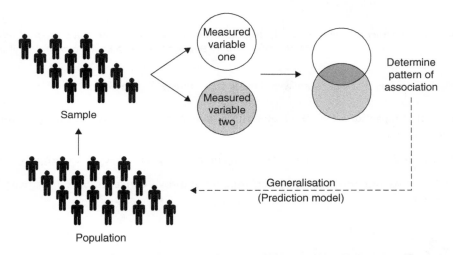

Figure 2.4   *The correlational research strategy allows for associations to be determined between two or more measured variables.*

The types of questions that can be answered using this strategy may include:

- Is there an association between social class and those who attend Badminton Horse Trials?

- Is the number of aerobic training miles completed in a year associated with sport-related injuries over the same time period?

- How does the long-term motivation of a sports team associate with the number of wins per session?

- Is there an association between lower-limb bilateral strength deficits and the number of falls in elderly women?

Research focus 2.3

In a study by García-Ramos and colleagues (2016), a correlational research strategy was selected to examine the association between vertical jump height and swimming start performance. Furthermore, the researchers were interested to examine whether such a relationship altered after a period at a high-altitude training camp. Although they reported that significant correlations between jump performance and swimming start time had previously been reported, the accuracy in determining changes in swimming start performance through the changes in jump performance after a short-term training programme had not been established.

A total of 15 performers were selected for this repeated-measures design, which incorporated a correlational research approach. The authors carried out a range of methods to collect the data, including unloaded and loaded vertical jump height (metres), and a 15-metre swimming test that required the performer to undertake a kick start from a starting block located 0.70 metres above the water. In addition, the swimmers completed a training programme prescribed by the coaches throughout a 17-day training camp. With numerical data from squat performance and swim start performance the authors conducted statistical analysis to determine the extent to which unloaded and loaded squat height related to swim starts before and after high-altitude training exposure. The degree of association between the selected measures provided the authors with an insight into how best to optimise swim start performance.

Survey research

The purpose of this research strategy is to describe the characteristics of a population. Whether that be another group, organisation or community, the approach allows the researcher to find out how the population is distributed on one or more variables (i.e. age, football team preference, attitudes towards school PE, motives). The researcher generates numerical or non-numerical data from people by way of scores, outcomes, ratings, conditions or opinions using data collection methods such as questionnaire, interview or observation (Figure 2.5). The researcher can begin to describe and explain phenomena and attempt to make representations to the wider population. As with other research strategies, the population is rarely studied; instead a sample is surveyed and a description of the population is inferred from what is found out.

The types of questions that can be answered using this strategy may include:

- How effective are community-based well-being initiatives in improving social and emotional health among isolated rural dwellers?

- What is the importance of athlete-centred education to the aspiring elite athlete and how may it support performance development?

- What were the attendee's perceptions of a new Active Living workshop series promoted by a primary care trust?

- What strategies are fitness centre managers developing and implementing to combat the fall in membership numbers?

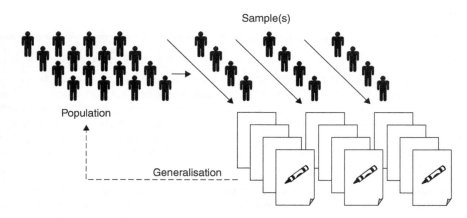

Sample(s)

Population

Generalisation

Figure 2.5   The survey research strategy allows for the collection of data from a large number of cases using methods such as questionnaires.

Research focus 2.4

In a study by Brown et al. (2017), a survey research strategy was undertaken to identify whether satisfaction gained from watching swimming at the London 2012 Olympic Games influenced future intentions both to watch and to participate in sport. Data were collected using a detailed questionnaire, administered at the Olympic Aquatic Centre during the 2012 Olympics ($n = 185$) and a regional leisure centre approximately 200 miles from London ($n = 135$). This approach was selected to assess any differences that could exist between those watching a live event and those watching it remotely at the centre. To assist data collection, six trained researchers were assigned to key locations around the Aquatic Centre, where respondents were randomly recruited to complete the questionnaire. At the leisure centre, respondents were approached as they entered the facilities. The study took place shortly after the Olympic Games, and the venue was the home of a high-profile Olympic diver and training centre for the national swimming and diving teams.

All respondents were asked to indicate their recent swimming participation (last 12 months), in addition to a series of indicators that reflected their behavioural intensity, such as the number of ticket purchases and extent of television watching. Furthermore, respondents were asked to rate their preference for a number of statements using a Likert scale (1 = strongly disagree through to 7 = strongly agree). Statements included *I will swim regularly for fun, I will attend swimming events as a spectator* and *I swim regularly for fitness*. All completed questionnaires were gathered, subjected to statistical assessment where appropriate and reported for an appraisal of the findings in relation to the initial hypotheses.

Observational research

The purpose of this research strategy is to capture, through a range of observational techniques, social behaviour as accurately as possible. The ability of researchers to use their senses effectively to record systematically observable phenomena or behaviour in a natural real-world setting allows for the study of people in their native environment in order to understand things from their perspective.

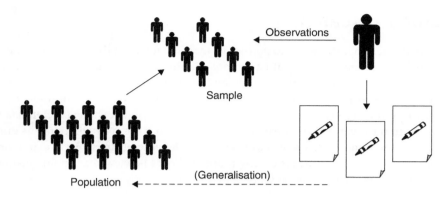

Figure 2.6   The observational research strategy provides a framework to observe behaviour to understand individual and group dynamics within a changing real-world setting.

Through systematic inquiry into the nature and qualities of observable individual and group behaviours we can learn what it means to function physically and socially within the world and/or interact with others to form social connections. Away from control and manipulation, the observational research strategy offers a gateway for the researcher to identify how social constructs and inter-relationships within and between people impact on social functioning (Figure 2.6).

The types of questions that can be answered using this strategy may include:

- What is the nature of the coach–junior athlete relationship in the presence and absence of parents?

- What are the movement dynamics of members within a newly built fitness centre and how may this influence placement of promotional material to different user groups?

- What are the actual, rather than reported, warm-up techniques of amateur golfers?

- What behavioural responses do school children exhibit when taught for the first time by a trainee sports coach?

 Research focus 2.5

Faber and colleagues (2017) selected a longitudinal observational research strategy to investigate the capability of four key movement characteristics inherent within the National Table Tennis perceptual-motor skills assessment tool. Youth table tennis performers between the ages of 7 and 10 were selected and observed at an annual national talent day over a period of 5 years. In total, data from 1191 youth players were recorded. All players were assessed under similar conditions based on four items: sprint, agility, speed whilst dribbling and throwing a ball. These items are used by the Netherlands National Table Tennis Association as part of their talent identification programme to evaluate a wide range of domains that are considered important precursors to successful performance in table tennis. Each player undertook a number of table-tennis-specific and non-specific movement tasks, during which trained observers recorded their performance using a standard observation template.

Case study research

The purpose of this research strategy is to portray, analyse and interpret the uniqueness of individual units – a person, class, family, event, situation, organisation or even a product. Each case should have boundaries – it should be an entity in itself. By capturing the complex contextual nature of the unit within a real-life setting, the researcher is able to present and represent an in-depth, detailed picture of one or more units or cases within the environment using a wide range of data sources. Bound tightly within the constructivist paradigm, the ability to make generalisations sits firmly with the recipient (i.e. the reader of the research) (Figure 2.7). Because of the subjective, interpretivistic nature of case study research, generalising any findings should be viewed as approximating future expectations rather than establishing causality or making predictions.

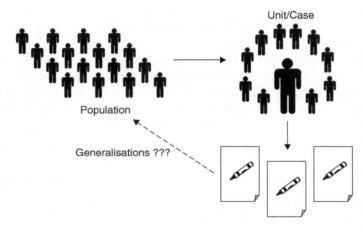

Figure 2.7   The case study research strategy involves collecting data, generally from only one or a small number of cases, to provide insight into particular situations and/or experiences.

The types of questions that can be answered using this strategy may include:

- What is the impact of a non-charter status football club on coaching provision across a wide age range?

- Does GolfMark improve junior development within a local privately owned club?

- What are the physical and mental preparatory strategies of a round-the-world sailor?

- What educational benefit does 'sports day' have within secondary education?

 **Research focus 2.6**

In a study by Rabelo et al. (2016), a case study research strategy was selected to explore the perceived versus intended training loads experienced by professional futsal players. The objective was to investigate whether the intended training load, prescribed by a coach, matched the perceived training load experienced by the players. Over a 45-week season, on a daily basis, the players' rating of perceived exertion (RPE) and coach's rating of intended exertion (RIE) were collected. To draw comparisons across the player's season, it was divided into four periods: pre-season, first competitive period, inter-competition period and second competitive period. Before each training session, the coach's RIE was recorded using a 0–10 Borg scale. This was based on a predicted load for the session, determined within a weekly training planner devised by the coach, and specific to the period of the season. Players' RPE was obtained using the same scale approximately 30 minutes following the completion of the training session to capture a global perceived level of exertion. Players made the judgement independently of the coach's intentions for the session and were not aware of the RIE made by the coach, or other players' RPE scores. Analysis of the data took place to identify the extent to which the planned intentions of the coach compared with the experiences of the players.

Ethnographic research

The purpose of this research strategy is to understand and describe a group or culture, accepting that all human behaviour occurs within a context. The word ethnography literally means 'writing about people' and broadly refers to the strategy of studying people for the purpose of describing their sociocultural activities and patterns. This approach essentially involves descriptive research methods as a basis for interpretation. It represents a dynamic picture of the way of life of some interacting social group and, as a process, is a science of cultural description. Inductive in nature, ethnography differs from other similar approaches (i.e. case study research) in that it attempts to collect information from an insider's perspective and make sense of the data from an external social science perspective (Figure 2.8).

Ethnography can be written in different styles and formats, typically describing group histories, geography of location, kinship patterns, symbols and rituals, political positioning, educational and social systems and the degree of contact between the investigated subculture and the main culture.

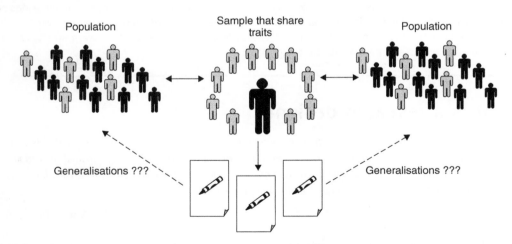

Figure 2.8   The ethnographic research strategy attempts to collect information from an insider's perspective and make sense of the data from an external social science perspective.

Employing methods that range from the literature content analysis of books, newspapers and electronic materials to individual interviews and observational strategies, the ethnographic approach attempts to gain a true insight from an insider's viewpoint and externalise it to social cultural dimensions.

The types of questions that can be answered using this strategy may include:

- What are the sporting experiences of Eastern European immigrants within inner-city locations?

- How has a change in gender acceptance impacted on women's experience of skateboarding?

- How may a community 'new-age' sports festival alter the perceptions of youth sport among elderly residents?

- Is social status a passport to private golf membership?

 Research focus 2.7

In a study by Cavallerio and co-workers (2016), an ethnographic research strategy was selected to gain an in-depth understanding of overuse injuries in 16 female rhythmic gymnastics. Over a 12-month period, the lead researcher immersed herself in a gymnastic club environment, observing and talking to key stakeholders and members. As a former gymnast and coach with over 15 years' experience, she shared a common cultural background with the organisation's coaching staff and performers, therefore she was granted *insider status*. She took on the role of an overt participant observer, marginally participating in club activities, whilst undertaking observations. This approach meant that she could access people and situations considered a potential barrier for an 'outsider'. Data were collated using a reflective journal, allowing for critical reflection on the researcher's role and interactions with club members and performers.

Secondly, a co-author acted as a critical friend, ensuring personal values, beliefs, thoughts and feelings did not alter interpretation of observations. A series of interviews, observational field notes, timeline logs and focus groups were conducted with gymnasts and their coaches, and as time progressed the research lens was narrowed (i.e. the questions became more focused) to ensure the researchers were able to channel their observations into a richer narrative (i.e. story).

What is a research design?

Research design is different from methods by which data are collected. Many research methods texts confuse research designs with methods. It is not uncommon to see research design treated as a model of data collection rather than a logical structure of the inquiry. But there is nothing intrinsic about any research design that requires a particular method of data collection.

(De Vaus, 2005, p9)

Consider tournament golfers for a moment. Before they step out on to the course for their round, they will have developed a plan to help them achieve the best score for that day. The player will have a detailed plan of the course layout, where the hazards are around each hole, the width of each fairway, the size and shape of each green, undulations and contours and each flag placement. They will even have an awareness of the general weather conditions for the day. Their plan will also contain detail about how each hole needs to be played, considering where the ball needs to be positioned on the fairway following the tee shot and what parts of the green they want to avoid.

As players function in different ways it is unlikely that the detail within each of their plans would be exactly the same. They will all show similar characteristics, however. Some players, for example, may be naturally more aggressive than others, wishing to take more chances and accept the risks. These players expect unpredictable situations to occur on the course and see this as an inherent aspect of playing golf. Other golfers may be more reserved and calculated. Meticulous in their planning, they like to ensure that their performance is as predictable and replicable as possible, working out exact shots, club selection and distances. Neither of these two approaches is wrong and the plan selected suits the needs of each golfer. By developing a plan before they go out on the course, the golfers can have confidence that their approach will help optimise their chances of producing their best results.

Developing a design for our research requires the same care and attention as the golfer takes before each round. If the question is to be answered successfully then the design must be well considered before you embark on any data collection. *Research design* refers to the logical and systematic structure or plan by which data collection can take place. Bryman (2015) defines research design as a framework for the collection and analysis of data, supported by the definition of Fraenkal and colleagues (2011), who see the design as a plan for collecting data in order to answer the research question. The design is, therefore, the blueprint for the study, providing the researcher with an overall guide as to how the research methods will fit together and how, when and where the data collection tools and techniques will be implemented.

The design is inextricably linked to the research strategy selected, which is directly linked back to the ontological and epistemological position held (Figure 2.1). Just as golfers create a plan based on their own philosophy towards playing the game and their objectives for the round, researchers also develop their plan based on their beliefs and the objectives of the research. The plan selected, therefore, sits firmly within underpinning assumptions, governed by the wider ontological viewpoint, but more importantly, by the objectives defined – in the case of the golfer, being 'how can I achieve the lowest score?' As can be seen in Table 2.1, five research designs allow for a flexible working approach.

How do research methods differ?

Once the golfers have their plans, they can then go out on the course and start playing. Their shot selection will relate back to their original plan and, therefore, depending on their overall *design,* each shot will be different and require different technique. The desired outcome for each means that the approach taken will produce slightly different end results and it is likely that these results will be slightly different each time performed. It is how players are able to implement the skills of using their tools, that is, their clubs, knowledge, experience and training, that will dictate the quality of their play and ultimately the overall score achieved. If the wrong club is selected, technique implemented or decision made (i.e. the player goes off-plan), then the desired outcome, that is, the objectives set at the beginning, will not be accomplished. Selecting a research method in essence is no different. There are many clubs (or methods) in our bag and selecting the right ones at the right time and then being able to use our skill and experience to implement them will dictate the quality and value of the data collected.

Table 2.1   Five research designs that create the plan within the research strategy (adapted from Bryman, 2015)

Research design	Description	Research strategy	
		Quantitative	Qualitative
Experimental	A research design that deliberately imposes a treatment on a case in the interest of observing the response. Within this design, a number of experimental conditions can be created (e.g. cross-over, repeated measures, within-subjects, between-subject design)	e.g. typically employs numerical data comparisons between an intervention/treatment case with a control case and requires research methods that allow for the collection of objective numerical data	Not typically employed within this paradigm
Cross-sectional	A research design that involves collecting data on one or more cases at a single point in time. Collecting quantifiable data in connection with two or more variables allows for patterns of association to be determined	e.g. can involve collection of numerical data from surveys, observational approaches or literature/content analysis on a case at a single point in time	e.g. non-numerical data collected by interviews, focus groups, observations that relate to a single point in time
Longitudinal	A research design where cases are assessed at several different time periods. Usually this design is used when interested in how people change over time	e.g. survey research on a case on more than one occasion or literature/content analysis relating to different time periods	e.g. mapping change over time through ethnographic research across periods, interviews on more than one occasion or through literature/content analysis
Comparative	A research design that involves studying more or less identical methods on two or more contrasting cases. Making comparisons implies the research can better understand social phenomena between cases/situations	e.g. survey research where a direct numerical comparison is made between two or more cases, such as cross-cultural research	e.g. making direct comparisons through ethnographic or qualitative interviews/observations on two or more cases/situations
Case	A research design where a case is studied intensively. A case may be individuals, programmes or any unit, depending on what is to be examined	e.g. numerically oriented survey research on a single case with a view to revealing important features about its nature	e.g. applying ethnographic, qualitative interviews to study a case intensively, whether an individual, team or organisation

It is not uncommon to see many research-related textbooks use research design and research methods interchangeably or confuse the two terms. *Research design* should be seen as the plan that guides us through the process of data collection, while the *research method* concerns the approach of how the data will actually be collected. Hitchcock and Hughes (2003) see research methods as techniques employed to gather data, consisting of listening to others, observing what people do and say, or collecting and examining documents which human beings construct. Methods should be viewed as instruments and techniques of research that involve a technical, practical and ethical dimension. As can be seen in Table 2.2, research methods can be categorised into six areas: clinical/non-clinical measurement, questionnaires, observations, literature/content analysis, interviews and focus groups.

Table 2.2   A broad range of methods are available to the sport researcher and are selected on the basis of what needs to be known from the world and people around us

Research method	Description	Sport-related example
Clinical and non-clinical measurement	Any instrument, technique and/or procedure used within the natural sciences to make accurate objective numerical measurements of phenomena	Collecting data by performing an incremental exercise protocol on a cycle ergometer to assess submaximal and maximal physiological responses
Questionnaire	Any instrument consisting of a series of questions and other prompts, used for the purpose of gathering numerical and/or non-numerical data from respondents	Collecting data by administering a series of linked questions to assess mood state during exercise (profile of mood states: POMS)
Observation	Any technique, associated procedure and data-recording instruments that allow for the systematic recording of observable behaviour of individuals or groups	Watching and listening to how a coach interacts with a group of beginner swimmers during their first formal poolside lesson
Literature/content analysis	Any technique and associated procedure that seeks to organise written, audio and/ or visual information into categories and themes related to the central questions of the study. This approach is especially useful in product and document analysis	Collating and analysing all newspaper, magazine, television and radio interviews conducted with members of the England cricket team over a 1-year period
Interview	Any technique and associated procedure that involves a conversation between two or more people (the interviewer and the interviewee) where questions are asked by the interviewer to obtain information from the interviewee	Meeting with recreationally inactive elderly women in order to assess their attitude to exercise
Focus group	Any technique and associated procedure where a group of people are asked about their attitude towards something. Questions are asked in an interactive group setting where participants are free to talk with other group members	Meeting and asking a group of exercise professionals about their views on the success of the general practitioner exercise referral scheme

Not being able to distinguish between design and method can lead to a poor research strategy and the inability to answer the research problem appropriately. Practically any design can be linked to any collection method, but this is dependent on the research question, so the art and science of research are to be aware of the relative strengths and weaknesses of each selected method and link them to the most appropriate design. By bringing together an understanding of design and method, the selection of the overall research strategy will emerge.

Research strategy selection

So far in this chapter, research strategies, research designs and research methods have been explored. To consider your research approach successful, all three of these aspects, underpinned by the associated assumptions linked to each position, must be brought together. Drawing on a research question already outlined earlier on in the chapter, we will see how we can apply Table 2.3 to help point us in the right direction.

Table 2.3   The selection of a research strategy begins with the question or problem. Each strategy can be linked to a corresponding design and method

Research strategy	Ontological position	Epistemological position	Methodological position	Research design	Research method
Systematic literature review	Objectivist/ constructivist	Positivist/ interpretivist	Quantitative and/or qualitative	Cross-sectional or longitudinal	Literature/content analysis
Experimental	Objectivist	Positivist	Quantitative	Experimental (true, quasi- or natural)	Can include one or more of the following: • Observation • Questionnaire • Clinical/ non-clinical measurement
Correlational	Objectivist	Positivist	Quantitative	Cross-sectional	Can include one or more of the following: • Observation • Questionnaire • Clinical/ non-clinical measurement

Survey	Objectivist/ constructivist	Positivist/ interpretivist	Quantitative and/or qualitative	Case, cross-sectional, comparative or longitudinal	Can include one or more of the following: • Observation • Questionnaire • Clinical/ non-clinical measurement
Observational	Constructivist	Interpretivist	Qualitative (but may include aspects of the quantitative approach)	Case, cross-sectional, comparative or longitudinal	Observations
Case study	Constructivist	Interpretivist	Qualitative (but may include aspects of the quantitative approach)	Cross-sectional, comparative or longitudinal	Can include one or more of the following: • Observations • Questionnaires • Focus groups • Interviews • Content analysis
Ethnographic	Constructivist	Interpretivist	Qualitative (but may include aspects of the quantitative approach)	Case, cross-sectional, comparative or longitudinal	Can include one or more of the following: • Observations • Questionnaires • Focus groups • Interviews • Content analysis

Let us start with a research question already mentioned: 'What is the nature of the coach–junior athlete relationship in the presence and absence of parents?' We can use this as an illustration to show how a suitable research strategy, with associated design and methods, can be selected. One of the first questions should really focus on what needs to be known in order to answer the question. That is, what knowledge do we need to acquire? In this case, we want to know about *behaviours* exhibited through the relationship dynamics between the coach and junior athlete, which may be verbal and/or non-verbal. We want to identify whether these alter during the two situations: when parents are present and when they are absent from the coaching situation. Does the parents' presence influence how the coach, athlete or both act and react to each other? It seems appropriate (and probably necessary) to conduct this in as natural and real-world a setting as possible so as not to influence artificially in any way the interactions we are interested in observing.

Reviewing the seven research strategies and referring to Table 2.3, it seems logical in the first instance to consider the experimental approach. This strategy allows us to manipulate something (i.e. whether parents are present or not) and assess the effect (i.e. how the coach and junior athlete behave in each other's company). But, as it is important to set our research within a natural setting and doing this would make it incredibly difficult to control all other factors, establishing causality would be very problematic. Positioning the question within the positivist paradigm may also limit the type of knowledge we are able to gain when we conduct the research project. We would be bound to collect quantitative data (i.e. numerically based) that, although would allow for some statistical analysis, may not enable us to find out about things that cannot be expressed through numbers, such as descriptions of body language, the meaning of hand and facial gestures and expressions or particular emphasis on words and phrases.

Looking at Table 2.3, we can recognise that some strategies may be better suited than others. Opting for a different approach we can begin to gain knowledge from the participants that would allow us to paint a more detailed picture than other approaches would permit. Some may consider it acceptable to approach this research question from an experimental perspective, particularly those who position themselves firmly in the objectivist camp. By applying another approach, however, such as the observational research strategy, we would reposition the research within the constructivist/interpretivist perspective, gaining qualitative rather than quantitative data. Opting for the observational research strategy, the researcher would be able to record, unobtrusively, behaviours exhibited by all (i.e. parents, coaches and athletes) in order to determine the social relationships, connections and influences that may exist. The selection of this approach would lead to a number of different research designs and methods that could be applied in order to build the research plan. This would lead to the selection of instruments, techniques and procedures to collect the data and then undertake data analysis.

So the question must drive the selection of the strategy and the strategy will provide a focus for the design and methods. Overcoming this hurdle in a research project opens up a gateway to effective data collection and project conclusions. The true value of the project can then be realised, enhancing not only the worth of the research to others, but also the researcher's own understanding of the overall research process.

 Learning activity 2.1

Read the range of research questions below. Using the knowledge gained from Chapters 1 and 2, and referring to Table 2.3, allocate a research strategy (design and method(s)) to each. Remember that more than one approach may be taken, so write down all you feel could be used. Consider the strengths and weaknesses of each strategy and rank order them in preference if there are more than two.

- What are the emerging political developments relating to the sport-tourism link in Cumbria?

- What are the ground reaction forces on take-off for a group of high jumpers?

- Why is the introduction of self-administered training plans found on the internet seen as a threat by professional fitness trainers?

- What type of cycling pedal cadence is the most efficient?

- How do the perceptions of emotional climate among injured athletes impact on their personal and social interactions within a sporting team?

- Will the introduction of a new coach lead to higher performance levels throughout the team?

- What are the feelings of older adults (> 65 years) about the introduction of local physical activity road shows?

 Chapter review

In this chapter we have considered the importance of research strategy and how each can be linked to different research questions. The choice of strategy and its associated research design(s) and method(s) provides researchers with a foundation for their investigations. Being able to appraise the selected strategy critically, justifying why it is more suitable than others and knowing its limitations will provide the researcher with an insight into the very nature of the knowledge, the process of collection and its overall generalisability and value. By using a range of sport-related research examples throughout this chapter you should now be able to:

☑ make the important distinction between a research strategy, a research design and a research method;

☑ explain the differences between the seven main research strategies and be able to list a range of sport-related questions that can be answered using each;

☑ list and describe the range of research designs and be able to link each design to an appropriate strategy;

☑ identify the different research methods that can be used to obtain data.

Further reading

Creswell, JW (2013) *Research Design: Qualitative, Quantitative, and Mixed Methods Approaches*. 4th ed. Los Angeles, CA: SAGE Publications.

This well-structured text will provide the researcher with a plain-talking overview on designing, planning and evaluating research. Covering the main aspects relating to research design selection, this text should be read by all those wishing to gain a deeper understanding of research design.

Jensen, E and Laurie, C (2016) *Doing Real Research: A Practical Guide to Social Research*. London: SAGE Publications. Part One: pp1–47.

This text offers a further commentary on research design, offering the reader a range of illustrations to clarify the point. Easy to access, this additional text supports the chapter.

Walliman, N (2010) *Research Methods: The Basics*. London: Routledge. Part One: pp5–28.

This opening chapter of a research methods text provides contrasting perspectives on research design. Although more aligned with Chapter 1 of this book, it is worth reviewing your knowledge on research strategy by reading this well-written selection.

3

Systematic review research strategy

Learning objectives

By linking your understanding of sport in practice to sport-related research examples, this chapter is designed to help you:

- identify the value of a systematic literature review strategy and place it into context using a range of sport-related research examples;
- understand how systematic reviews are planned, conducted and reported;
- recognise the research methods that systematic reviews require.

Introduction

Systematic literature reviews in the field of sport, exercise and health have increasingly replaced traditional narrative reviews and literature commentaries as a way of summarising the growing body of research evidence. The use of such a research strategy among students is typically uncommon primarily due to a lack of familiarity with this research approach, the perceived complexity and the lack of procedural understanding. Undertaking a systematic review, however, can be immensely valuable and allow the researcher to develop a multitude of research and employability skills.

Systematic reviews attempt to bring the same level of rigour to reviewing research evidence as that which was applied in producing such evidence in the first place. The systematic review procedure differs from a traditional literature review as it explicitly focuses on an objective, replicable, systematic and comprehensive search of literature and research evidence, and includes a transparent audit trail of methods and processes. Systematic reviews should be based on a pre-determined protocol so that they can be replicated if necessary.

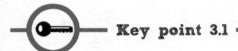 **Key point 3.1**

In the field of sport, exercise and health, the systematic review procedure has been widely used in assessing primary-research evidence. Areas that may be covered include:

- physical activity guidelines;

- health policy;

- exercise take-up and adherence in sport;

- leisure participation and policy;

- injury prevention strategies and models of best practice;

- physical performance assessment methods;

- effectiveness of exercise therapy;

- physical activity programmes for special populations;

- psychological perspectives of sport, health and exercise.

Examples of systematic reviews in the field of sport, health and physical activity are:

- Burton, E, Farrier, K, Lewin, G, et al. (2016) Motivators and barriers for older people participating in resistance training: a systematic review. *Journal of Aging and Physical Activity*, 1-41.

- Capostagno, B, Lambert, MI and Lamberts, RP (2016) A systematic review of submaximal cycle tests to predict, monitor, and optimize cycling performance. *International Journal of Sports Physiology and Performance*, 11 (6): 707-14.

- Colonetti, T, Grande, AJ, Milton, K, et al. (2017) Effects of whey protein supplement in the elderly submitted to resistance training: systematic review and meta-analysis. *International Journal of Food Sciences and Nutrition*, 68 (3): 257-64.

- Slimani, M, Chamari, K, Miarka, B, Del Vecchio, FB and Chéour, F (2016) Effects of plyometric training on physical fitness in team sport athletes: a systematic review. *Journal of Human Kinetics*, 53 (1): 231-47.

- Stojanović, E, Ristić, V, McMaster, DT and Milanović, Z (2016) Effect of plyometric training on vertical jump performance in female athletes: a systematic review and meta-analysis. *Sports Medicine*, 1-12.

- Truelove, S, Vanderloo, LM and Tucker, P (2016) Defining and measuring active play among young children: a systematic review. *Journal of Physical Activity and Health*, 1-32.

Systematic literature reviews: what are they?

Systematic reviews are literature-based research studies that can be used to answer a number of questions we may have generated throughout the course of our studies. In a systematic literature review, primary evidence from scientific studies is first located, then evaluated and finally synthesised using a strict scientific strategy, which must itself be reported in the review. Similar in approach to other research strategies detailed within preceding chapters, the systematic literature review research strategy follows a logical set of principles and procedures. Synthesising information that establishes facts in an unbiased manner ensures that new conclusions can be generalised. The ultimate aim is to provide new information that has value within the field of sport, health or exercise and may be used with confidence for decision-making, guideline creation, recommendation and best-practice models, policy development and evaluation.

 Research focus 3.1

In a systematic review conducted by Lanhers and colleagues (2017), the authors' objective was to review systematically the effect of creatine supplementation on upper-limb strength performance. Accessing a number of databases (i.e. PubMed, Cochrane Library, ScienceDirect and EMBASE), a number of key words were used (*creatine supplementation* and *performance*) to focus the search.

The authors' search was not restricted to specific years or languages, and all randomised controlled trial studies needed to include experimental designs that contained a control and placebo. Further selection criteria included studies with healthy males or females as participants, independently of age, imposing any creatine dose, extending over various intervention periods, with or without strength training and without a history of weight loss induced by a restrictive diet. Given the focus of the systematic review, a key inclusion criterion was a description of strength performance at baseline and following supplementation or placebo. Finally, the duration of exercise when performance was measured had to be no longer than 180 seconds.

The authors included 53 studies in their final analysis, concluding that creatine supplementation is an effective means of increasing upper-limb strength performance for exercise durations less than 3 minutes.

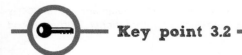

Key point 3.2

Academic literature review

A standardised review that summarises a number of different primary and secondary research studies, theories or ideas and draws conclusions to support, guide and justify the development of a research question or problem.

Systematic literature review

A review of evidence on a clearly formulated question that uses systematic and explicit research methods to identify, select and critically appraise relevant primary studies and to extract and analyse data from the studies included in the review.

Meta-analysis

A review of evidence that applies statistical techniques to combine the results of studies addressing the same question in a summary measure.

Why are systematic reviews important?

There are two main practical reasons for the importance of systematic reviews: first, the limitations of the traditional academic literature review that researchers undertake as part of a research project and, second, the added power brought by synthesising the results of a number of smaller studies into one. Traditionally, a literature review is a subjective assessment using a select group of materials to support an (often pre-determined) conclusion. In contrast, the systematic review attempts to be *systematic* in the identification and evaluation of materials, *objective* in its interpretation and *reproducible* in its conclusions. The term systematic in its most basic of definitions describes a system or approach concerned with classifications. Applying this to research, the term provides a basis by which research studies can be reviewed and classified by way of set criteria linked to the research question(s).

Key point 3.3

The most important activity during the planning of a systematic review is formulating the research question(s). Here are six types that may be addressed.

1. assessing the effect of an intervention on an outcome;
2. assessing the frequency or rate of a condition;

3. determining the performance of a diagnostic instrument, piece of technique or an assessment protocol;

4. identifying whether a condition or event can be predicted;

5. assessing economic/social value of an intervention, procedure or initiative;

6. identifying cost and/or risk factors.

Smaller primary studies we encounter in peer-reviewed journals (see Reflection point 3.1, later) may appear to have a rigorous research approach and practically significant or insignificant findings. However, when pooled together with other primary studies of a similar nature, the results from a number of smaller studies may lead to more conclusive generalisations both in confirming a beneficial outcome (e.g. sodium bicarbonate on short-term high-intensity exercise or the level of physical activity necessary to bring about health benefits) and in eliminating ones of negligible benefit (e.g. the impact of ginseng on endurance performance or the role of stretching on injury prevention). Politically, systematic reviews are also important for larger organisations such as the National Health Service (NHS) or Sport England (see Key point 3.1). For example, the NHS Research and Development Strategy concentrates on the successful utilisation of research findings from systematic reviews rather than the generation of original research which may often be unable to provide definitive answers.

Internationally, the stimulus for systematic reviews has come from the Cochrane Collaboration (www.cochrane.org), a worldwide group of subject and methodological specialists who aim to identify and synthesise primary research studies – normally randomised controlled trials in all aspects of health, but also including aspects of sport, leisure, physical activity and exercise.

Why perform a systematic review?

The key reasons for performing a systematic review include the ability to:

*   summarise existing evidence concerning a treatment or technology;

*   identify any gaps in current research in order to suggest areas for further investigation;

*   provide a framework/background in order to position new research activities appropriately;

*   inform policy and decision-making about an organisation and the delivery of a service (e.g. the health care service).

The advantage of the systematic literature review approach over the more academic literature review is that this well-defined research strategy makes it less likely that the results of the literature analysis are biased. This approach can also provide information about the effects of some phenomena across a wide range of settings and methods. However, the systematic review may require considerably more effort than a literature review, due to the much larger number of primary research studies that need to be evaluated in depth.

Research focus 3.2

In a systematic review conducted by Okubo et al. (2016), the authors' objectives were to examine the effects of stepping exercise interventions on fall risks and incidences in older people. The methods involved searching a number of comprehensive databases (e.g. PubMed, EMBASE, CINAHL, Cochrane) using a range of selected terms and words chosen based on the research design, training intervention, outcomes (falls and fall risk factors) and participant age. Inclusion criteria applied to those studies identified upon initial search included randomised controlled trials, clinical trials conducted in all settings and those studies that targeted ageing populations aged over 60. Studies investigating disease-specific samples were excluded.

Given that systematic review focused upon stepping exercises, studies with at least one treatment were included. In the context of this study stepping exercises were defined as *training of single or multiple volitional or relative steps in an upright position in response to an environment challenge*.

From extraction and synthesis of data the authors found 16 eligible studies. Analysis revealed that both reactive and volitional stepping exercise reduces falls among older adults by approximately 50%. The researchers concluded that findings might be due to improvements in reaction time, gait, balance and balance recovery, although not strength.

Key point 3.4

Systematic reviews meet several associated objectives that may not always be possible through the application of other research strategies (Murlow, 1994; Gough et al., 2017). They can benefit us by:

- reducing the quantity of data to a single review;
- helping us plan research, make suitable purchases, design research studies and create user guidelines;
- making efficient use of existing data;
- ensuring generalisability of large datasets;
- checking consistency (and inconsistency) across studies;
- quantifying outcomes statistically with meta-analysis;
- improving the precision of services, procedures, techniques or interventions;
- reducing bias that may occur from reviewing limited (selected) numbers of studies.

Features of systematic literature reviews

Systematic reviews seek to identify all relevant published and unpublished evidence and select studies or reports for inclusion based on an assessment of quality. By synthesising the findings from individual studies in an unbiased way, interpretation of the findings can provide a balanced and impartial summary. Features that distinguish a systematic literature review from a formal literature review include:

- a review protocol that specifies the research question and the methods that will be used to perform the review;

- a defined search strategy that aims to detect as much of the relevant literature as possible;

- documentation of the search strategy (i.e. within a methods section) so that the reader can assess the rigour, completeness and repeatability of the research process;

- explicit inclusion and exclusion criteria to assess each potential primary study;

- specific information that was obtained from each primary study.

The systematic review process

Guidelines which structure the review process can be placed into clear stages and offer the researcher a framework by which a timeline of activities and milestones can be developed. As with all research strategies, each stage is systematically and logically positioned to follow on from the last and prepare the researcher for the next. The following eight stages act as a starting point, which can be used as a progression-monitoring tool.

1. identification of the need for the review;

2. background research and problem specification;

3. requirements of the review protocol;

4. literature searching and study retrieval;

5. assessment of studies for inclusion on basis of relevance and design;

6. assessing the quality of the studies;

7. data extraction and synthesis;

8. report structure and review.

Briefly, as illustrated in Figure 3.1, developing a systematic review requires the logical completion of a number of steps.

1. *Defining a research question.* This requires a clear statement of the objectives of the review, intervention or phenomenon of interest, relevant groups and subpopulations (and sometimes the settings where the intervention is administered), the types of evidence or studies that will help answer the question, as well as appropriate outcomes. These details are rigorously used to select studies for inclusion in the review.

2. *Searching the literature.* Published and unpublished literature is carefully searched for the required studies relating to an intervention or activity (on the right groups, reporting the

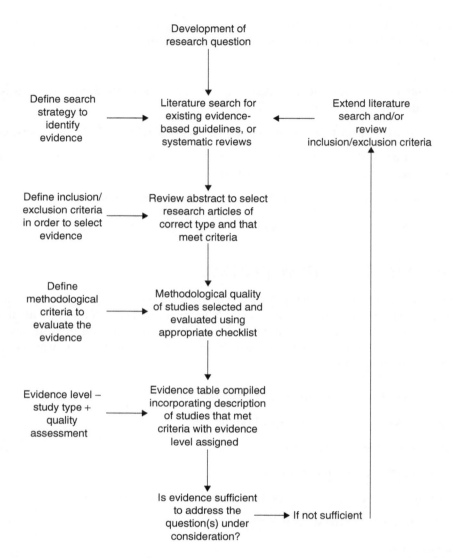

Figure 3.1 *The effective implementation of a systematic review research strategy requires a number of clearly defined stages to ensure objectivity, transparency, reliability and comprehensibility.*

right outcomes, and so on). For an unbiased assessment, this search must seek to cover all the literature, and not be limited to databases, websites or journals out of convenience. In reality, a designated number of databases should be searched using a standardised or customised search filter. Furthermore, the grey literature (material that is not formally published, such as institutional or technical reports, working papers, conference proceedings or other documents not normally subject to editorial control or peer review) is searched using specific databases or websites. Always asking the opinion of your supervisor on where appropriate data may be located is a gateway into a wide range of literature.

3. *Assessing the studies.* Once all possible studies have been identified, they should be assessed in the following ways. Each study needs to be assessed for eligibility against inclusion criteria. At this stage it is typical that all full text papers that meet the inclusion criteria are retrieved. Following a full-text selection stage, the remaining studies are assessed for methodological quality using a critical appraisal framework. Poor-quality studies are excluded but are usually discussed. Of the remaining studies, reported findings are extracted on to a data extraction form and a list of included studies is then created.

4. *Combining the results.* The findings from the individual studies are combined to produce an overall summary. This combination of findings is called evidence synthesis and the data are usually presented in tabular format.

5. *Placing the findings in context.* The findings from the collation studies need to be discussed to put them into a practical context. This will address issues such as the quality and spread of the included studies, the likely impact of bias, as well as the applicability of the findings.

Development of a review protocol

The review protocol is a written document that contains background information, the problem specification and the research strategy of the systematic review. The first stage of any review research is to develop (with tutor approval) the protocol structure. In essence, this is the design and methods of the systematic review. Remember that the value of a systematic literature review over other academic literature reviews is the fact that this approach should be unbiased, so documenting the research strategy ensures transparency and reproducibility. When you undertake this first step, any review should be free of researcher bias, therefore providing a more consistent and generalisable piece of research. For example, without a structured review protocol it is possible that the selection of individual studies or the analysis may be driven by research expectations and not a structured unbiased and systematic research method.

Components of a protocol include:

- background – the rationale for the study need;
- review questions – what exactly is to be answered as a consequence of the research;
- search strategy, including search terms and resources to be searched;
- study selection criteria and procedures – which studies will be included in, or excluded from, the systematic literature review. It is often wise to pilot the selection criteria on a subset of primary studies before starting the main project;
- study quality assessment checklists and procedures – the development of quality checklists will aid in the assessment of individual studies;
- data extraction strategy – this defines how the information required from each primary study will be obtained;
- synthesis of the extracted evidence – the purpose is to clarify whether or not formal statistical techniques could be applied to the data;
- project timetable – this should define and document the entire review schedule.

Generation of a search strategy

It is both necessary and important to the whole systematic review process to determine and follow a search strategy. The development of such a strategy is usually an iterative process: one attempt will rarely produce the final strategy. Strategies are built up from a series of preliminary searches, evaluation and discussion with your supervisor. The benefit of preliminary searches is that the researcher is able to identify previous systematic reviews and assess the volume of potentially relevant studies. Furthermore, undertaking trial searches using various combinations of search terms derived from the research question will allow the researcher to scope out the size of the study base and provide justification for the need for the study.

A list of key terms and words can be created by breaking down the research question. Take, for example, the studies outlined in Table 3.1, which describes the objectives of the systematic review, the databases used and the search terms and words applied. The researcher may also wish to consider synonyms, abbreviations or alternative spellings (i.e. American spelling) that can be used in the search as well. Some studies limit searches to one language, while others place no restrictions, thereby increasing the search field. Once some research studies have been accumulated, the search for references the authors have cited can act as a further method of finding related articles. Once a few connected articles have been located, these will soon link together. This approach will assist the researcher in obtaining a wide and varied range of research for the systematic review.

Table 3.1   An example of how the search terms and words should be linked to the research objectives

Author	Study objective	Databases used	Search terms and words used
Burton et al. (2016)	To identify motivators and barriers to older people participating in resistance training	CINAHL, PsycInfo Medline (ProQuest), PubMed, SPORTDiscus (ESBCO), SCOPUS (between 1975 and 2015)	Resist*, train*, strength train*, weight train*, progress*, barrier*, motivate*, facilitat*, belie*, deter*, old*, elder*, age*, aging*, community
Colonetti et al. (2017)	To evaluate the effectiveness of whey protein supplementation in the elderly undertaking resistance training	Medline, PubMed, EMBASE, Cochrane Controlled Trials Register (until 2015)	Resistance training, whey protein, elderly (synonyms were also used within the search strategy)
Truelove et al. (2016)	To examine the key concepts used to define and describe active play among young children	Medline, CINAHL, JSTOR, PubMed, SCOPUS, ScienceDirect, and ProQuest (until 2015)	Preschool child, preschool*, preschool-aged children, early childhood, early years, physical activity, locomotor activity, physical exertion, active play, active movement, outdoor play
Capostagno et al. (2016)	To investigate the development and use of submaximal cycling to predict and monitor cycling performance and training status	Medline and SCOPUS	Cycling, cyclist, cyclists, test, submaximal, sub-maximal, sub maximal, athletes, trained, well-trained, elite

Reflection point 3.1

Relevant research databases where sport science-related articles may be found:

- CINAHL (www.ebscohost.com)
- Google Scholar (www.scholar.google.com)
- Medline (www.ebscohost.com)
- PsycInfo (www.apa.org/psycinfo)
- PubMed (www.ncbi.nlm.nih.gov/pubmed)
- SMARTT (www.smarttjournal.com)
- SPORTDiscus (www.ebscohost.com)
- The Campbell Collaboration (www.campbellcollaboration.org)
- The Centre for Evidence-Based Medicine (www.cebm.net)
- The Cochrane Library (www.cochrane.org)
- The NHS Centre for Reviews and Dissemination (www.york.ac.uk/inst/crd)

It is also worth going on to journal websites as they often have access to search facilities through previously published abstracts. Simply type the journal name into a web-based search engine to find a range of freely accessible primary studies. Journals that may be of interest include:

- *Human Movement Studies;*
- *International Journal of Coaching and Sport Science;*
- *International Journal of Sport Physiology and Performance;*
- *International Journal of Sports Medicine;*
- *Journal of Aging and Physical Activity;*
- *Journal of Applied Biomechanics;*
- *Journal of Applied Sport Psychology;*
- *Journal of Electromyography and Kinesiology;*
- *Journal of Science and Medicine in Sport;*
- *Journal of Sport Management;*
- *Journal of Sports Sciences;*
- *Journal of Strength and Conditioning Research;*
- *Medicine and Science in Sport and Exercise;*
- *Psychology of Sport and Exercise;*
- *Sociology of Sport Journal;*
- *Sports Medicine.*

Primary study selection process

The study selection procedure is intended to identify those primary studies that provide direct evidence about the research question and will help the researcher to answer it successfully. In order to reduce the likelihood of bias, the criteria used should be decided upon during the protocol construction, although they may need to be refined after initial trial searches. As the inclusion criteria ultimately determine which studies will be included in the review, it is inevitable that the researcher will have a dilemma as to how broadly or narrowly to define the criteria. To offer some advice: it is far better to start broadly and be liberal, capturing a large range of studies. Following an initial broad review, refinement can then be made to narrow the searches to a more specified focus.

The selection of studies should be viewed as a multi-staged process and can be followed by referring to Figure 3.2.

As can be seen from Figure 3.2, the process of study selection should be viewed as multiple parts, interconnected in a logical manner. Thorough consideration of these parts and how they fit together will influence the overall quality of the review. Initially, selection criteria should be interpreted liberally, so that unless a study identified by electronic and hand searches can be clearly excluded based on title and abstract, a full copy should be obtained. The next step is to apply inclusion/exclusion criteria based on issues such as:

- journals;

- authors;

- settings;

- participants/volunteers;

- research design;

- sampling method;

- date of publication.

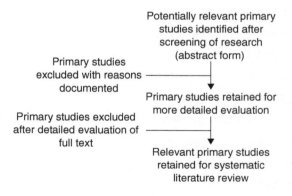

Figure 3.2   Flow diagram of study selection process.

As shown in Research focus 3.3, Brinkley and co-workers used a number of inclusion criteria in order to narrow down their initial database searches. By applying their search strategy to locate the primary articles and then implementing inclusion and exclusion criteria they were able to obtain 18 out of 50 primary studies that fulfilled their study requirements.

 **Research focus 3.3**

In a systematic review conducted by Brinkley et al. (2017), the authors aimed to synthesise the evidence on the benefits of team sports for individual (e.g. fitness and health), group (e.g. teamwork relations) and organisation health (e.g. sickness absence). Literature search inclusion was for the period between April 2000 and April 2015 and included a wide range of common search databases (EBSCO, PsycARTICLES, Medline, PubMed, SPORTDiscus, EMBASE, Web of Science and CENTRAL: Cochrane Central Register of Controlled Trials). Selected keywords used for searches included a series of combinations over 50 separate terms. Some included were workplace, work site, organisation, group, team, sport, physical activity, exercise, programme, RCT, longitudinal, survey, questionnaire, health, benefit, weight, cardiovascular. Specific inclusion criteria identified before data analysis were: (1) all studies met their definition of team sports; (2) studies used 'team sport' as a variable; and (3) at least one of the study outcomes was concerned with employees' well-being and health for the individual, group and organisation.

Initial data extraction resulted in a total return of over 56,767 articles. This was reduced to 50 after the removal of duplicates and abstract-only articles. Additional manual searching resulted in a further six articles. Close scrutiny of the 56 using the inclusion criteria resulted in a final sample of 18. This final sample of selected studies was reviewed based on: (1) the location, year and research design; (2) research objectives addressed; (3) demographics of participants/organisation; (4) type of team sports participated in; (5) methods of data collection and outcome measures; (6) methods of analysis; and (7) results/findings of the studies. The authors concluded that participation in a range of team sports has beneficial effects, not only to individual health and well-being, but also for the group and organisation as a whole.

Quality assessment checklists

The assessment of quality during the study selection process ensures that the primary research evaluated fulfils a critical level of acceptance into the systematic review. This is important to ensure that studies are of an acceptable scientific standard before proceeding with detailed data extraction. A quality checklist is quite simply a data collection instrument derived from a consideration of factors linked directly to the nature of the research question. Checklists provide an objective assessment of the primary research evidence, thereby reducing the amount of researcher bias during the data collection stages. As shown in Key point 3.4, a checklist is simply a range of questions that allow the researcher the chance to evaluate a paper's general suitability quickly. With a quick search of the internet, the researcher should be able to locate several more that can be adapted to suit the particular requirements of the research project. Each checklist will have some measure of suitability or quality, either expressed simply as 'yes' or 'no', or providing more depth as expressed on a scale for each item listed. Whatever the nature and structure of the checklist, pilot study evaluations should be conducted to ensure that it evaluates what the researcher intends to evaluate.

Learning activity 3.1

There are a number of reasons why a quality checklist is important when undertaking a systematic review. Try and consider what these are and why assessment of quality is important. How may it benefit the systematic review process and the applicability of the findings?

It is important that researchers not only define the quality checklist in the study protocol but also explain how the data generated from the checklist will be used. Such data can be used in two different ways, so clarity at this stage is necessary. One way data can be used is to construct detailed inclusion/exclusion criteria. Data collected prior to the main project, such as during a pilot study, can be obtained from a separate checklist to assist the researcher in deciding which primary studies will be included within the main project. The second way is to assist analysis and synthesis. In this case the data are used to identify subsets of the primary study to assess whether differences in the quality of the primary research are associated with the outcomes reported.

It is often the case that primary research studies are very limited in the amount of detail presented. As many journals place word limits on research submissions, the level of detail needed for effective quality assessment may not be reported. This means that it is not always possible to determine the quality of a primary research study. It is very tempting to assume aspects of the reported study, such as sample type, design issues and method procedures, even though they have not been reported. It is also tempting to assume that, because something wasn't reported, it wasn't done. This assumption may be incorrect, so it is the prerogative of the researcher to obtain as much information as possible. Most peer-reviewed articles published in sport-related journals include author contact details. It may be the case that additional correspondence is required to clarify and obtain further detail. The role of the researcher is to construct and apply a quality checklist that addresses methodological quality and not reporting quality.

Key point 3.5

This assessment should be completed for each study included and then the assessments should be aggregated in a results section and also discussion/conclusions for each section. Overall review summaries and any discussion of the limitations of the review should also include some summary of the aggregated information as well as transparent discussion of the limitations of this tool. Where studies give no or little information, tick 'unclear'. It is not usually good practice to make assumptions. If this is the case for significant numbers of studies then this will be a major limitation of the review.

Study no. / title / authors

No.: _____

Title: _____

Author(s): _____

Source: _____

Relevance assessment

Is the study laboratory-based? Y/N/where? _____

Is the field of the study relevant to the research topic? Y/N/unclear _____

_____

Name field, i.e. primary/secondary/other (specify) _____

_____

_____

Are the aims of the study relevant to one of the questions within the research topic? Y/N/unclear

_____

Quality appraisal

Is the study reporting a process of structured inquiry? Y/N/unclear _____

_____

_____

If yes, is it transparent and replicable? Y/N/unclear _____

_____

_____

Is the study design appropriate to answering the question? Y/N/unclear _____

_____

If not structured inquiry, tick which applies:

Discussion/opinion piece ❏ Non-systematic secondary review/analysis ❏ Other ❏ Please specify

_____

Ethical issues

Does the study report whether informed consent to participate was obtained from participants? Y/N/
unclear _____

Does the study report whether representatives of the target population were involved in the design/
steering of the study? Y/N/unclear _____

Describe any other ethical problems with the design or conduct of the study. _____

_____

_____

_____

Search documentation (search process)

The process of performing a systematic literature review must be transparent and reliable. This is achieved by understanding the research methods needed in undertaking the review. The researcher must ensure that all primary studies accessed are documented in sufficient detail within the research report so that readers are able to assess the thoroughness of the search. Table 3.2 provides

Table 3.2   Documenting each search ensures transparency and reliability in the research methods used

Data source	What needs to be documented?
Electronic database/digital library	• Name of database • Search strategy for the database (words used, number of articles found) • Date of search • Years covered by search (include rationale for choice)
Journal hand searches	• Name of journal • Year searched • Any issues/volume not searched (reasons provided)
Conference proceedings	• Title of proceedings • Name of conference (if different) • Journal name (if published as part of a journal)
Unpublished research sources	• Research group/researchers contacted (name, contact details) • Research websites searched (date, URL, detail provided)
Other sources	• Date searched/contacted • Website, publication date, location • Any specific conditioning pertaining to the search

a structured template to follow. In such documentation, the researcher should specify the rationale for the selection of the electronic databases, journals, conference proceedings or other data sources to be searched.

For example, if the researcher wished to use a database, a record of the database name, search words used, date of search and years covered by the search (with justification) would need to be clearly documented. For example, if researchers were interested in finding primary research studies focusing on golf fitness, they might use the database SPORTDiscus, using the terms 'golf', 'fitness', 'exercise' and 'physical activity' within the search; they might have performed it on 9 August 2017 and the search covered the years 1990–2017. The rationale for covering these years might have been that no golf-related research in fitness existed before 1990. Making the process transparent by documenting it increases the reliability of the strategy.

Data extraction from primary studies

The objective of effective data extraction from the primary studies included is to obtain the required information accurately that enables the research question to be answered. This is often a straightforward process once a data extraction form is in place. The data extraction form must be designed in such a way to collect all information needed to address the review questions and the study quality criteria. In most cases, data extraction will define a set of numerical values that should be extracted for each study (e.g. number of participants, research design and methods used, type of intervention, treatment size and effect). Such numerical data are important in any attempt to summarise the results of a set of primary studies and are a prerequisite for larger meta-analysis studies that apply techniques to evaluate primary studies statistically.

Reflection point 3.2

Content or literature analysis refers to any technique and associated procedure that seeks to organise written, audio and/or visual information into categories and themes related to the central questions of the study. The major feature of the content analysis method is objective, system-atic and quantifiable analysis of the overt content of documents (i.e. primary research studies). Content analysis attempts to provide a solution to establishing meaning by rigorous specifica-tion of the frequency, similarity and differences within text that can be extended to the content of research studies. Further to quantification, content analysis provides the researcher with qualita-tive synthesis that can establish concepts, themes and frameworks bound within the content of the material analysed.

There is no one correct way of developing a data extraction form. However, most forms are often similar in structure and can be adapted from one review to another, taking due account of the dif-ferences in the categories being used. Simply typing in 'extraction form' or 'extraction template' into web-based search engines will reveal a number that can be viewed and adapted to suit the researcher's needs.

Key point 3.6

Creating an extraction template within a spreadsheet is one of the simplest ways of ensuring all the data are kept together and can be easily reviewed and compared. If you assign rows to the categories you wish to use or information you want to know from the studies, and columns to the studies themselves, you can begin the process of data extraction fast and effectively.

Keep all data in one easily referenced sheet, with included and excluded studies documented on different worksheets. In this way, the spreadsheet can act as a historical record of decisions that you take during the review process. The added benefit of using spreadsheets is that they can be e-mailed to your supervisor for quick review and comment without having to spend time examining every single form that has been completed. Both you and your supervisor will save time and increase productivity.

The data extraction form should be structured logically to help data entry. With most research method instruments, it is often best to pilot test them first. This may help identify data that are not needed or missing, and confusion around coding categories can be clarified. Extraction and record information from each study can then be uniformly organised and managed.

Make sure the form also contains general pieces of information such as the date of extraction, who did it, if it was someone different, the bibliographic details of each study and the source where the information came from. It is also worthwhile leaving additional space for writing general notes about the study to ensure that questions and reminders can be captured in a systematic way during the analysis.

Synthesis of extracted data

Data synthesis simply involves collating and summarising the results of the primary studies included from the data extraction form(s). Synthesis of the data can be both non-numerical and descriptive (qualitative) and/or numerical (quantitative). The process of carrying out data synthesis should ensure that data are presented in a succinct manner. Presented by way of tables, each should be structured to highlight the similarities and differences between the included studies. An evidence table, as can be found within the research articles outlined within this chapter, provides a very clear and effective way to present data extracted from a range of primary studies that meet the inclusion criteria. From a critical perspective, it should be possible to assess qualitatively the reasons for differences between studies. The key elements in the approach to data synthesis may include the following characteristics:

- population;

- interventions;

- settings of research;

- environmental, social and cultural factors that may influence compliance;

- nature of outcomes measures used, their relative importance and robustness;

- sample size for each study (may also include intervention group size, control group size, male:female ratio).

Structuring the contents of a systematic review

Preparation of the systematic review report requires as much care and attention as the rest of the research process. Being able to write the report in a concise manner is an integral part of a systematic review. Clear structure and content will ensure the reader is able to judge the validity of the research and evaluate the scientific rigour of the research methods used.

As documented in Table 3.3, the report structure for a systematic review is really no different to that of any other research study. As would be expected, no lengthy literature review is needed, only a short account of the background to the research question. The systematic review must contain a section that reports the research strategy, namely the design and methods. It is mainly this aspect that distinguishes it from a traditional literature review, so it is vital that the methods are described in sections similar to that found within the review protocol. Detail of the search process

Table 3.3   Understanding the content and structure of a systematic review will help you to identify the differences when compared to a traditional literature review

Section	Subsection	Comment
Title		Short, informative and based on the question being asked. It is important to state that the study is a systematic review
Abstract	<ul><li>Context</li><li>Aims/objectives</li><li>Research strategy</li><li>Findings</li><li>Conclusions</li></ul>	A structured summary is important in any research project and permits the reader to assess quickly the quality, relevance and generality of the systematic review
Background		Description of the problem being investigated with an indication why the systematic review is needed. Specific statements that clearly identify each review question
Review questions Review strategy (include design and method)	<ul><li>Data search strategy</li><li>Study selection</li><li>Study quality</li><li>Assessment</li><li>Data extraction</li><li>Data analysis</li></ul>	This should be based on the research protocol and include detail regarding the overall strategy applied. This will include information about the type of design and the methods of data collection
Included and excluded studies		A clear representation of the criteria used, the point at which studies were excluded and a detailed coverage of all those included/excluded should be apparent
Findings		Numerical results can be presented as tables and graphs (e.g. similarities, differences, frequency of agreement) Non-numerical results can be presented as summaries of each paper included in a tabular form
Discussion	<ul><li>Principal findings</li><li>Strengths and weaknesses</li><li>Meaning of findings</li><li>Recommendations</li></ul>	Discuss the evidence considering the bias associated with systematic reviews. Make it clear to what level the findings imply causality by discussing the level of evidence. What are the implications of the review for practitioners/researchers?
Conclusion		Summarise the content referring specifically back to the initial research questions. Were these answered? To what extent? Future directions?

and strategies, inclusion and exclusion criteria, assessments of relevance and quality of primary studies, data extraction and synthesis techniques should be included. The majority of the report will be found in the discussion where the principal findings will be discussed, along with their meaning and linked recommendations.

Chapter review

In this chapter it has been shown that the rigorous and extensive search criteria adopted in the systematic review procedure, alongside the comprehensiveness and quality control ensured by both the researcher and the review process itself, mean that it is a highly relevant and appropriate research strategy. Used to assess the evidence base objectively and transparently in relation to the existing body of research evidence, the systematic review strategy provides a research approach that develops not only important research skills linked to literature searching and evaluation, but also a gateway to the growing body of scientific evidence that now exists in the field of sport. By using a range of sport-related research examples throughout this chapter you should now be able to:

☑ distinguish between a systematic literature review and more traditional literature review;

☑ identify when and why a systematic literature review strategy may be used to answer sport-related research questions;

☑ appreciate the logical set of guidelines that can be applied to plan, conduct and report a systematic review;

☑ understand the value of a review protocol and how its structured framework aids effective data collection;

☑ acknowledge the research methods used within this approach to ensure objectivity, transparency and reliability.

Further reading

Boland, A, Cherry, M and Dickson, R (Eds) (2013) *Doing a Systematic Review: A Student's Guide*. London: SAGE Publications.

Gough, D, Oliver, S and Thomas, J (2017) *An Introduction to Systematic Reviews*. 2nd ed. London: SAGE Publications.

Petticrew, M and Roberts, H (2005) *Systematic Reviews in the Social Sciences: A Practical Guide*. Chichester: Wiley Blackwell.

These books are worthwhile additions to anyone's library, providing a practically oriented explanation of the systematic review process. They are clearly presented and well structured; developing a search strategy will be easier once you have read them.

Centre for Reviews and Dissemination (2009) *Systematic Reviews: Guidelines for Undertaking Reviews in Healthcare*. York: York Publishing Services. Available online at: www.york.ac.uk/inst/crd/system atic_reviews_book.htm.

This free online resource from the University of York is indispensable to students wishing to undertake a systematic review as part of their studies. Packed full of valuable information, each section logically explains the process in detail, providing a detailed examination of the review protocol design.

4

Experimental research strategy

By identifying research situations for which an experimental research strategy would be applied, this chapter is designed to help you:

- grasp the basic concepts that underpin an experimental research strategy and identify the relative merits of this approach;
- identify how an experimental type and design impact on the validity of research findings;
- link research design with appropriate data collection and analysis techniques.

Introduction

For the researcher interested in sporting behaviour and its causes, an experimental research strategy presents an ideal approach. Through observation of the sporting world around us, many research ideas emerge that lend themselves to experiments. By applying the scientific method of inquiry, the experimental strategy enables the researcher to discover the effects of presumed causes. What causes an increase in maximal oxygen uptake after training? Or, what is the effect of topspin on a tennis ball? The key feature of experiments is that, through the deliberate alteration of something, the researcher is able to see what happens to something else. This is something people do all the time, for example, going to the gym to get fitter. The experimental approach, however, differs from this causal relationship, as it makes a deliberate attempt to make observations free from bias.

The purpose of this chapter is to provide clear explanation as to when and how the experimental research strategy should be applied to answer particular research questions. An outline of the key features of the experimental strategy will establish a framework by which the researcher can identify different experimental types and designs. Through the understanding of experimental research methods, appropriate data collection and analysis techniques can form part of the overall strategy. Although it is not the intention of this chapter to explore statistical techniques relevant to experimental research, an overview of how design and suitable statistical techniques link together will be covered. By the end of the chapter you should have grasped a step-by-step approach to experimental research.

The importance of experimentation in sport research

Through the study and practice of sport, problems emerge that necessitate an experimental research approach in order to find a solution. As covered in Chapter 1, selecting the most suitable research strategy depends heavily on the nature of the research question. The experimental research strategy is a quantitative approach designed to discover the effect of presumed causes. By the very nature of deductive research, the application of the scientific method of inquiry attempts to test theory by subjecting it to different conditions. Experiments in sport provide the researcher with that very opportunity.

Examination of sporting behaviour and attempts to discover the underpinning causes to the effects observed enable the researcher to test theories, such as how we fatigue during exercise, or how we experience peak flow during performance. Aside from the theoretical testing that is an inherent part of experimental research, a practical, more applied perspective also has an important place within sport-related experiments. By discovering the causes of improved aerobic fitness, increased muscle mass or reduced concentration, for example, new training approaches, enhanced performance tools, more specific exercise guidelines or additional assessment strategies may be generated.

 **Key point 4.1**

Experimental research can be defined as research that attempts to identify cause-and-effect relationships between phenomena.

Establishing causality through experiments

One of the key characteristics of the experimental research strategy is that of cause and effect. Quite simply, the overall purpose of any experiment the researcher conducts is to determine with as much confidence as possible what may have caused an effect. The effect may be an increase in strength, a lowering of heart rate, a quickening of reaction or a slowing of pace. Whatever the effect happens to be, the experimental strategy attempts to determine what the cause was by deliberately altering one thing (e.g. training, recovery, caffeine consumption or intensity). By altering only one thing (i.e. variable), while trying to keep all other things (variables) constant, the researcher can begin to gain confidence that if an effect is seen it is more likely to be due to the thing that was altered. In comparison to qualitative research approaches, covered in later chapters, tightly controlled experiments are the only means by which cause and effect can be established.

It has already been noted that an experimental approach differs from a non-experimental one in that the researcher can establish cause and effect by deliberately altering or manipulating variables, while trying to keep all other variables constant or controlled. Such cause can be thought of as the independent variable and the effect the dependent variable. Experiments require the precise control of all variables except the independent variable.

Characteristics of the experimental approach

The experimental research strategy has a number of characteristics that distinguish it from other research strategies. In the attempt to discover the causation between phenomena, a number of conditions need to be met. These include control, randomisation and manipulation.

Experimental control

The concept of control within the experimental approach can take many different forms and have different usages within this methodological approach. Control refers to eliminating the influence of any extraneous factors or variables that could affect observations made on the outcome (the dependent variable). The purpose of control is to enable the experimenter to isolate the one key variable which has been selected in order to observe its effect on some other variable. Control within an experiment, therefore, allows the researcher to conclude that it is the cause, and nothing else, which is influencing the effect.

Being able to control external variables apart from the one under investigation (the independent variable) will provide confidence that change to the outcome variable was not down to other variables. For the researcher wishing to conduct experimental studies, control may take the form of:

- being in total control of the events that the participants experience;

- controlling the groups so that one does not experience the independent variable;

- controlling the variables so that the consequences of the independent variable can be clearly seen separated from other factors.

Key point 4.2

'Cause and effect' refers to the link between one event (called the cause, A) and another event (called the effect, B), which is a direct consequence (the result) of the first (the cause). When determining a cause-and-effect link between two events, probability testing, that is to say, statistical tests, allow for a degree of certainty to be attained. This degree of certainty, or probability score (P), provides the researcher with an indication that the effect is a consequence of the cause; so therefore A probabilistically causes B if A's occurrence increases the probability of B.

Randomisation

Randomisation within the experimental research strategy eliminates the influence of extraneous variables acting on one group and not on another. Randomly assigning participants to different groups or treatments provides the researcher with a degree of confidence that each group will be representative of the population from which it was drawn. It therefore has implications for generalising results of the experiment back to the population. Random assignment provides assurance that the extraneous variables are controlled and the bias across groups reduced.

Consider an experiment in which half the participants are in an exercise condition and the other half are in a no-exercise condition. Suppose that the participants are also different in a third factor, such as annual income. If the researcher wished to investigate the causal relationship between exercise and anxiety, for example, randomly assigning participants into the conditions would eliminate the influence of income differences between the conditions. Not randomly assigning participants to groups means that annual income may have an impact on anxiety, which could mask any causal relationship between exercise and anxiety. Ensuring that participants are assigned to different groups in a random way increases the internal validity of the experiment.

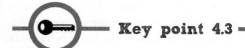

Key point 4.3

One of the easiest ways to assign participants randomly to groups is by allocating a number to each one, so say 1-20, and then asking a friend to call out a number between 1 and 20. You could either place the first ten numbers called into one group and the next ten numbers to another, or every other number. Although basic, this provides a quick and effective way of randomly assigning participants into your groups.

Experimental manipulation

If you create change within a controlled setting and then observe the resulting effect, you may be able to establish what the true cause of the change was. The implication of change in this context therefore is extremely important and distinguishes the experimental approach from other research strategies. This approach deliberately introduces change, which forms the core of the experiment, and such change is termed manipulation. Consider the flight of a football for one moment. The flight of the ball off the boot can make a number of different shapes, which are all caused by single or, more likely, multiple factors. These include the design of the boot, the boot material, the location of impact, the angle of impact and the speed of impact.

From an experimental perspective, the researcher may start by changing or manipulating these in isolation, keeping all other factors constant to see how they alter ball flight. Changing the material, for example, from leather to a rubberised compound may cause less ball spin off the boot and therefore reduce slice. Alternatively, changing the location of impact on the boot through relocation of the laces, for example, may cause the ball to travel faster for the same impact speed. Through manipulation and control, the researcher can begin to identify what causes alterations and therefore develop new approaches.

If researchers wished to explore the impact of agility-specific drills on a group of junior hockey players, they could apply manipulation to their study. The researchers could manipulate the type of practice (e.g. agility versus non-agility), the group (e.g. boys versus girls), or both. If, however, they were interested in how different types of music alter 5k running performance in elite runners they could manipulate the type of music (e.g. fast versus slow) that the runners listen to. Manipulation in this context refers to the purposeful change in one variable so that the effect on one or more other variables can be observed. This process allows the researcher the opportunity to begin testing theories and existing models, make improvements and predict future events or occurrences. With research questions wishing to determine whether any meaningful change exists between groups, conditions and/or across periods of time, the manipulation of one factor or variable can provide the researcher with an opportunity to determine the extent of an effect.

 Reflection point 4.1

Validity is an important issue when it comes to applying the experimental approach to research. The two types that probably have the most impact on your research at this stage of your understanding are internal and external validity. Table 4.1 gives explanations and some practical examples that will help your comprehension. These will be mentioned again throughout the chapter so it is important you understand what they mean and how they can impact on your research findings.

Another way to view manipulation within the experimental approach is through the deliberate administration of a treatment to a group in order to observe the response. The word treatment basically refers to something that the researcher imposes on to participants. For example, researchers may administer a co-ordination practice drill to one group and no practice drill to another to see how the drill changes the response – the junior players' hockey performance. Or they may administer a training programme, a sport drink or a different piece of sports equipment to a group. The main aim therefore is to attempt to keep all aspects of the situation constant except one; that being

Table 4.1   The meanings and applications of validity

Validity type	Description	Example
Internal validity	Provides the researcher with a level of confidence that the independent variable caused a change in the dependent variable	Julie conducted a laboratory experiment to investigate the impact of sound on reaction time. She ensured that as many factors as possible were kept constant for all assessments apart from the one she was interested in – sound. In this instance Julie had a *high level of internal validity* as any change in reaction time would be a consequence of the type of sound and no other factor
External validity	Concerns the degree to which the conclusions in the research study would hold for other persons in other places and at other times	Henry conducted a field-based experiment to investigate the impact of membership promotion type on recruiting new gym goers. He wished to ensure that his study was set in as natural an environment as possible so that he could generalise his findings. He recognised that due to the research setting and the *high degree of external validity* he was unable to control for many factors and this would lower his confidence in concluding that the promotional type caused change in new gym members

To find out more about the meaning and application of validity within the experimental strategy a number of resources can be consulted. Research Methods Knowledge Base (2006) offers a no-nonsense explanation regarding validity in research. Alternatively, for a more thorough grounding, the textbook of Christensen et al. (2014) *Research Methods, Design, and Analysis* and Cozby and Bates's textbook, *Methods in Behavior Research* (2012) offer a clear overview of the definition and practical implications of validity when the experimental strategy is applied.

the one thing the researcher wishes to investigate or change (the effect the treatment has on a group of objects or participants). This approach allows the researcher, in a very controlled way, to establish whether a meaningful effect caused by the treatment impacts on those involved in the research.

 Learning activity 4.1

Read through each of the research projects (below) devised by students studying courses relating to sport and exercise science. Try and identify the independent variable and dependent variable for each study by highlighting each in a different colour. *Remember, the independent variable is what you wish to manipulate or change and the dependent variable is what you will be measuring.*

- Two groups (basketball vs. volleyball) completed a standing vertical jump to assess vertical distance (in metres) jumped.

- Three groups of pistol shooters (novice, intermediate and expert) were assessed for reaction time (milliseconds) during a manual tracking task.

- One group of darts players were assessed for accuracy (millimetres) before, during and after ingestion of caffeine.

- Four groups of school children (ages 4–6, 7–9, 10–12, 13–15 years) completed three tests (trials 1, 2 and 3) to assess peak heart rate (beats·min⁻¹) recorded during the hop, skip and jump game.

- Two groups of postgraduate sport science students completed seven 1.5-mile runs and had their rating of perceived exertion recorded immediately before, mid-way and on completion of each run.

- One group of well-trained cyclists completed five indoor 40-km cycling time trials during which power output (watts) was recorded at 10-km intervals.

- Six groups of second-year sport science students completed four tests during which motivation to work was assessed before and after hypnosis.

- One group of MSc sport coaching students completed three statistics exams with anxiety assessed before, 30 minutes during and 1 hour after each test.

Types of research experiment

For researchers undertaking experiments, it is a necessary part of the strategy to decide upon an experimental approach that will match the objectives of the research study. This means that they need to develop a plan that includes the research design type and the data collection and analysis methods. Before we discuss the different research designs, it is worth considering the three types of experiments and how they can be linked to sport research. The three are: true, quasi- and natural experiments.

True experiments

So far in this chapter we have focused on an experimental type that permits the researcher to control, in principle, all extraneous factors and variables except one – the one that is manipulated. Such an experimental approach is known as a true experiment and is considered the strongest approach of all experimental types. Providing a high degree of internal validity, the true experiment provides the researcher with the greatest level of confidence that any change observed in the dependent variable is a consequence of the independent variable and nothing else. In order to ensure internal validity, therefore, true experiments tend to occur in artificial settings, such as the sport and exercise science laboratory. However, the attempt to attain a high degree of internal validity will impact on the external validity of the study. This means that a true experiment may not reflect a real-life situation; the artificial environment distorts the real-life nature of observations.

The ability to move experiments outside the laboratory (e.g. on to the football pitch or within a school playground) allows for a more natural setting (field experiment). When the external validity of the study is increased, the findings may have more ecological significance, but control of many extraneous factors may not be possible. Such an approach can still be referred to as a true experiment but may be less ideal. As with a controlled laboratory experiment, the independent variable is still deliberately manipulated. However, it is not possible to have such tight control over all variables. If researchers wished to conduct a study in a natural setting, therefore, they must be aware of the external factors that, in addition to the independent variable, could change the dependent variable. The researcher must decide whether the benefit of increasing external validity, by setting the research in a more natural environment, outweighs the reduction in internal validity.

Research focus 4.1

In a study by Bloms et al. (2016), a true experimental approach was selected to examine the effects of caffeine ingestion on squat jump height and jump execution in collegiate athletes. The study deployed a single-blind, randomised, cross-over design, where athletes consumed either caffeine (5 mg·kg⁻¹) or a placebo. In this study the independent variable was the condition to which the athletes were exposed (supplement vs. placebo) whilst the dependent variable (what was measured) was their performance (peak force and height) produced during three vertical and countermovement jumps.

In total, 25 athletes, aged between 18 and 23 years, were randomly assigned to one of the two conditions. Of all the athletes, 16 were not regular consumers of caffeine, whilst nine of the participants consumed caffeine on a regular basis in the form of coffee, energy drinks or pre-workout supplements. The treatments (either caffeine or placebo condition) were provided to the athletes 60 minutes before their jump assessments. Once they had completed their jumps, a period of 1 week passed, following which all athletes returned to the testing facilities and the other treatment was given to them (cross-over design). They then repeated the jump assessments as they had done on their first visit.

The results of the study indicated that, when exposed to a caffeine dose equivalent to 5 mg·kg⁻¹ body weight, jump parameters significantly increased compared to the placebo condition. The execution of the squat and countermovement jump following the experimental treatment enhanced both height and execution of jumping.

Quasi-experiments

There are occasions when it is not possible to control, in principle, the influence of all extraneous variables as in the true experiment. Such an experimental type is known as a quasi-experiment. As with the true experimental type described above, this approach allows the researcher to examine the impact of an independent variable on a dependent variable, but causal inference is much more difficult. In most research instances, the use of a quasi-experimental approach results from the inability or lack of need to assign participants randomly into groups. This may be the case, for example, when the researcher wishes to compare particular groups (e.g. one school class against another).

Research focus 4.2

In a study by Larsen and colleagues (2016), a quasi-experimental approach was taken to assess the feasibility of standardising an exercise prescription for cognitive improvement, without reducing the fitness benefits of exercise. This between-group design started with a non-randomised sample of 49 females (mean age 48 years) who self-allocated themselves to one of three groups based on their own class time preferences. The three independent groups (independent variables) were treadmill-based walking, floor/step aerobics or stretching classes that took place over a period of 7 weeks. For this approach a number of dependents were measured. These included a cognitive test battery to measure executive function, attention, processing speed and a learning test (memory and recall). In addition, a single-stage submaximal treadmill walking assessment was used to measure cardiorespiratory fitness (maximal oxygen consumption). All participants completed these assessments at pre-intervention, mid-point during the intervention and following completion of the classes. Throughout the course of the experiment, the number of participants reduced from 49 to 27 by the post-exercise class assessment (aerobics = 8; treadmill = 9; stretching = 10).

Findings revealed that those participants who self-selected the floor/step aerobics class may experience greater cognitive gains, whilst still finding cardiorespiratory fitness benefits. Given that groups were determined based on class time preference, rather than a randomised allocation, this quasi-experimental approach may have resulted in bias towards a particular exercise intervention.

Natural experiments

A third type is known as a natural experiment and involves naturally occurring events rather than naturally occurring groups. This means that the researcher does not manipulate the independent variable like the true experiment; rather, a deliberate change is introduced that occurs naturally within the research setting for which the researcher is not responsible. Natural experiments, by their very nature, have low internal validity due to the inability of the researcher to control extraneous factors during the study. Because of this, the results of natural experiments are often difficult to generalise back to the population from which the study sample was drawn.

 Research focus 4.3

In a study by Grandjean et al. (2002), a natural experimental approach was taken to examine an unintended 'experiment' on world-class gymnasts at the 2000 Olympics. During the women's all-around final, the vault apparatus was initially set 5 centimetres too low, potentially undermining the athletes' self-confidence. The 18 gymnasts who vaulted early in the competition became an unknowing experimental group. The remaining 18 vaulted after the error was corrected, becoming a randomised control group. For this between-group pre–post-test design there was only one independent variable: group. Both groups had pre-test scores (from preliminary rounds) and post-test scores (from the final) on each of the four apparatuses: vault, bars, beam and floor. From analysis of the data it is clear that the vault error had little, if any, effect on later performances or on the final standings. The researchers concluded that elite athletes in a closed-skill sport apparently learn to concentrate so well that most can recover from a mishap and refocus successfully for the next effort.

 Learning activity 4.2

On reviewing the previous section you should now be more aware of how each experimental type has both advantages and disadvantages when it comes to considering the internal and external validity of the research. Now read carefully the studies outlined below and attempt to allocate the most appropriate

(Continued)

(Continued)

experimental type to each. Remember that there may be more than one answer, so consider how the chosen experimental type and the associated degree of validity may impact on the accuracy of any inferences made as well as the applicability of the findings.

Study one

What does it take to win the London Marathon? An examination of champions' performance times over the last ten events.

Experimental type: _____

Study two

The effectiveness of seated leg exercises on lower-limb anterior cruciate ligament recovery time.

Experimental type: _____

Study three

The impact of ankle strapping on medial and lateral heel stability during the pedal cycle.

Experimental type: _____

Study four

The effect of multi-lateral versus unilateral reverse running on blood lactate recovery curves.

Experimental type: _____

Designing the experiment

When considering the design of an experiment it is important for researchers to keep in mind the impact of diminished internal validity on the ability to support the conclusion that the independent and dependent variables were causally linked. If the degree of internal validity within the selected design is threatened, that's to say, it is low, then it is difficult to be confident that the independent variable caused any change in the dependent variable. Based on this premise, the researcher needs to be aware that the selected research design, based on the research question, can have a significant impact on the conclusions and inferences made.

Simple quasi-experimental designs

Probably the simplest experimental design is the *one-group post-test design*. This is considered quasi-experimental as it lacks an important element of a true experiment: a control or comparison group. For this approach the dependent variable is measured once in a single group (i.e. within-group) following a treatment (Figure 4.1). Consider a single group being given a pharmacological supplement over the course of 6 weeks and then having their exercise ability assessed. Although some valuable

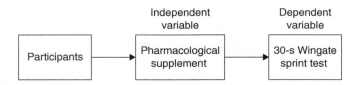

Figure 4.1   A single one-group post-test quasi-experimental design.

scientific data are produced, the omission of a pre-test before the treatment means that it is very difficult to know if the treatment changed the participants' ability or the change was a consequence of other extraneous factors not controlled for. Therefore, without a control group, it would be hard to say whether the same effects would have happened in the absence of the treatment. As a consequence, the internal validity associated with such a design is considered very low.

Advancing the first design further, it is sometimes the case that the researcher wishes to evaluate change in a dependent variable within the same group across two occasions (Figure 4.2). By measuring participants before and after the introduction of a treatment a comparison can be obtained. This type of within-group approach is aptly named the *one-group pre–post-test design* and can be referred to as a repeated-measures design. This approach, although not featuring a control group, is still considered quasi-experimental, but internal validity is increased as the researcher now has a pre-test comparison to make observations against. Let's suppose the researcher wanted to investigate whether a 4-week plyometric strength-training programme increased the ability to throw a shot put from athletes' dominant side. A group of participants would be selected and they would complete the pre-test throw, then they would be given the plyometric training programme to complete. After the 4 weeks their performance would be reassessed (i.e. post-test).

Unlike the previous two quasi-experimental designs, the non-equivalent control group design employs a separate control group (i.e. between-group or independent group design), but the participants in the two conditions are not equivalent (Figure 4.3). Take the example of a sports nutritionist

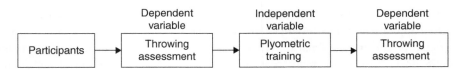

Figure 4.2   An illustration of a within-group pre–post-test design.

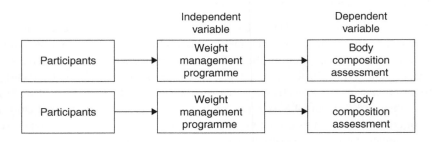

Figure 4.3   A between-group non-equivalent control group design with one independent variable (i.e. weight management programme).

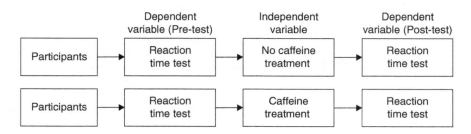

Figure 4.4 A between-group non-equivalent control group pre–post-test design with two independent variables (i.e. group and treatment condition).

who wanted to investigate the impact of a dietary programme on weight management. All overweight members of a local health club, as recorded on their personal record sheets, were identified and recruited to the study. Those members who actively volunteered became the experimental group and those who did not, by default, became the control group. Although this approach provided a control group for comparison, because of the selection differences between groups, problems arose because those who volunteered may have differed in some important way from those who did not. This design would therefore make it difficult to know whether any change in the dependent variable was a consequence of the independent variable or not.

To some extent, the design presented in Figure 4.3 can be extended to incorporate a pre–post-test component (Figure 4.4). Although an extremely useful quasi-experimental design, this is still not as robust as a true experiment, as the participants have not been randomly assigned, therefore introducing bias. As illustrated in Figure 4.4, although the change in the dependent variable can be assessed across each group, the groups may, by way of selection process, have characteristics that impact on that change (e.g. originate from an office where a high amount of coffee is drunk).

Simple true experimental designs

From the designs presented so far, quasi-experimental designs lack suitable participant randomisation and often appropriate control. With non-randomised allocation and the lack of control or comparative group, the threat to internal validity is increased and inference made difficult. Eliminating selection differences through the random assignment of participants to groups as well as the inclusion of a between-group factor provide a control or comparison group, and the researcher can begin to improve the degree of internal validity and ensure more confidence in the causal relationships between the independent and dependent variables.

Similar to the post-test-only design (Figure 4.1), the between-group post-test design involves the random assignment of participants into either an experimental or control/comparative group. Used to eliminate any systematic bias, randomisation of participants in such design will reduce the impact of extraneous variables on the dependent variable. This is also known as an unrelated design because the two groups are not related to each other; they are separate and treated as two distinct groups. In the example illustrated in Figure 4.5, one randomly assigned group wore thermal clothing during 30 minutes of cold-water submersion, while the control wore only their swimming costume. After the time was completed each group's core temperature was recorded.

As has already been noted regarding the one-group post-test design, this approach allows the researcher the opportunity to measure the dependent variable only once in each group and neglects

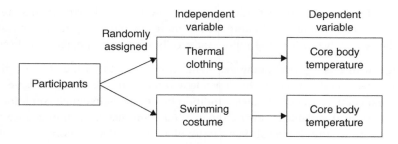

Figure 4.5   An illustration of a between-group post-test design with one independent variable (i.e. clothing condition).

any pre-test assessment. This thereby lowers the internal validity of the study. If the researcher had measured core temperature in each group before submersion then a pre-submersion value could be compared with the post-submersion value. If the researcher were therefore to find that both groups' core temperature changed by the same amount as a consequence of the 30-minute submersion, then they would have a high degree of confidence that the thermal clothing had no or little impact on the maintenance of core body temperature.

Take another research example. Suppose a researcher wished to investigate the impact of high-intensity fatiguing exercise on muscle activation patterns. By randomly allocating participants to two groups (experimental and control) the researcher firstly recorded all participants' lower-limb electromyographic patterns during a flexion and extension movement on an isokinetic dynamometer. Following this, the experimental group completed a 30-second Wingate test and the control group remained static on the ergometer. After the 30-second test each once again performed the flexion and extension movement and the electromyogram was recorded (Figure 4.6).

Repeated-measures design

Consider an experiment investigating the relationship between hydration status and cognitive functioning in competitive sailors. In independent group designs (i.e. within-group), as outlined and illustrated above, participants would be randomly assigned to one of two groups (i.e. dehydrated state or euhydrated state) and once in this state they would undertake a cognitive functioning test. In a repeated-measures design, the same individuals participate in all the conditions, meaning that participants are repeatedly measured on the dependent variable after being in each condition.

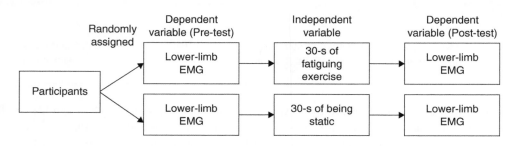

Figure 4.6   A between-group pre–post-test design with two independent variables (i.e. group and activity condition). EMG, electromyogram.

The advantages of this approach over others are that fewer research participants are needed and costs can be kept to a minimum. In addition to these more obvious strengths, the repeated-measures approach can be extremely sensitive to finding statistically significant differences between groups.

A major problem with this approach, however, stems from the fact that the order in which the conditions are presented could impact on the dependent variable. In the example above, suppose that all participants experienced the dehydrated condition before the euhydrated condition. Although a change in the dependent variable following the manipulation may be a consequence of the hydration status of the participants, it may also be a result of an order effect. Performance in the cognitive function tests may improve due to learning of test or becoming more familiar with the procedures. There is also the chance of a fatigue effect caused by insufficient time between the two conditions.

There are two approaches to dealing with such problems. To counteract any potential fatigue effect, the researcher can create a procedure in which the time interval between conditions is of sufficient length. The balance between being too short and too long needs careful consideration both in terms of impact of the dependent variable as well as participant availability. The second relates to the order effect. In repeated-measures design this can be resolved by *counterbalancing* the order of conditions. As shown in Figure 4.7, the participants would be randomly allocated to two groups. Each group would undertake both conditions but in a different order: group one undertakes order 1 and group two undertakes order 2. In essence, all participants are doing exactly the same, but the order has changed. By applying this approach to the repeated-measures design it is possible to reduce the impact an order effect may have on the dependent variable.

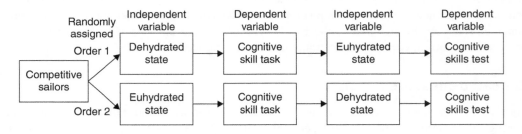

Figure 4.7   A counterbalanced within-group repeated-measures design with one independent variable (dehydration status).

 **Key point 4.4**

A counterbalanced approach is a method of controlling for order effects in a repeated-measures design by either including all orders of treatment presentation or randomly determining the order for each participant.

An understanding of the basic structure of experimental designs, the impact such design has on the threat to internal validity and the link between the research question and the within-, between- or repeated-measures approach enables the researcher to use these models as building blocks to create more elaborate approaches to experimental research design. Irrespective of what design is created, however, the issues relating to the control of extraneous variables that may impact on the ability to conclude causal links between the independent variable and dependent variable will always be the researcher's challenge.

It is important to remember that each design has its strengths and weaknesses that will impact on the researcher's selection decisions. The choice of a pre-test, a control group and the randomisation of participants will influence the validity of the study and affect the ability to determine causality confidently.

Reflection point 4.2

The simple experimental designs presented within this chapter act as a starting point for the evolution of more complex experiments. By understanding the building blocks of basic research design within an experimental research strategy, you can be led to more elaborate research questions.

Increasing the number of independent variables or levels, as they are sometimes referred to, the researcher can begin to understand much more about the cause-and-effect relationships between independent variables and dependent variables. Experimental designs, such as a 2×2 factorial design that combines both within- and between-group models, are not uncommon in undergraduate research. This approach involves two independent variables/levels (e.g. sex and vertical jump score), each consisting of two groups or conditions (e.g. sex (male and female) and vertical jump score (pre-training and post-training)), hence 2×2. In this design the first level (sex) is a between-group factor and the second (jump score) is a within-group factor. If you know this information about the experimental design you will be able to determine, in advance of data collection, the most suitable statistical test to use (see Figure 4.8 on page 80).

If you want to find out more about complex experimental designs, such as the factorial design, then look at the recommendations listed in the Further reading section, later in this chapter.

Learning activity 4.3

Without looking back through this chapter, try and recall the three key characteristics of the experimental research strategy. Once you have done this and entered them into the grid below, re-read the two research summaries in Research focus 4.1 and 4.2 and evaluate each against the three characteristics. For each one indicate below whether the characteristics are met or not by placing a tick or cross in the corresponding space.

Characteristic	Bloms et al. (2016)	Larsen et al. (2016)
1:		
2:		
3:		

Collection of data in experiments

A further component of the experimental research strategy, and one that comes after the selection of the research design, concerns decisions about the data collection methods – methods that require the researcher to select appropriate instruments or techniques that are then implemented via a set procedure or protocol to ensure efficient and effective data collection.

Presentation of the independent variable

An important starting point for the researcher is to consider how the independent variable will be presented and how the dependent variable will be measured. In some studies, researchers become involved in the presentation of the independent variable, and their active participation is required in the administration of the variable which is to be manipulated. Consider the researcher's involvement in a study that implements a training programme, sandwiched between two 5 maximum repetition tests. In this instance the researcher may be fully involved with the presentation of the independent variable to the participants, monitoring and recording testing and training to ensure accurate accounts are made. This approach has advantages as the researcher is able to ensure familiarity and consistency in the presentation of the independent variable. The limitation, however, is that researcher bias can impact on the presentation. This may have an unwanted effect on the dependent variable.

One way around this is to present the independent variable in a way that reduces bias. Consider a study that aims to identify the effect of caffeine compared to placebo on 2000-metre rowing performance. In this instance researchers may choose firstly not to inform the participants as to which solution they are receiving (i.e. single-blind). The value of this approach is that the participants will not be influenced by knowing that one is the caffeine and the other a placebo. To advance this further, researchers may also wish to remove their own influence by also becoming 'blind' to the solutions each participant is receiving. Known as a 'double-blind' approach, a third person would organise the solutions, labelling each *A* and *B*, devising a testing schedule and then providing it to the researcher. In this way, the researcher presenting the independent variable cannot impose bias on to the procedure or participants in the study.

Measurement of the dependent variable

The selection of instruments and their associated procedures for the measurement of the dependent variable will be dictated by what behaviour the researcher wishes to measure. The researcher in sport has a wide and varied range of clinical and non-clinical measurement tools available, spanning broad areas of physiology, biomechanics and psychology. Sport-specific ergometry, video capture systems, cardiorespiratory devices, sport-specific questionnaires, field-based assessment tools and force platform technology are among only a few different instruments that, when applied in a reliable and accurate manner, can produce a sensitive measure of the dependent variable.

The dependent variable in experiments typically falls into three broad categories: self-report behavioural and physiological. Self-reporting measures are used to measure quantifiably such things as attitudes, emotional states, confidence and motivation levels, or perceived ratings of exertion.

Rating scales (e.g. Likert scales) with assigned descriptions are the most common and allow the researcher to convert ratings into numerical responses. Behavioural measures are direct observations of sporting behaviour, often using video or notational tools and, as one can imagine, are endless in number. These can be verbal and non-verbal and are recorded to produce numerical quantification of behaviours (e.g. time spent in different zones on court). The final measure is physiological in nature and refers to the recording of bodily responses. Indicators from a physiological perspective may include temperature, heart rate, oxygen uptake, blood markers (e.g. lactate), blood pressure and lung function. From a biomechanical viewpoint, measures may include measures of ground reaction force or movement kinematics.

It is sometimes desirable for the researcher to measure more than one dependent variable in order to build up a more concrete view of the sporting behaviour in question. For example, measuring participants' endurance capacity on a treadmill may require the measurement of velocity, oxygen uptake, heart rate, rating of perceived exertion and blood markers. What this approach creates is the question of importance and order. When more than one dependent variable is measured, the order in which measurements will occur and their associated importance need to be recognised. All dependent variables in the example above may have been of equal value and collected all at the same time period. There may be cases when one measurement leads on to the next and the researchers should be aware of the impact on each subsequent measure as well as their overall importance to the study.

Linking design with an analysis approach

The analysis of numerical data collected from experiments provides the researcher with the opportunity to decipher the meaning behind the numbers. Analysing experimental data using statistical analysis methods often incites unnecessary fear among many novice researchers. In reality, once the experimental design is decided upon, the selection of data analysis techniques, whether basic descriptive statistics or more complex procedures, is relatively straightforward. What is important – and most novice researchers do not do this well – is to decide on the analysis method prior to data collection. The point of undertaking statistical analysis on the collected data is that the researcher can determine whether differences across groups or conditions are due to chance or a consequence of a cause. Remember, the whole point of the experimental approach is discovery of cause and effect. Does the independent variable, which is the one that the researcher manipulates, affect the dependent variable? Subjecting the data to statistical analysis reveals to the researcher the likelihood of any effect measured being caused by the independent variable and not just by chance occurrences.

What tends to confuse most when it comes to data analysis is not so much the mechanics of statistical analysis but rather the process of matching the research design, which is related to the research question, to the type of analysis that needs to be performed. A wide range of software packages now makes it easy for the researcher to put data in, press a few buttons and get something back. It may not always be the case that this is understood, but the mechanics are simplified.

As illustrated in Figure 4.8, the relationship between research design and statistical analysis tests can been seen. Specific tests are best suited to analysis data collected using specific types of design. Whether a between-group or within-group design, one independent variable or more, or a number of different groups to compare, the decision tree process allows the researcher to consider the type of statistical analysis test whilst designing their study.

To provide practical examples to illustrate the effectiveness of the decision process, let's consider an earlier quasi-experimental design (Figure 4.5) that was constructed to investigate the effect of

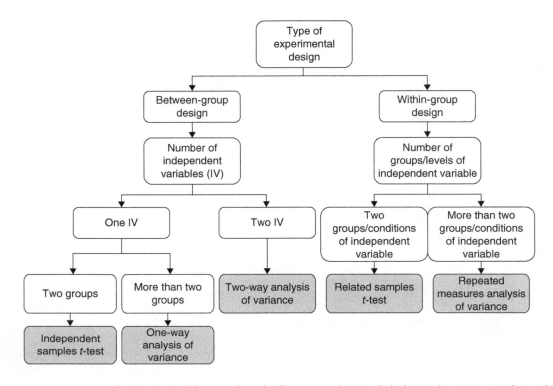

Figure 4.8   Decision tree for selecting appropriate statistical tests based on experimental research design. IV, independent variable.

clothing on body temperature following 30 minutes' submersion in cold water. In this design, participants were allocated to one of two groups (thermal clothing or swimming costume). In this between-group design there were therefore two groups that did not experience the other condition during the experiment. The independent variable for this study was the type of clothing worn. By applying these three basic design features to our decision tree, that is: (1) between-group design; (2) one independent variable; and (3) only two groups, the resultant statistical test will be an independent *t*-test.

Next consider the example illustrated in Figure 4.7. In this study, the researcher wished to examine the impact of hydration status on cognitive functioning. The design was a repeated-measures approach where the same participants took part in all conditions. This design can be considered a within-group design. There was one independent variable, the hydration status, which comprised two conditions (dehydrated and euhydrated). By again applying the basic design features to our decision tree, that is: (1) within-group design; and (2) two conditions, the resultant statistical test will be a related *t*-test.

 **Learning activity 4.4**

Refer back to the three Research focus boxes (4.1, 4.2, 4.3) earlier on in the chapter. Applying your understanding of experimental research design gained from this chapter and working logically through the decision tree illustrated in Figure 4.8, attempt to determine which statistical test you would use. It may help to consider the following:

- Is the design a within- or between-group design?
- How many independent variables are there?
- How many groups or conditions are being compared?

Research focus 4.1: Bloms et al. (2016)

Based on the experimental design, the statistical test would be:

_____

_____

_____

Research focus 4.2: Larsen et al. (2016)

Based on the experimental design, the statistical test would be:

_____

_____

_____

Research focus 4.3: Grandjean et al. (2002)

Based on the experimental design, the statistical test would be:

_____

_____

_____

_____

 Chapter review

Throughout this chapter we have investigated when and how to apply the experimental research strategy in order to examine a wide range of sporting behaviours. Examination of the importance of internal and external validity in experiments helps to verify the cause-and-effect relationship between measured variables. In constructing the experiment, selecting the most appropriate design will allow the researcher to draw accurate and truthful conclusions while allowing for a degree of generalisability. Whether a between-, within- or a combined-group approach is required, being able to make the link to the most suitable statistical technique will guide the researcher to make the right analysis and interpretation. By using a range of sport-related research examples throughout this chapter you should now be able to:

(Continued)

> *(Continued)*
>
> ☑ recall a definition for the term experiment and explain why it is different from non-experimental approaches;
>
> ☑ list the strengths and weaknesses of this strategy and identify how it can be used to answer specific research problems;
>
> ☑ name the three core experimental types and provide sport and exercise science-specific examples for each;
>
> ☑ construct a suitable research design based on a range of sport-related research questions.

▬▬ **Further reading** ▬▬

Christensen, LB, Johnson, B and Turner, LA (2014) *Research Methods, Design, and Analysis.* 11th ed. London: Pearson Education. Part IV.

Advancing on from the basics, part IV of this textbook will offer you a much more thorough grounding within experimental research approach and design construction. Set out in a clear manner, each chapter ends with internet site recommendations, practical tests and learning activity challenges.

Cozby, PC and Bates, SC (2012) *Methods in Behavior Research.* 11th ed. New York: McGraw Hill Higher Education.

Montgomery, DC (2012) *Design and Analysis of Experiment.* 8th ed. New York: John Wiley.

These valuable books should be on the shelf of everyone wishing to undertake experimental research. The key themes outlined within this chapter are further advanced, and complex research designs are clearly examined to help students understand and apply these approaches to their own research projects.

Keeble, S (1995) *Experimental Research 1: An Introduction to Experimental Design.* The Open Learning Foundation, Churchill Livingstone.

This is an extremely practical text with lots of useful learning activities. It will guide you through a more detailed perspective on the experimental approach with particular reference to experimental design.

Field, A (2017) *Discovering Statistics Using IBM SPSS.* 5th ed. SAGE Publications.

Ntoumanis, N (2001) *A Step-by-Step Guide to SPSS for Sport and Exercise Studies.* London: Routledge.

Both of these textbooks provide the reader with a thorough grounding in statistical data analysis. They provide practical illustrations on how to conduct and interpret the SPSS findings. Whether you are a first-time user or are more experienced at using SPSS, you will find these books of particular value.

Keeble, S (1995) *Experimental Research 2: Conducting and Reporting Experimental Research.* The Open Learning Foundation, Churchill Livingstone. Higher Education.

The second volume in the series takes you through reporting experimental research, which is particularly useful when you come to write up your experimental project work.

5

Correlational research strategy

Learning objectives

In developing an understanding of why correlational research is of value, this chapter will explore how a correlational research strategy can be applied to answer sport-related research questions. By identifying research situations for which this strategy may be applied, this chapter is designed to help you:

- explain the basic concept of a correlational research strategy;
- identify the relative merits of this approach and identify how to apply it to sport research;
- describe the pattern and strength of an association by way of scatter plots and analysis techniques.

Introduction

Sport is full of links and connections. Consider the connections between fitness and endurance success, fibre type and strength, motivation and sporting achievement or wealth and sporting opportunities. The list is endless and highlights the relationships that exist between phenomena in a sporting context. In wishing to understand more about sporting behaviour and how phenomena relate to each other, the researcher can apply a correlational research strategy that not only enables the degree of relationship to be determined, but also prediction to occur.

Non-experimental approaches to research, such as this strategy, do not attempt to manipulate variables in order to assess the resulting effect; rather they observe or measure phenomena in order to study the relationships between them. This is achieved by asking people to describe their behaviour, directly observing behaviour, recording physiological responses or, rarely, examining records, such as national census data. It is the very act of determining the degree to which variables associate with each other that provides the researcher with opportunities to discover the intricate interwoven relationships that occur in sport.

The value of association in sport research

We constantly make associations between phenomena encountered through our sporting and academic experiences. It may be assumed, for example, that time spent studying will be associated with better grades, time spent in the gym will be associated with stronger arms or time spent reading will be associated with more knowledge. We would like to think that all of these are true and time invested reaps positive reward.

Similarly, we know through our own experiences that if we increase our training load, while considering the correct nutrition and allowing plenty of time for recovery, we should begin to see beneficial developmental changes in our physical status. We also know however that many other factors could play a contributing role in explaining improved fitness irrespective of our training commitment. The application of the correlational research strategy allows the researcher to investigate whether these relationships or associations between sets of measured characteristics, or variables, exist and to what extent they agree or disagree with each other. The degree to which two or more phenomena vary can begin to provide the researcher with an indication as to the extent to which such variables are associated or related.

 **Key point 5.1**

The correlational research strategy, also called known as a non-experimental approach, uses measurements of variables to determine whether variables are related to one another.

In a study by Imai and Kaneoka (2016), a correlational research strategy was applied to examine the relationship between the trunk endurance plank test and a series of athletic performance tests in youth football players. Fifty-five participants performed prone and side plank tests (dependent variable), as well as seven different performance tests: the Cooper test, the yo-yo intermittent recovery test, the step 50 agility test, a 30-metre sprint test, a vertical countermovement jump, a standing five-step jump and a rebound jump (independent variables). All measurements were conducted over a 2-day period, with each day beginning with a 10-minute warm-up preceding the start of the assessment. The relationships between the individualised plank test scores, the combined scores and the performance tests were deduced using a Pearson correlation coefficient.

Findings revealed that for combined plank test scores (prone and side) a significantly positive relationship was found with the yo-yo intermittent test ($r = 0.71$, $P < 0.001$), whilst there were only moderate correlations when related to the Cooper test ($r = 0.57$, $P < 0.001$). Poor correlations were identified for all other remaining athletic performance assessments when related to plank scores. Based on the results of this study, the researchers indicated that the trunk endurance plank test may be a good indicator of the yo-yo intermittent assessment.

Characteristics of correlational research

Throughout the study of sport and exercise, a wide range of phenomena is encountered. Such things as physical attributes recorded during physical activity, scores from questionnaires, movement patterns noted during exercise or observations during play can help the researcher describe and explain different types of sporting behaviour. Through the process of data collection of such wide-ranging variables, the researcher can begin to develop an understanding of how these may relate to each other. This approach to research can lead to questions about how such associations can be used to predict future sporting behaviour.

The ability to make meaningful associations and predict outcomes inherently infers that the researcher is attempting to generalise to a wider population. Through the choice of this strategy, by its very nature, the researcher is being guided to make inference, or generalisation, to a population from which the study sample was drawn.

Aaron, in his final year of a Physical Activity and Health degree, wished to examine the association between Pilates class attendance and class-based self-confidence in a group of sedentary elderly females (> 65 years). Based on previous theory, he hypothesised that participation in these group exercise classes would increase individual self-esteem and self-efficacy and result in a greater feeling of self-worth.

(Continued)

(Continued)

Aaron identified eight groups that ran weekly classes in and around his university city and recruited 63 participants for his study. Each class ran for a period of 12 weeks and throughout he monitored attendance of all participants, giving them a score of 1 to 12 dependent on the number of sessions they attended. At the beginning and end of the 12-week period he administered a self-reporting numerical questionnaire to determine their levels of self-confidence. To determine the extent of change across the period he subtracted the end score from the initial score to generate a change value for each.

The attendance score (independent variable) and confidence change score (dependent variable) for each participant were plotted on a scatter plot. After visual inspection of the plot and application of a Pearson's correlation coefficient statistical test, Aaron found there was a strong positive association between attendance and self-confidence ($r = 0.91$, $P < 0.001$). Aaron's findings were summarised in his results section in the following way: there was a significant positive linear relationship between attendance at group-based Pilates classes and class-based self-confidence (Pearson's product moment correlation, $r = 0.91$, $n = 63$, $P < 0.001$).

Can cause and effect be claimed?

The purpose of applying the correlational research strategy to sport is to assess whether an association exists between phenomena of interest. As a result, the researcher can become informed on how selected variables alter when looked at together. What the correlational approach will not allow the researcher to do, however, is suggest a 'cause-and-effect' assumption between measured variables.

Consider the example of a researcher finding that scoring more points during a basketball game increased with the aggressiveness of the player. From this, the researcher could draw three conclusions. The first and most straightforward conclusion is that being more aggressive means the player scores more. The second is that scoring more points means the players become more aggressive. The final conclusion could be that something else not measured, a third variable, has caused both the scoring of more points and the development of aggressive tendencies. For example, the player's stature (i.e. height) may be associated with aggressiveness as height gives the player more confidence, but it may also be associated with more scoring opportunities and therefore more points. It can be difficult to discern the true cause from the measured effect. What can be concluded is that some relationship has or has not occurred between the measures, but what cannot be assumed is that aggressiveness causes more points, or more points cause aggressiveness.

To illustrate this further, assume another researcher identified that golf handicap seemed to be lower the longer a player spent practising. Again, three conclusions could be drawn from this. Firstly, those players who practise more play better golf and therefore lower their score. Secondly, scoring less may make players feel more confident and motivated about their game and therefore they practise more. Or thirdly, an unmeasured variable, such as a reduction of overtime working hours, may impact on both variables. Working less overtime may make players more relaxed, which impacts positively on their golf score, but also they have more free time to practise their golf game.

Making conclusions based on the associations observed and measured clearly involves the assumption that many unmeasured variables are also likely to impact on how the findings are evaluated. As researchers are unable to measure all of these within one single research project, they must therefore accept the fact that certain phenomena can impact on the associations and they should not claim that a cause-and-effect relationship exists. What they can determine, however, is the strength of agreement between the two variables they have selected.

Reflection point 5.2

When collecting data from either a laboratory or real-world setting, it is important to recognise the data fitting into two camps. One is that the data can be in the form of numbers (i.e. quantitative) on the nominal, ordinal, interval or ratio level of measurement. So, for example, the number of football players within teams across different age groups (nominal), the score of an anxiety test scale (ordinal), ground temperature at golf tournaments (interval) or the running speed at lactate threshold (ratio). The other camp sees the data in the form of personal qualities or characteristics that cannot be given a number. Examples come from data collected from patients who provide their opinions on the effectiveness of a physical activity referral scheme or a hockey referee's reasoning for the penalty corner in a match. Because our data may fall into either of these camps, we must make sure the correlational approach can be applied.

The researcher should only apply the correlational research strategy when collecting data that can be expressed as numbers. Although quality or qualitative data may allow for some degree of informal association between phenomena, the researcher cannot apply any numerical method of association between the variables. Choosing to select variables, which may be biological (e.g. physiological characteristics such as age, body mass, stature or resting heart rate) or psychological in nature (e.g. intelligence, personality or attitudes), presents the researcher with a range of data that may help to understand the intricate links that exist within sport.

Learning activity 5.1

Based on your most recent series of practical sessions, recall eight phenomena (i.e. variables) that you encountered – these may be biographical, physiological or psychological variables you either measured or discussed. Next, based on your current understanding, suggest a variable that may be related to the phenomenon encountered.

Phenomena encountered   **Related phenomena**

For example:

Anxiety levels during competition   *Years of competitive experience*

1 _____   _____

2 _____   _____

3 _____   _____

4 _____   _____

(Continued)

(Continued)

5 _____   _____

6 _____   _____

7 _____   _____

8 _____   _____

Design of a correlational study

Generally, a correlational study is a quantitative method of research in which two or more quantitative variables from the same group of individuals are compared in an attempt to determine if there is a relationship between the two variables (a similarity between them, not a difference between the means). Theoretically, any two quantitative variables can be associated (for example, hair length and 5k run time) as long as the researcher has scores on these variables from the same individuals. It is important to note, however, that selecting variables to associate must be grounded in previous research and rational logic. Collecting and analysing data when there is little reason to think the two variables would be related to each other is really a waste of time!

 Research focus 5.1

In a study by Dawes and Spiteri (2016), a correlational strategy was selected to examine the relationship between pre-season testing performance and playing time within a men's basketball team. The rationale for the study was based on the uncertainty of how effective pre-season assessment of players' physical attributes could be used as a marker of on-court performance. Evidence existed that had previously examined the relationship between performance test and court performance, but the researchers wished to examine the efficacy of pre-season measures as a marker of playing times at different competitive levels.

Performance data for ten male players were used within the study. Six weeks before their first league match, each player was required to undertake a series of physical assessments. These comprised anthropometric measures, lower-body power, change of direction speed and sprint speed assessment, anaerobic capacity test, assessment of aerobic capacity and upper- and lower-body strength tests (dependent variables). On-court time (minutes) played for each athlete across the season was retrieved from the World Wide Web on their university's athletics page (independent variable).

Pearson correlation coefficient of the measured variables (dependent variables vs. independent variables) results indicated significant correlations between playing time and lower-leg strength (predicted one-rep max (1-RM) bench press: $r \geq 0.71$) and upper-body strength (1-RM back squat: $r \geq 0.74$). The authors concluded by suggesting coaches should emphasise the importance of resistance training to develop both upper- and lower-body strength in increasing on-court playing time.

Selection of participants: more is better than less!

With all quantitative studies, the greater the number of participants, the more value the study will have. The reason is that the closer the sample size is to the overall population size, the stronger the inference will be. For a correlational study to be of real value the researcher should be aiming to have 30 participants or more as this will increase the validity of the research. However, this is often problematic due to assignment requirements, length of time given to do the project, personal time constraints, cost-associated factors and willing volunteers. This being the case, an attempt to get at least 12 individuals will provide the researcher with a useful set of data that should allow for some meaningful conclusions.

Learning activity 5.2

Referring back to Student case study 5.1, Aaron was asked to construct both a null and alternative hypothesis.

Based on your understanding of these terms, note down below what Aaron would need to write:

Null hypothesis

_____
_____
_____
_____

Alternative hypothesis

_____
_____
_____
_____

Determining associations between variables

Phenomena the researcher evaluates can *relate* in either a positive, negative, curvilinear or neutral way. Considering the type of associations between measured variables helps the researcher to understand how one variable co-varies with another. This ability to collect data from two separate variables using a range of data collection methods, organise them so as to unravel a story and then apply data analysis techniques to interpret the story will ensure the researcher can insightfully report the research findings and make sense of the data.

Positive associations

In a positive relationship, increases in one variable are accompanied by increases in a second variable. Consider the example of researchers who wished to determine the strength of a relationship between vertical jump height (variable *A*) and lower-leg isokinetic strength (variable *B*) across an entire cohort of netball players. Based on previous research findings, the researchers assumed that both should increase in association with each other. Following the study they found that as variable *A* increased so did variable *B*: as vertical jump score increased, isokinetic strength also increased.

Further suppose that researchers wished to discover the relationship between running miles and spend on running shoes. They approached a running club and found out the amount of training and competition miles each member had undertaken in the past 12 months (variable *A*) and also asked how much money each member spent on running shoes over the same period (variable *B*). It is likely that, as the amount of hours spent running decreases, then so should the wear and tear on their shoes, and therefore the amount of money spent replacing them. Findings revealed that this was indeed the case. The runners who were training more spent more money on shoes as they were wearing them out quicker.

Two examples of positive associations are shown in Figure 5.1.

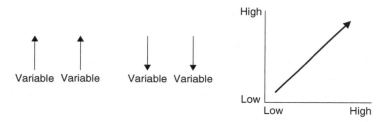

Figure 5.1   Positive associations are found when changes in one variable are accompanied by same-direction changes in another variable.

Negative associations

In negative associations, increases in one variable are accompanied by decreases in another variable. Consider the example of a student who was interested in evaluating the association between ball velocity (variable *A*) and driving accuracy (variable *B*) in high-handicap golfers. Relating the two variables revealed that, as ball velocity increased, the golfer's ability to drive the ball straight deteriorated. Concluding that a negative association existed between the two variables, the student's project supported the notion of a speed–accuracy trade-off in golf driving. Further suppose a researcher wished to determine whether the number of freely accessible open-air playgrounds (variable *A*) was associated with levels of childhood inactivity (variable *B*). Through survey and observational data collection processes, findings revealed that as the number of available playgrounds increased, reported childhood inactivity levels decreased.

Two examples of negative associations are shown in Figure 5.2.

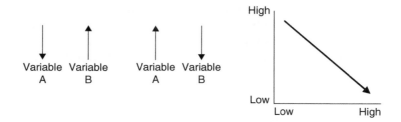

Figure 5.2   Negative associations are found when changes in one variable are accompanied by opposite-direction changes in another variable.

Curvilinear associations

In a curvilinear association, increases in the value of one variable are accompanied by both increases and decreases in the values of another variable. In other words, directional changes occur at least once. Some classic curvilinear relationships from a sporting context are the inverted-U theory (Figure 5.3a), relating to arousal and performance, blood lactate response to incremental exercise intensity (Figure 5.3b) and the length–tension relationship in muscular force.

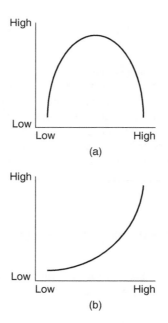

Figure 5.3   Curvilinear relationships are found when increases in one variable are accompanied by both increases and decreases in other variables. (a) Classic inverted-U and (b) exponential.

Neutral associations

Many phenomena that can be measured in sport simply have no association with each other (Figure 5.4). For example, peak racket head velocity measured during a tennis serve (variable *A*) is likely to have little to no association with running velocity at lactate threshold (variable *B*), or similarly, a basketball player's scoring average over a season should have a neutral association with the length of his shorts!

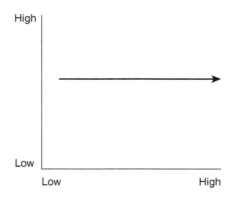

Figure 5.4   Neutral associations are found when changes in one variable are not accompanied by changes in another variable.

Reflection point 5.3

Reflecting back on previous sections should remind us of the importance of showing how two variables are *related* and the direction of such a relationship. Remembering that this does not justify the claim of a causal relationship between the measures should make us consider the full range of conclusions that can be made. There may be a causal relationship, but other explanations usually exist. Remember that the variables may be related because both have a causal relationship with a third variable. So, in Figure 5.4, if you find that *A* is associated (i.e. correlated) with *B*, any of the following explanations covered in Learning activity 5.3 may explain the *cause* underlying such a relationship.

Learning activity 5.3

Consider each of the studies described below, where a positive or negative association was found and a range of explanations is given to support the findings.

Study one

A study of hockey players showed that the longer they had been playing together as a team, the more similar their opinions on social and political issues were.

Positive or negative?

Positive.

Explanation A

Players who have been in teams longer could become more similar *or* being more similar may lead to more longevity in the team.

Explanation B

Similar life experiences may have made them develop similar beliefs *and* made them more likely to stay together.

Study two

An intelligence test was given to all the children in a gymnastics group. The results showed that the longer children had been in the group, the lower their IQ scores.

Positive or negative?

Negative.

Explanation A

The gymnastic environment has an adverse effect on cognitive development.

Explanation B

More intelligent children did not regularly attend the gymnastic group.

Study three

In a study of British cities, a relationship was found between the number of elite swimmers and the number of swimming pools.

Positive or negative?

Positive.

Explanation A

The availability of pools stimulates a greater interest in swimming, which will lead to an increased number of elite performers.

Explanation B

The number of both swimming pools and elite swimmers is related to the size of the cities.

(Continued)

(Continued)

Study four

A football coach found that the more training sessions players miss, the lower their performance level during matches seems to be.

Positive or negative?

Negative.

Explanation A

Absent players miss training opportunities to develop.

Explanation B

Players with multiple responsibilities (jobs, family obligations) find it difficult making it to training and also have trouble finding time to train.

The importance of scatter plots

It is often easier to interpret the meaning of collected data when they can be viewed visually. When determining the relationship between two measured variables, a *scatter plot* is the typical way to evaluate the nature of such an association. The term scatter plot simply means a way of showing scattering of pairs on a graph made up of a *y*-axis that goes up the side and an *x*-axis that goes along the bottom.

Consider Student case study 5.1. The purpose was to investigate the association between exercise class attendance and class-based self-confidence. The researcher wished to evaluate whether the participant's self-confidence (e.g. self-esteem, self-efficacy and self-worth: variable *A*) was dependent upon attendance at a 12-week Pilates group (variable *B*) and sampled 63 elderly females across a range of groups. With the *y*-axis representing one variable (change (Δ) in self-confidence scores) and the *x*-axis the other (number of classes attended), a scatter plot can represent each participant's points in a visually clear way. As illustrated in Figure 5.5, each point provides a co-ordinate that locates each participant's position. Once all of the data, that is, all of the 63 participants' scores, are plotted the researcher can begin to identify the nature of the association.

Using a scatter plot, the researcher is able to identify visually the type of relationship between the two measured variables. Referring back to the study on basketball players and aggression, the researcher can conclude that a positive relationship exists and three conclusions can be made.

1. As aggression increases players score more points.

2. Scoring more points makes players more aggressive.

3. A variable not measured may have caused both the scoring of more points and an increase in aggressiveness.

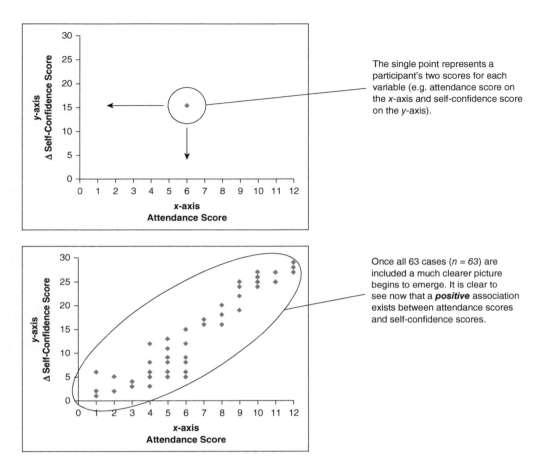

The single point represents a participant's two scores for each variable (e.g. attendance score on the x-axis and self-confidence score on the y-axis).

Once all 63 cases (*n = 63*) are included a much clearer picture begins to emerge. It is clear to see now that a ***positive*** association exists between attendance scores and self-confidence scores.

Figure 5.5   The construction of scatter plots is an effective visual way to assess the nature of the association between measured variables.

Using software packages such as Microsoft Excel, Minitab or SPSS for Windows to create a simple scatter plot, the ability to assess the nature of the association visually begins to offer more insight into the way variables may or may not be associated.

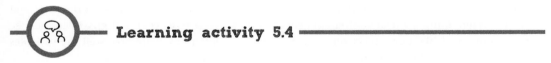

Learning activity 5.4

From what you have learnt so far in this chapter, read each study description below and draw an arrow on the graph to reflect the direction of the relationship. It may help to label the axes first.

Study one

Observing a professional football game, Charlie found that as the noise level of the crowd increased (x-axis) the concentration (y-axis) of the players decreased.

(Continued)

(Continued)

He concluded that the direction was?

Based on Charlie's study, what three conclusions can be made?

1. _____

2. _____

3. _____

Study two

Collecting data across a series of break times, Emily found that the more sports equipment provided to the children (*x*-axis), the more time they spent running around (*y*-axis).

She concluded that the direction was ?

Based on Emily's study, what three conclusions can be made?

1. _____

2. _____

3. _____

Assessment of association strength

The determination of association direction begins to inform researchers about the nature of the relationship, but doesn't tell them all they need to know about relative strength between the measured variables. Determining the relative strength between the two gives researchers a degree of confidence as to how one variable may impact on the other. So being able to evaluate how well the variables relate to each other indicates the degree of association between measured variables.

When the measured variables that are to be correlated are classified as continuous data (i.e. interval or ratio levels of measurement) it is common to select a data analysis technique known as a *Pearson's product moment correlation coefficient*. When data are regarded as discrete (i.e. ordinal level of measurement), the *Spearman rank order correlation coefficient* is applied. There are occasions when this is not always the case, for example, when the interval or ratio data from one or both of the variables do not possess a normal distribution. When this occurs, it is common to put the data into rank order (i.e. convert to ordinal-level data) and perform a Spearman correlation coefficient. For more details on why this is done and how to achieve this, see Further reading at the end of the chapter.

The correlation is a useful approach that will provide the researcher with a coefficient value (more often known as an *r* value). This value will always range from −1 to +1 and reflects the strength of association between our variables. At either end of the extremes, −1 and +1 mean that there is a perfect negative or positive relationship between our measures, that is, all of the points fit perfectly in a straight diagonal line. Figure 5.6 shows that when a perfect relationship exists (i.e. Pearson's *r* value of −1 or +1) all the points on a scatter plot form a line.

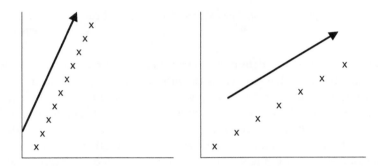

Figure 5.6   As can be seen from these two scatter plots, all of the points form a perfect diagonal line, although at different angles. Both would result in a correlation coefficient value of +1 as they are both positive.

These scatter plots simply illustrate what the plots will look like in order to obtain a perfect correlation. In the real world, however, it is rare to find such a perfect relationship and more common to see positive or negative trends in our scatter plots that provide a correlation value of somewhere above −1 and below +1 (Figure 5.7).

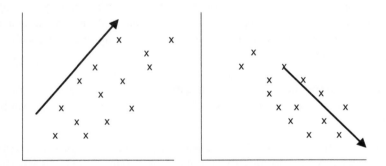

Figure 5.7   Both of these scatter plots show directional trends, whether that is a positive or negative trend. What we see differently here is that not all of the points form a perfect diagonal line.

Typically, as the points start to spread out, the strength of the association gets closer to 0.0. This indicates that the two variables are becoming more weakly associated. There are exceptions, however, as illustrated in the far-right example in Figure 5.8. Here all of the points are on the same line; however they all share the same value on the *y*-axis. This means that, although one variable is increasing (*x*-axis), the other variable is not. This will result in a neutral or no relationship between the measures.

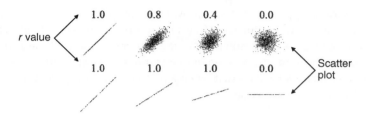

Figure 5.8   Visual inspection of a scatter plot can begin to reveal the approximate strength of a relationship.

When using statistical packages to determine the *r* value for the relationship, it is common to be presented with a significance value (known as the probability or *P* value). Such value provides the researcher with a means of accepting or rejecting our null hypothesis. Based on criteria, often set at a 95% level of confidence, the *P* value will indicate the degree of significance in the association. Without over-complicating the issue here, if the *P* value is less than our critical value (usually 0.05, that is, 95% divided by 100%), then the researcher can conclude that there is a significant correlation between the variables. So if *P* is less than (<) 0.05, the null statement can be rejected, therefore accepting the alternative hypothesis. Alternatively, if the *P* value is found to be more than (>) 0.05, the null hypothesis is retained. (If you wish to know more on the theory, consult the Further reading at the end of the chapter.)

Presentation of correlational findings

The ability to present coherent and accurate findings is fundamental to a successful project. It is often the case that a lot of hard work and time is devoted to organising, planning and conducting the correlational project for it to fall at the last hurdle because of inadequate or inappropriate communication of findings. Aspects relating to the design, analysis and interpretation should end up in the research strategy and findings section of your work. In a comprehensive account the following points should be considered.

- The type of association – was it positive or negative? And what was the strength of the relationship? The correlation coefficient value should be included (the *r* value) to support the results statement.

- A clear scatter plot to depict visually the association between the measured variables. Make sure that both axes are labelled and the correct units of measurement are included. Think about how the reader will view this so ensure it is well presented – this can make a big difference!

- If significance has been found, make sure to include this. More importantly, though, make sure the meaningfulness of the significance is determined. Is it of practical value to the reader?

- A statement within the discussion that simply and effectively explains whether the null hypothesis has been accepted or rejected. This will indicate to the reader the researcher's key conclusions based on the findings.

Chapter review

Throughout this chapter we have investigated when and how to apply the correlational research strategy. By measuring phenomena without the need for manipulation the relationships between variables can be discovered. Although the researcher cannot be certain of cause and effect, the degree of agreement in the form of a correlation coefficient can be determined. The application of the correlational research approach to solving sport-related problems offers the researcher opportunities to uncover relationships about behaviour that may impact on future performance and achievement. By applying a range of sport-related research examples throughout this chapter you should now be able to:

☑ describe the basic concept of the correlational research strategy and provide a range of examples with the field of sport;

☑ list the strengths and weaknesses of this non-experimental strategy, justifying when and when not to use it;

☑ describe the four types of relationships that can exist between variables and link these to appropriate means of determining significance in the association.

Further reading

Field, A (2013) *Discovering Statistics Using IBM SPSS*. 4th ed. London: SAGE Publications.

This text will provide the interested reader with a detailed explanation of the statistical importance of the correlational approach. It provides practical illustrations of how to conduct and interpret SPSS findings. More experienced users of SPSS will find this chapter particularly useful.

Ntoumanis, N (2001) *A Step-by-Step Guide to SPSS for Sport and Exercise Studies*. London: Routledge.

This book provides a valuable description of how to conduct a correlation in the SPSS package within a sport and exercise science context.

William, C and Wragg, C (2004) *Data Analysis and Research for Sport and Exercise Science: A Student Guide*. London: Routledge.

A 'how to' approach to relationships within the field of sport and exercise studies that will help you to understand some of the more complex aspects of the correlational strategy.

6

Survey research strategy

Learning objectives

It is the process of surveying what is around us that allows us to begin to make sense of our physical and social world and how we operate within it. Through the recording of beliefs, feelings, motives, preferences, occurrences, thoughts or opinions we can start to understand more about sport. By identifying research situations for which a survey research strategy would be applied, this chapter is designed to help you:

- describe the characteristics of a survey research strategy;
- define and explain the linked stages of survey research;
- explain the importance of survey design and sampling techniques to improve this research approach;
- identify the range of data collection methods that can be applied to the survey strategy.

Introduction

When we think about the word survey, several thoughts often spring to mind. We've all at some point taken part in a survey or surveyed something in order to gain a better insight or view. We may have in the past been stopped by a researcher wanting us to complete a survey about something or had to survey the surroundings so that we could locate someone or something. We've maybe questioned our tutor in order to gain some feedback about our biomechanics assignment, quizzed a friend about the football result from the weekend or asked for our lecturer's opinion on our exercise psychology research idea. Whatever the instance, we have used a range of techniques to gather information from people or things in order to find out something of interest.

The value of survey research in sport

Imagine you've been stopped outside a sports stadium following a game by a researcher who wants to know about your match day experiences. She shows you a short typed-out questionnaire pinned to a clipboard and asks you to read the top and complete the nine questions. You survey the questions, read the instructions and complete the tick-box questionnaire. Passing the clipboard back, you leave the researcher with some insight into opinions and feelings about your day's experience.

Take another example: you are out on the golf course with a tricky second shot to a closely guarded green. You survey the landscape around the green to see where the best place would be to hit your next shot. You want to avoid the deep bunker on the left, the tree on the right and the water past the green. Your ability to gain an overall view of the layout in front of you will help you make the correct decision. After completing your survey, you execute the shot and it lands safely on the green.

Key point 6.1

Survey is defined as a systematic gathering of information from a sample of individuals for the purpose of describing the attributes of the larger population of which the individuals are members.

These two examples, the first viewed as collecting a range of opinions from someone, and the second taking in an overall view of something, give instances of surveys. In the context of this chapter the term survey simply refers to the act of collecting information in a systematic way. The purpose is to describe single or multiple attributes of either an individual or larger group. In essence, the researcher wants to get the views, opinions, motives, plans or feelings of a group who represent a bigger group; this might be in the form of numbers or words. And systematic because the researcher is following a research process that has clear logical steps. Collecting a range of attributes, the researcher attempts to describe basic characteristics or experiences of the group (sample) that then makes generalisations back to the larger population from which the sample has been drawn.

Whilst on her study placement at a local hospital trust during her Sport and Exercise Science degree, Laura was asked to undertake a study with a small group of stroke patients ($n = 15$). Nursing staff had noticed that regular ward exercises, playing board games and talking about past exercise and sporting habits were having positive benefits for the well-being of the patients whilst they were recovering. Laura had been involved in ad hoc support within the ward and the nurses felt that if she could find out more from the patients, family members and consultants, this would support a case to the trust manager to provide more formal arrangements. This was in the form of a paid appointment offering additional rehabilitative provision to the patients.

Laura selected several research strategies to gather sufficient evidence. Firstly, acting as an observer participator, she undertook an observational strategy to record current practice within the ward. This involved making detailed notes, plans and accounts of all interactions and activities (verbal and non-verbal), continually monitoring behaviours whilst she was present. Additionally, she undertook a survey research strategy as she wanted to collect opinions and reflections from patients, family members who regularly visited and nurses on the ward. This would enable her to gain a deeper sense of what was valued, patients' perceptions and what additional provision and resources could be offered. She also interviewed the consultants to assess the extent of impact of existing activity on patient rehabilitation. Finally, Laura undertook a review of the literature, including existing evidence in her report.

From the evidence Laura had collected, she was able to present her observations to the nursing team. It was clear from her information that the nurses' informal observations were confirmed, and that the patients were recovering quicker and having a more positive outlook following their stroke, whilst family members were reassured that they were involved in progressive enrichment activities. Consultants were noticing considerable difference in patients' psychological well-being, and although not measured, there did seem to be anecdotal impact on reducing time in hospital.

Why conduct surveys?

Factors such as age, gender, marital status, previous education or sporting interests, as well as behaviours, individual preferences, beliefs and opinions, offer insight into who people are and what they may be thinking or feeling about a given issue. Intended to probe the individual's point of view, the survey allows the researcher to describe people and what they experience. Although there are many research strategies, it is often the case that survey research is really the only strategy for asking questions the researcher wants individuals to answer.

Survey research offers researchers the opportunity to find out about individuals' attributes, behaviours, beliefs, preferences and/or opinions on something or someone. Depending on the nature of the research question, they may be interested to find out about quantities or qualities. This activity is intended to start you thinking about how you may construct simple questions in order to find out more about the individual and whether individuals share the same opinions – therefore qualitative. Being able to gain information from the sample is at the heart of survey research and will enable you to achieve your objectives.

Select one topic that you have recently covered in a unit or module. It may be 'performance profiling an athlete', 'the use of open questions when coaching' or 'video analysis and player performance development', for example. Once you have chosen your topic area, imagine you're going to ask a fellow student a series of questions about the topic. Using the headings below construct two questions for each that will aim to find out more about the student's thoughts and opinions. Base one question from a qualitative perspective and the other from a quantitative perspective.

Belief   Preference   Feeling

So, for example, if we had selected 'performance profiling an athlete' as our topic area, we might ask the student from a qualitative perspective the following questions:

- How do you *believe* performance profiling impacts on athlete improvement?

- Why might you *prefer* to work with the coach and athlete together rather than separately?

- How do you *feel* your answer to the last question impacts on the performance profiling process?

From a quantitative perspective, we might ask the following:

1. Do you *believe* performance profiling impacts on athlete improvement?

    Strongly disagree   Disagree   Neutral   Agree   Strongly agree

2. Indicate your *preference* of the number of athletes you would be comfortable working with during a single session.

    1   2   3   4   > 4

3. How do you *feel* your answer to the last question impacts on the performance profiling process?

    Don't know   No impact   Low impact   Medium impact   High impact

Listen to the responses and see how each answer informs you about the respondent's thoughts and understanding. Think about how the use of such questions can open up to you a wide range of possibilities when you want to find out about individuals. Which questions do you consider to be open and which closed? What impact does this have on the depth of response?

Based on your standardised questions you could now ask more students in your group and begin comparing responses. Are they all the same or do they differ? Which students/questions differ and why may that be the case? Which individuals in particular seem to offer similar answers? Is there a reason for this? Do you think their views reflect the general consensus of the class? What about the whole year group?

Measurement concepts

Like other approaches, survey research involves setting clearly defined objectives for data collection, constructing a suitable research design, preparing a reliable and valid collection method, administering and scoring the instrument, analysing the data and reporting the findings. Similarly to other research strategies covered in this book, survey research allows for the collection of both qualitative and quantitative data. The generation of numerical data can mean causal links between measures may be established, offering the opportunity to make statistically supported generalisations to larger populations.

Depending on the data collection methods used, collection of qualitative data may provide a more enriched perspective of individual qualities and characteristics. Constructing appropriate data collection instruments allows the researcher the opportunity to collect relevant data to answer the key research question. With an appreciation of the relative merits of both, survey research offers a non-experimental quantitative and qualitative approach that suits the multi-disciplinary nature of sport.

Although survey research can be applied to simply describing a population, such as the number of football clubs with chartered status, the particular support needs of elite athletes or the motives for exercise adherence, we may also be interested in making planned comparisons between groups or occasions, such as the motives for exercise adherence in two separate locations. We may wish to look at changes over time, such as surveying a sports team before and after a series of coaching sessions to gauge their opinions on its success. It may be that we wish to know the effects of some behaviour – for example, those who take protein supplements to increase muscle mass compared to those who do not.

 Research focus 6.1

In a study by McManus et al. (2017), a survey research strategy was selected to describe the nutritional practices of a female recreational runner who completed 26 marathons in 26 consecutive days. Given that detailed information documenting the habits and feeding patterns during multi-day endurance events is limited, the study's purpose was to provide a picture of the practice, changes in body composition, dietary intake and performance outcomes across the period.

To begin the case study, an initial needs analysis was performed capturing the existing literature within this area. This was used to develop a client action plan that would form the data collection phase. A number of key sport science support interventions were provided that focused on: (1) periodised training advice; (2) sports psychology support; (3) nutritional strategies to support training; (4) strategies to optimise immune function; and (5) event food planning to support nutritional habits throughout the marathon. Over the 12-month case study period, a number of physiological assessments, face-to-face and e-mail/telephone meetings and one-to-one support sessions were held. Both quantitative and qualitative observations were recorded and used to evaluate the success of the interventions strategies.

Findings revealed that across the 26 marathons the total energy intake reached 99,570 kcal and 112.9 litres of fluid were consumed. Total distance completed was 1097.07 km, in a total time of 165 hours 30 minutes 01 seconds. Mean marathon time was 6 hours 21 minutes 55 seconds (5:09:14-7:30:00): both moving and total time slowed down over the 26 days. Anthropometrical assessments performed 19 days prior and 11 days post the 26 marathons reported a reduction in body mass of 4.6 kg (62.4–57.8 kg). The authors concluded that the case study provides clear evidence of the importance of effect and managed nutritional education in the lead-up to and during multi-day endurance challenges.

Characteristics of survey research

Survey research is uniquely placed among the broad array of strategies because of the useful ability to describe the characteristics of a large population from a quantitative, qualitative or mixed-research approach. With the additional benefit of being able to conduct relatively inexpensive surveys, especially self-administered ones, accessing locations via the internet, e-mail or telephone, and the standardisation of the method, survey research is a popular approach to the study of sport. The ability to obtain large sample sizes that improve generalisability as well as the flexibility in deciding how the survey will be administered open up a wide range of sport-related research questions.

The survey approach can have immense value if it is the researcher's intention to record the prevalence of attitudes, beliefs and behaviours in people. When considering how people display these characteristics through their involvement in sport, the survey strategy can be used to capture a wide range of perspectives within and between different populations of people. Whether through evaluation of a change over time, differences between groups or causal links between characteristics, the survey strategy provides an opportunity to delve deep into the perceptions and realities of the world within a sporting context.

Approaches to survey research

Survey research can be approached in a number of ways. From a natural scientist's perspective, subscribing to an objectivist ontological position, the purpose would be to survey people in order to quantify numerical aspects of their physical dimensions, such as age, mass or stature, or social dimensions, such as motivation levels, self-esteem or anxiety. Subscribing to such ontology that views knowledge generation through the collection of universal, observable facts not impacted upon by social factors, the natural scientist would survey and record, deductively testing a theory through the creation of set hypotheses.

From a social scientist's perspective, taking a constructivist ontological position, social dimensions would not be objectified in such a way. Rather, social phenomena would be considered accessible only through the interpretations of the individuals involved. Clearly, such a survey approach taken by the natural scientist that considers the collection of numerical data to describe social dimensions would be viewed as illegitimate by the social scientist. Instead, a survey approach that allows the researcher to interpret the meaning, significance and value of things, events and people would provide a more culturally determined set of social phenomena.

The distinctions raised above are important as they have an impact on the approach to survey research. Although the researcher does not necessarily need to subscribe to one or other approach, it is important to acknowledge their impact on the research question and selected methodology. As the collected survey data may or may not be numerical, depending on the type of instrument used and how the questions are constructed, the choice should be carefully considered in relation to how the researcher views reality and gains knowledge from it.

Causality and survey research

It is important to remember that, with any research strategy, the survey approach has a number of considerations that may impact on the validity and reliability of the findings. The first key point relates to the assumption of causality, discussed in Chapter 4. As mentioned, a survey can be used to collect quantitative data (i.e. numerical data from a questionnaire) and therefore can be submitted to statistical analysis to test a theory.

Suppose a theory states that the longer we socialise with others, the closer our values become. Taking an objectivist approach, we decide to test this within a sporting context. We set up our survey research to assess whether the length of time hockey players spend together as a team relates to their values on teamwork. We choose to sample a large range of hockey teams and get players in each to complete a questionnaire survey. This would be specifically designed to find out about their time spent together as a team and their views on working in a team. Once we have numerical data from the survey, we carry out analysis that reveals a negative association between the amount of time spent together as a team and values on teamwork.

When we apply the three types of explanation to our interpretation of the associations, we arrive at the following conclusions:

1. Because of our different values on teamwork we spend more time together as a team.

2. Because we spend more time together as a team we develop different values on teamwork.

3. Another factor that was not measured altered the time spent together and values independently of each other.

From our survey findings we can conclude that the theory (the longer we socialise with others, the closer our values become) was not supported. However we are unable to be conclusive about the reasons why: the answer could be 1, 2 or 3! When we select this survey approach investigating causality between attributes we must therefore tread cautiously when interpreting our findings (see Chapter 5 for more details).

If we take a constructivist approach here, we might opt for a different survey approach, such as an interview or focus group, which allows us to obtain greater understanding of the players' experiences, how their cultural background impacted on the team and why conflicts may have arisen. These views of reality from the players who experienced it, recorded through instruments that capture subjective interpretation of the social world they function in, is in contrast to the objectivist approach of a natural scientist who would view reality as universal, objective and quantifiable.

Such strength of the survey approach, however, can actually be a disadvantage. With such rigidity in method and design, the lack of flexibility could hinder exploration of deeper social issues that a social scientist may wish to investigate. Thinking carefully about your overall research question and the type of data you want to obtain when examining your chosen sporting topic can help you select particular research methods that offer slightly more flexibility.

 Learning activity 6.2

The art of undertaking successful survey research is the ability to set out a very clear plan before you start data collection. Establishing a plan enables researchers to align their research question with the most suitable design, population and sampling strategy, research method(s) and data collection tool(s).

A framework set up early in the research process gives the researcher the opportunity to develop ideas and adjust the plan in accordance with the work brief and academic expectations.

 Reflection point 6.1

When you read through the stages of survey research try and create a plan in the form of a table or list. Use the questions outlined below, as well as aspects from other chapters. Chapter 8, examining case study research strategy, for example, outlines guidance on creating a case study protocol, which may be very useful.

1. What will the survey goals be? How do these link to the research question?

2. What survey design will be used? How will the choice be justified?

3. Who will be selected to take part in the research? What sampling technique will be applied?

4. What data collection method(s) will be used? How will this be constructed? What type of data will be collected (i.e. quantitative, qualitative or both)?

5. How will the selected instruments be administered?

6. How will the data be analysed? How will the research be presented? e.g. poster, scientific report, presentation, video/web blog, audio recording, newspaper article, summary sheets?

A step approach to survey research

When undertaking any research study, the process of breaking down the whole into parts will make survey research more achievable. Remember, research involves undertaking a systematic, logical process of inquiry. As with all other research strategies covered in this book, survey research requires just as much diligence in planning. If you develop a structured survey research plan before you start practical data collection, you will be in a much better position to evaluate the research process continuously. This will help you to foresee and resolve any problems well in advance. The knock-on effect will be the improved ability to communicate the chosen design and data collection methods clearly.

Establishment of the survey goals

Guided by the research question, the decision to select the survey research strategy will be governed by a series of underpinning requirements from the researcher. These will focus on the need to use a methodology that asks people about themselves with the hope of generalising from the study sample to the wider population. The first stage in conducting the survey research based on the research question will be to develop survey goals. This early stage is important and ensures the vital connection between goals and a more refined and specific research question. Equally importantly, it will allow the researcher to reflect, making sure that undertaking this approach is really the correct choice, or whether a different strategy would be better suited to the research question.

The process of defining the survey goals will draw attention to what knowledge the researcher wants to gain from people and should lead to the development of more specific and meaningful questions. Several important questions need to be asked, to begin the process of survey research formation.

The first question relates to *who* is going to be surveyed. At this point, having a vague idea about who the sample will be and their likely characteristics and attributes gives the researcher the chance to plan access to the participants and allows for a sampling strategy to be considered (both of these topics are explored in more detail later on in this chapter). The researcher may want to find out athletes' perceptions of and attitudes towards physiological sport science support services offered at a university, the level of weekend members' satisfaction of provision at a local premier fitness centre, parents' opinions of a new basketball kit for the under-9s team, inactive people's motives for watching sport on television or school teachers' opinions about the government's drive to increase PE within the National Curriculum. Irrespective of the general question, having an idea about *who* is to be surveyed (e.g. athletes, gym members, parents, non-active people or teachers) leads to what knowledge is to be collected.

The next question researchers can ask themselves relates to what characteristics they wish the sample to have. Is their age important for the study? What about gender? Do they have to have a certain amount of experience, or come from particular local areas or schools? Does their occupation matter? Considering *who* at this stage will really help researchers to plan their approach and create the design and sampling strategy.

The third question relates to what knowledge needs to be obtained from participants. Based on the overall study question the researcher should be able to narrow this down into more purposeful objectives. There may be an interest in exploring opinions, beliefs, motives and/or attitudes towards some aspect of sport, establishing the frequency of events/occurrences at particular locations or determining associations between habit and prevalence, such as the link between smoking and inactivity. Once you know this, a more structured and meaningful plan can emerge.

Consider the researchers who wished to explore athletes' perceptions and attitudes towards physiological support. Once they had decided exactly who they were targeting, they began to establish more specifically what knowledge they wanted to obtain. For this study they focused on athletes between the ages of 18 and 35 years who had a minimum of 2 years' experience working within a support system. They were interested in topics relating to the support process, the personnel providing the support, the quality and value of the feedback, the relevance of the assessments and external support networks. Since they were clear about the sample and the knowledge required, the researchers could then move to the design stage.

Research focus 6.2

In a study by McNeill and Meade (2017), a survey research strategy was applied to describe those specific processes that caddies employ that professional golfers find most effective in managing and facilitating their psychological performance. Six professional golfers were selected for the study, all of whom were competing at either regional or European level. Players ranged from 27 to 57 years old and had between 7 and 40 years of experience playing competitive golf.

The researchers undertook semi-structured interviews, devised from previous literature. The topics for discussion with the players focused on: (1) the perceived advantages and disadvantages of having a caddy; (2) how players and caddies come together; (3) expectations of each other; (4) good and bad experiences; (5) when caddies are most important in a round; (6) caddie involvement in decision-making; and (7) reacting to mistakes.

Through transcription, content analysis and subsequent construction of connected topics and themes, the researchers concluded that the thematic structures and dialogues revealed similarities among players. Of significance was the perception that an effective caddie can have a significant and measurable effect on performance. The role of the caddy goes far beyond carrying a bag, and experts perceive the relationship between professional golfers and their caddy as being vital for a successful performance at such a high level.

Selecting a survey design

By articulating the survey goals clearly and concisely, a more structured start to survey research will occur: if the researcher begins with muddled goals and is unable to develop meaningful questions, any findings collected and interpreted will also be muddled. The goals will inevitably link to the survey design and data collection methods, so being thoughtful at this stage will ensure the research process is a success.

Establishing goals in accordance with the overall research question starts opening the envelope of research design. When choosing the correct design for the research, the main questions that need to be asked relate to when and how often the survey will be given and to how many groups (irrespective of how the groups were selected or the size – see later, when we discuss sampling).

Reflection point 6.2

Consider the five studies below. Read them carefully and think about these questions: when and how often will the survey be given and to how many groups?

1. A community-based health centre wanted to develop a series of Exercise for Life workshops for residents in the local area. In 2016, a student on work experience conducted a survey on a random sample of people to find out what they would like to see covered in a series of six workshops.

(Continued)

(Continued)

2. A student working on a placement for the local health authority wanted to know how much knowledge people had acquired from the series of Exercise for Life workshops that had now been running for over 4 years. Surveys were conducted with random selections of attendees from workshops in 2014, 2015, 2016 and 2017, and the findings were compared.

3. The health centre has continually updated its workshop content in line with the changing attitudes of the local community. In 1995, a similar programme existed, called Get Fit 4 Life. Over the course of the year over 1000 people attended. Every 5 years since, the health centre has been monitoring attitudes by surveying a different random sample of people from the 1995 delivery. This approach means that some people may be surveyed more than once and others not at all.

4. Wanting to understand how the knowledge and attitudes of those participants attending the very first series of workshops had changed, a researcher surveyed a random sample of attendees from the 2013 series and has continued to survey them at the same time of year ever since.

5. For a 4-month period in 2017, a series of Active Living workshops was also running at the same time in a neighbouring health centre. A survey comparing participants' knowledge and attitudes towards exercise and diet will be conducted at the workshop's completion from a random sample attending each class.

When you review the examples, you should see a difference in how each has been constructed. Each requires a survey research strategy, but the design is not the same for all. In fact, as shown in Table 6.1, each one requires a different design type. Work through Table 6.1 and re-read the five studies. By asking the questions 'when was the survey given?' and 'how often was the survey given?', further insights of the survey design can be obtained.

A cross-sectional survey design offers a real insight into people's beliefs, opinions and/or preferences at a given point in time. A survey to find out which seats offer the best view at Wembley Stadium or people's thoughts on government expenditure in hosting the next Olympic Games are examples that use a cross-sectional approach. If the researchers want to find out about change, then longitudinal designs can be used. That could be a trend design, where they survey a group of coaches in summer, another in autumn and another in winter; a cohort design, where they select a sample of children, for example, from a Key Stage 3 class in 2014 and the following year when they have moved to Key Stage 4 take another sample from the same group; or a panel design, where they select a sample of hockey players and survey them at the beginning, middle and end of the season.

If the researchers wanted to compare groups, so for example, those who only used static machines in the gym compared to those who only used free weights, they could select a comparison design. Bear in mind that making contrasts between groups can also fall under the banner of the experimental research strategy and such design may take on similar characteristics to that found in Chapter 4.

Table 6.1 By linking the design to the research question, the research plan for the survey approach can be determined (extracts from Fink, 2012)

What was the survey finding out?	When was the survey given?	How often was the survey given?	How many groups was the survey given to?	What were the results?	Design type
Preferences for workshop content	2016: a year before the start of the workshop series	Once	One: a random sample from the local area	Description of preferences	*Cross-sectional* (data are collected at a single point in time)
Knowledge acquired from workshop attendance	Same time of year in 2014, 2015, 2016 and 2017	Four times	Four random samples of participants from different workshops	Estimate of changes in knowledge	*Longitudinal: trend* (surveying a particular group over time)
Attitude to health and well-being	Started in 1995 and every 5 years after that (2000, 2005, 2010, 2015)	Five times	Five random samples of attendees from the 1995 programme	Estimate of changes in attitude	*Longitudinal: cohort* (surveying a particular group over time, but the people in the group may vary)
Attitude and knowledge towards diet and exercise	Same time of year in 2014, 2015, 2016 and 2017	Four times	One: the same sample	Estimate of changes in attitudes and knowledge	*Longitudinal: panel* (surveying the same group over time)
The merits of the two workshop series	Once in 2017; after the completion of the workshops	Once	Two groups: (1) the Healthy Lifestyle attendees and (2) the Active Living attendees	Comparison of attitudes and knowledge	*Comparative* (contrasting one group with another: see experimental research strategy)

Sample importance to survey research

Selecting the sample for a research study is often the one aspect the researcher spends least time considering but is probably the most important part of the design. This aspect tends to be taken for granted, not given the attention it deserves. A thoughtful and well-planned sampling approach can have a significant impact on the quality of the overall study. Also, once researchers understand the importance of sampling and the varying techniques that can be used, they can begin to articulate the strengths and weaknesses of the selected approach. Being able to discuss these issues within the research report will demonstrate to others a critical awareness of the impact of the research design and, in particular, sampling on the overall survey's findings.

A sample refers to a part of something that shows the quality or character of the whole. In the context of this text, the sample is a representation of the target population the researcher wishes to investigate. A clear explanation of the target population allows for purposeful generalisations to be made. For generalisations to be made, the beliefs, behaviours, opinions and preferences of the selected sample should reflect those of the population from which they have been drawn.

Sampling from a target population

The first stage in selecting an appropriate sample is to have a clear picture of the target population. Suppose the researchers are interested in examining experienced football referees, elite runners, active elderly women, PE teaching assistants or pre-adolescent inactive children. Being able to define the target population will allow them to begin the process of selecting an appropriate sample from the population. Take the first example: they want to survey experienced football referees to establish their views on the use of pitch-side technology during matches. They want to identify whether referees feel that such technological assistance would help or hinder them in their capacity to officiate a match fairly.

To start this process, the researchers would need to consider what their operational definition is for the target population. If their particular focus is on experienced referees, then a starting point may be how they are defining the term experienced. Should an experienced official have refereed a certain number of games across a wide range of playing standards? If so, how many games and to what standard? Should experienced officials possess particular refereeing awards and badges? Or should they have a certain number of years' experience at refereeing? It may be that all these are important and the researchers need to take them all into account when defining the target population. It is through having a clear picture of the target population that they can start to establish the type of sampling technique they wish to use.

Once a target population has been selected based on an operational definition it then becomes possible to consider the sample. It may well be the case that the population is so small that all members can be sampled. The researcher may be interested in surveying all 11 employees of a small sports clothing company and therefore it is relatively easy. It is often the case, however, that the target population is made up of many more members and therefore attempting to sample all would be unrealistic in terms of both time and resources. Consideration therefore has to be given to how a sample can be extracted from the target population.

 Learning activity 6.3

Identify three different specific populations you may encounter during your daily sporting activities and that relate to your broader research topic area. These may be coaches, referees, parents, PE teachers, sport officers, tutors, students, performers or assistants. Consider their gender, age, physical and mental ability level and experiences. So, for example, you may have encountered secondary school PE teachers or junior tennis players.

Now try and describe the three populations in as much detail as possible. Think about the characteristics they share. What specific skills may they have or need? What environments do they regularly encounter? What activities do they participate in? What physical attributes do they have in common? Do they share social and cultural experiences that group them together? Are you able to describe these?

Make sure to compare your three populations and take time to reflect on how they may or may not be different. What features, qualities and/or characteristics are you using to differentiate between the populations? How may an understanding of your target populations impact on your research? And how easy will it be to obtain a sample from your selected population?

Development of a survey sampling frame

How well a sample represents the target population depends on the *sampling frame*, the specific technique used to select the sample and the sample size. Once the population of interest has been defined, the next stage is to determine the sampling frame – the list of units within the target population from which the sample will be drawn. These units could be people, places (e.g. schools, sports fields, leisure centres) or things (e.g. coaching records, attendance logs, equipment use). Ideally, the sampling frame will be identical to the target population. So, if researchers wanted to sample leisure centres they would ensure that their list contains all possible leisure centres that fit within their target population operational definition. The importance of this is that each unit in the sampling frame has an equal chance of being included within the sample.

Often, however, this is not the case. For example, a researcher may wish to survey local opinion on the recent closure of a swimming pool by taking a sample of the community (the target population of interest), but does so by only surveying people who were on the swimming pool's membership register (the sampling frame). In such a scenario, the sampling frame may not represent the population as the register will be biased, as it is based only on those who used the facilities.

The goal, therefore, is to locate or construct a list that includes all members of the target population. However, this can be extremely problematic, particularly within the scope of an undergraduate research project. Consider students who wanted to target students across a local network of sport colleges. In this instance, they may be able to obtain registers for all those who attend classes, thus are able to generate a representative sampling frame. However, it may be the case that other students wanted to target their local sports centre. Although they could obtain a list of all memberships, many others who are not registered may use the facilities.

Sampling techniques

This links nicely to sampling techniques. Remember that the process of sample selection should reflect the characteristics and qualities of the target population selected. Using appropriate sampling techniques, the researcher can ensure that the sample is representative and therefore corresponds as closely as possible to the population. To maximise this, all members of the target population should have an equal chance of being selected for the sample. Because the ability to generalise from a sample is limited by the sample frame, it is important that, within any research report, the process undertaken to determine the sampling frame is detailed, indicating the likely chance each unit has of being included within the sample.

Sampling techniques are typically divided into two types. The first is referred to as *non-probability* sampling. In this approach samples are selected based on a judgement regarding the characteristics of the target population and the needs of the research question. With these techniques, outlined in Table 6.2, the researcher is less confident that the chosen sample reflects the target population. This will impact on the precision of estimate, that is, our ability to make estimations about the population based on the study sample. When a non-probability sampling technique is used, some members of the target population could have a greater or lesser chance of being selected than others. With this approach, the researcher is increasing the likelihood that the chosen sample will not represent the population. This being the case, the survey's findings may not be applicable to the target population.

Table 6.2   The advantages and disadvantages of sampling techniques

Sample type	Description	Advantages	Disadvantages
Non-probability Purposive sample	Selecting units purposely based on specific qualities or characteristics that relate to your research question	• Inexpensive • Using best available information	• No estimates of accuracy • May miss important elements
Volunteer sample	Actively asking members of the target population to take part in the survey. The sample is based only on those willing to volunteer for your study	• Co-operative respondents • Easy to access	• Not representative of population • May have biased opinions
Haphazard sample Snowball sample	Selecting units due to their ease of contact and availability Previously identified members identify other members of the population	• Available sample • Reduces time and cost • Can quickly lead to a large study sample • Can all have similar qualities and characteristics	• No relation to population necessary • Sample may not suit study needs • All members of the sample may be very similar, distorting generalisability
Convenience sample	The use of a group of individuals or units who are readily available	• Easy to acquire a study sample • Can be useful as a pilot study sample	• Not representative of population • May introduce unwanted bias
Quota sample	Selected based on the proportions of subgroups needed to represent the proportion in the population	• Willing respondents • Allows for a quick process	• May only represent the population based on superficial characteristics
Probability Simple random sample	Every unit in the population has an equal chance of being selected using a random table of numbers	• Sample should accurately reflect population • Sampling error can be calculated	• Potentially expensive • Sampling frame required

Stratified random sample	The target population is grouped according to meaningful characteristics or strata	• Ensures random representation of contrasting groups based on their qualities/ characteristics	• Often requires large sample sizes to produce statistically meaningful results
Systematic sample	Every xth unit on a complete list of eligible units is selected. For example, every even, odd, fifth, tenth unit is selected from your sampling frame list	• No need to assign numbers to participants' names and then look them up (as in random sampling)	• If inherent ordering is apparent, may bias sample
Cluster sample	Natural groups or clusters are sampled, with members of each group subsampled afterwards	• Allows for more concentration of sample by first grouping unit together (clustering)	• Labour- and time-intensive • Requires a large initial population

The second technique is known as probability sampling and provides a statistical basis for saying that a sample is representative of the target population. In this approach each member of the population should have a known probability of being included within the sample, implying a random chance of being selected, therefore ensuring objectivity in choice of sample. As outlined in Table 6.2, a range of probability sampling techniques can be deployed, depending on both the research question and the nature of the target population. If the researcher wants to increase the likelihood of the sample reflecting the selected target population, then this approach should be selected. What this means in plain talk is that, although the researchers cannot be completely confident that the sample represents the target population exactly, they can determine the amount of error associated with an estimate of the population.

Consider a sample of 30 physical training officer recruits from 200 trainees at the RAF physical training centre. They may well show very similar qualities and characteristics compared to the overall target population. If the researchers use a random sampling approach, each member of the population has an equal chance of being selected and, therefore, the sample should resemble the population. Surveying all 200 trainees would offer the best solution in eliminating error, but this is often unachievable. Instead, we have to accept that there will always be some degree of discrepancy.

The researchers cannot be completely confident that the sample they have drawn truly reflects the overall opinions and behaviours of the entire group and, depending on the sampling techniques, may actually increase the differences between the two. So, the greater the sampling error associated with the selected sample, the lower the precision of estimation back to the population. Trying to make generalisations from a sample of 30 back to the overall group of 200 can become extremely problematic and it is easy to make incorrect assumptions about the target population based on the survey's findings.

No matter how the sample is drawn from the larger population, therefore, the sample will always misrepresent the population to some extent. It is possible to determine this amount of misrepresentation, known as *sampling error*. By calculating such error, the researcher can estimate the degree to which the sample and the target population differ. Calculating the sampling error enables us to be more confident in the predictions and generalisations made as a result of the survey findings. A wide range of resources on the internet can help establish the sampling error within a research study. Additionally, listed at the end of this chapter, further readings direct you to texts that guide you through this process.

Unless the researcher is able to sample the entire population, sampling error cannot be avoided. It can be reduced, however, by obtaining a sample of sufficient size. This brings us to the final factor that will determine how well the sample reflects the target population: *sample size*. The sample size simply refers to the number of units that need to be surveyed for the study. The most appropriate way to establish the correct sample size is to apply statistical calculations that can easily be found by typing in 'sample size' into any popular internet search engine. Although heavily dependent on resources and time, increasing the size will certainly increase the accuracy of the sample. However, for every unit added to a sample comes the additional resource drain on time and money.

Researchers must, therefore, decide whether such sampling techniques and the implications of the findings match what they are attempting to solve through the research. For many projects, the opportunity to have a large sample population may not be practical or realistic. Nevertheless, understanding the sampling technique and its effect on sampling error will assist the researcher in drawing conclusions about the survey data.

 Learning activity 6.4

How you select the sample from the target population can have a significant impact on the nature of your conclusions and scope of the recommendations. Applying the knowledge you have gained so far in this chapter and referring back to Table 6.1, consider how each sampling technique would impact on the research scenario below.

You want to explore why the fitness suite satisfaction level is low among weekend gym members compared to those who attend during mid-week. The centre has already conducted a question-naire with all members (target population) and recently purchased new equipment for the fitness suite. For your research study you will undertake interviews and conduct a number of focus groups to find out more about the reasons for the initial questionnaire findings.

Insert within the questions below the different probability and non-probability sampling techniques covered. Replace the blank space with 'haphazard', or 'random', for example. Try and answer the questions in relation to the research scenario above first. Once you have done this, apply these to your own research question.

- If I chose a _____sampling technique, how would I select my sample?
- Will gym members be willing to participate if I chose the _____ sampling technique?
- If I chose a _____ sampling technique, would I be able to generalise my findings?
- What are the limitations/advantages of choosing the _____ sampling technique?

Selecting a data collection method

The most important question that must now be asked is: what will be the most appropriate data collection method(s) for the research study? This decision will be directly related to the research problem that you are attempting to solve, but also influenced by the sample that has been selected, physical resources, time availability, facilities and cost. The research method, comprising collection technique and procedure, allows the researcher an opportunity to record data needed to answer the research question. As the choice of methods can have a large impact on overall survey findings, the ability to think smart will maximise the quality of the data.

Standardisation is the key characteristic of survey research methods that provides a degree of consistency in the instruments used. Consistency here refers to assessment across participants to ensure comparability in findings from everyone involved. It doesn't mean that everyone has to provide the same answers to the questions. Rather, the instrument used and the procedure undertaken to administer the questions should be the same for everyone. Whether that be a questionnaire, a series of interview questions or a focus group, without such standardisation, analysis of trends and patterns of data within or between samples would be meaningless. Without uniformity of approach any differences observed within a sample may be down to the procedures and tools used rather than underlying population differences.

Suppose researchers were interested in children's physical activity levels and the identified problem focused on why many young people seem to reduce their physical activity levels once they finish compulsory schooling. Through a process of narrowing the problem down, the researchers would form a specific question, say: what is the impact of local amenities and events on continued activity involvement in this target population? The researchers have been able to get access to a local sample of 30 post-16 school leavers aged 17–19 who have all volunteered to take part in the research study. They opted for a cross-sectional design and applied a volunteer sampling strategy. At first, they obtained details about all that was locally available to the school leavers so that they could create specific questions.

At this point, the researchers decided on the technique and procedure that would best capture the school leavers' thoughts on this matter. They knew that there were a number of instruments and techniques that could be used, namely questionnaires, interviews or focus groups, and a range of ways these could be administered to the group – face-to-face interviews, individually or in groups (focus group); telephone interviews; self-completion questionnaires on printed paper or questionnaires administered electronically via the internet or e-mail. They wanted to make sure they got as much quality information from everyone by allowing them the opportunity to explore openly all of their thoughts on the issues. They were aware, however, that they had a very short timescale and would be collecting and analysing all the data alone.

If you were in this situation what choice would you make? How would your choice impact on the quality of your data? Is one instrument or technique better than any others on this occasion? Would you be able to use more than one? And, if so, how would you organise this? How best could you administer or conduct this to ensure quality in your responses? Is one approach quicker than any others, considering the time constraints? Is one instrument or technique easier to evaluate than the others? How might this impact on the findings in relation to your initial research question? These are all important questions to think about when considering which research method to opt for.

Data collection instruments

How we gain information from people via the questions we ask them can have a significant impact on the quality of their responses. Just think back to the last time you filled out a self-completion questionnaire, for example. It may have been an end-of-year sport biomechanics unit evaluation or part of someone's final-year dissertation. In either case, the data collection instrument used may have required you to provide an answer to a pre-determined question, probably by ticking a box or maybe writing a few lines.

Based on your own experiences consider the following questions. How easy was it to fill out? Were you able to understand all of the questions? Was anyone available to help you if you didn't understand? What did you do if the answer you wanted to give did not fit the answers provided? Was there space for you to add extra comments? Were all the questions closed?

How about an interview? You may have had one in order to get on your sports course, or as part of a 'careers in sport' module. This may have been individually or in a larger group. To be successful here requires a clear understanding of the questions asked so that you can effectively communicate your answer. General or more specific open-style questions allow you to give more subjective answers. The interview gives you and the interviewer much more freedom and flexibility in the way it unfolds.

Think about the last time you had an interview and consider these questions. How did the questions link? Did they allow you to evolve your answers? How were you supported if you didn't understand a question? Were the questions more open than closed? Did you feel you had the freedom to express your thoughts and opinions? Did you have the opportunity to elaborate on the interviewer's questions? What feedback, verbal and non-verbal, did you receive during the interview? How did this make you feel? If there was more than one of you, were you able to put your point of view across? Did the interviewer engage all participants in the process? Were some members more dominant than others? Were your views shared by others?

Reflecting on our own experiences is an important process and will help us in our decisions. What is important is that ultimately the decisions made should ensure the researcher is able to maximise data in order to answer the research question. The questions the researcher wants to ask the participants through the instruments used can influence the type of responses obtained. Whether a questionnaire, interview or both are chosen and how these are administered will dictate the nature of the participant's responses. Add to this the style of questions asked, whether open or closed (open questions allow respondents to reply however they wish, while closed questions generate fixed answers), and instruments can be selected to provide the researcher with a large degree of response variation.

Table 6.3 illustrates the range of data collection techniques that can be used to collect data. In addition, the type of procedure that is applied to administer the instruments will impact on the nature and scope of responses received from participants.

Table 6.3   Typical data collection methods used during survey research

Data collection procedure	Data collection technique	Advantages	Disadvantages
Face-to-face (individual/ group)	Questionnaire, interview, focus group	• Personal contact allows for checking in understanding • Allows for elaboration if not clear • Flexibility of questions • Rapport building	• Time associated with administration and analysis • Interviewer bias can impact on responses • Cost of travel, printing, etc.
Self-completion web-based/ electronic/ e-mail	Questionnaire	• Cost saving • Ease of editing/data mining • Fast delivery time to respondents • Potentially quicker response times • Novelty through use of images, colour, fonts on web pages	• Samples could be linked (access) • Confidentiality • Layout/presentation issues • Need for very clear instructions • Obtaining e-mail addresses • Respondents need computer access • E-mails easy to delete
Self-completion paper-based/ mail	Questionnaire	• Allows respondents to answer at their leisure • No researcher bias involved	• Time associated with delivery to and from • Level of understanding • Detailed instruction required • Response rate
Telephone	Questionnaire and interview	• People can be contacted fast over the phone • Can lead to a better response rate than mail surveys	• Lengthy calls can cost • Lacks familiar personal approach • Responses can be misinterpreted • Difficulty in recording accuracy of responses – introduces bias

Responses to questions

An important point to consider once you have selected a data collection approach is whether the type of instrument selected matches the type of response required. Consider researchers who were interested in establishing adults' attitudes to the impact that aggressive behaviour in football, shown on television, has on children who watch and play it. In order to collect the data, they decided to choose a self-completion questionnaire that required the adults to answer a series of closed questions and rate their responses on a scale of 1 to 5 (i.e. Likert scale). They administered the questionnaire and, following data collection, presented the findings numerically. Because they opted for closed questions using a number scale to record attitudes, they found it difficult to explore fully the reasons why the adults felt the way they did.

The fact they followed a quantitative approach means that the researchers may have inadvertently missed the opportunity to identify the adults' subjective deeper experiences. If they had taken a qualitative approach, they might have gained greater understanding of their numerical responses. In this instance, numerical representation of attitudes failed to reveal all. Because of the way in which the questions had been constructed, the adults were unable to communicate fully their attitudes and opinions to the researcher. Although some nice data were collected with the self-completion questionnaire, the way in which the instrument had been set up (i.e. closed questions) did not really allow the researchers to answer their research question fully.

A better approach may have been to include several open-ended questions, allowing the adults the opportunity to explain and expand on their answers. Time, resources and the researchers' ability permitting, they could have constructed individual face-to-face or focus group interviews providing a more enriched account of the adults' true feelings and beliefs. Words that express their subjective thoughts could have provided a better picture than numbers. The type of data analysis that would have taken place would not have been descriptive or statistical, but qualitative, exploring narrative and content. For example, recording the interviews and then transcribing, coding and interpreting the data would have offered a different insight. The extra time and effort spent on this could have provided a much clearer picture of the attitudes of the adults and led to more meaningful conclusions.

 Learning activity 6.5

Take your time when constructing the data collection approach. You may be lucky and be able to use questionnaires that have already been constructed, such as those commonly used in sport and exercise psychology or physical activity. If this is the case, make sure you know how the questionnaire functions, what data it will produce and how you will analyse and interpret the data. Which ontological view does this approach fit and does it link to what you want from your research?

If you have to construct your own instrument or develop a focus group of interview questions, don't be put off, as this is a straightforward process. Refer to the Further reading at the end of this chapter for a range of texts to support you in this. Your most important ally is your tutor, so make sure you seek support soon in the research process. If you indicate at the beginning on your research plan that an instrument needs developing, you will give yourself plenty of time to construct, pilot and amend your instrument and technique ahead of the main research study.

To help you in this process you may want to ask yourself the following questions.

- Will respondents easily understand the questions? How will you check this?
- How long will the instrument or process take? How many questions?
- Do respondents know how to indicate a response? Will this be explicitly indicated?
- Will respondents understand what they have to do? Will there be clear, standardised explanation?
- Will privacy be respected and protected? How will you ensure this?
- How will information be recorded and collected? What technique will enhance accuracy?

Conducting the survey

The administration of the survey, whether it is a postal questionnaire, face-to-face interview or focus group, must be carefully considered before you start. Typically with survey research, you should have already undertaken a pilot study to enhance the instrument and familiarise yourself with techniques such as asking questions, taking notes and recapping. It is at this point that researchers must recognise their own skill set and knowledge base and be realistic about their level of experience in conducting surveys. Seeking and receiving additional training and advice from a tutor may therefore be paramount.

You will probably find that there is often a reluctance to take part. This can be for a number of reasons, ranging from scepticism, competitiveness or survey fatigue to dislike of form filling, lack of time and lack of privacy. How and where the survey is conducted can therefore have an important impact on the number of responses and involvement with the research. Asking people in the high street on a busy Saturday afternoon about their views on a local swimming pool development may not provide the findings hoped for. Similarly, trying to explore a golf coach's thoughts on the coach–player relationship in his golf shop may be awkward for him and his members. The setting, therefore, will impact on the quality of input from the respondent.

The interviewer's manner and style when approaching people will dictate the nature of their responses. How the interviewer communicates, both verbally and non-verbally, throughout the data collection process may alter the respondent's perceptions, thoughts and opinions. Researchers must ensure neutrality throughout, not attempting to direct responses or force their own opinions on respondents. Interviewer appearance is also important: would you feel more comfortable talking to a smartly dressed professional student or a scruffy, sports-kit-wearing student? Think about how others may perceive you and the impression you make. How might this impact on the successfulness of data collection? What impact will this have on the respondent's willingness to support your research?

If you are administering a questionnaire, how you send it could impact on the success rate. The issues of response rate and non-responders are of particular importance when using questionnaires and therefore implementing strategies can help increase the rate of return. Response rate is calculated by dividing the total number of returned questionnaires by the total number administered, then multiplying the answer by 100. So, if a researcher sent out 50 questionnaires to a local junior football club and received 29 back then the response rate would be $(29 \div 50) \times 100 = 58\%$. In an ideal situation we would have a response rate of 100%, but this very rarely happens, particularly as the sample size goes up.

Structuring the survey report

Irrespective of how survey research is presented, whether it is a poster, scientific report, presentation, video/web blog, audio recording or newspaper article, the structure should follow a similar pattern and include the key aspects of the selected research strategy. With a clear expression of objectives linked to the research question, the project must justify the reasons why a survey approach was applied in comparison to all others. The researcher must make reference to the target population, providing an appropriate operational definition. The sampling frame, sampling technique and likely sampling error should also be included. The selection of research design (e.g. cross-sectional, longitudinal) needs to be expressed and justified, as well as the data collection instruments and the procedures relating to their administration. This should include the total number in the sample, attrition rate (if applicable) and the process of survey collection. Finally, the data analysis techniques likely to be used (descriptive or statistical) should be discussed in detail.

 Chapter review

Throughout this chapter the wide-ranging survey research strategy has been encountered and dissected. This non-experimental research approach, which employs questionnaires and interviews, attempts to understand more about people's sporting attitudes, beliefs, opinions and demographics. Through the implementation of selective sampling techniques, instrument design and administration, the researcher is able to establish relationships between factors and determine how attitudes change over time. Covering both social and natural sciences, the survey research approach offers flexibility in design and method while maintaining a logical systematic structure throughout. It is for this very reason that the survey strategy is incredibly valuable to the researcher interested in sporting behaviours and their meanings. By using a range of sport-related research examples throughout this chapter you should now be able to:

☑ explain the key characteristics of the survey research strategy;

☑ define and explain the linked stages of survey research;

☑ understand the importance of survey design and sampling techniques to improve this research approach;

☑ identify the range of data collection method(s) that can be applied to the survey strategy.

Further reading

Andres, L (2012) *Designing and Doing Survey Research*. London: SAGE Publications.

De Vaus, D (2013) *Surveys in Social Research*. 6th ed. New York: Routledge.

These comprehensive books take the reader through the complete survey research process. Although lacking in relevant sport-related examples and illustrations, *Designing and Doing Survey Research* and *Surveys in Social Research* will offer all that is needed for anyone undertaking survey research.

Bryman, A (2015) *Social Research Methods*. 5th ed. Oxford: Oxford University Press.

This is a particularly useful research methods textbook that complements this chapter well. Packed full of practical activities, clear diagrams and comprehensive explanations, aspects relating to data analysis and survey instrument construction are of value to the reader planning on undertaking a survey strategy.

7

Observational research strategy

 Learning objectives

By identifying research situations in which an observational research strategy would be applied, this chapter is designed to help you:

- review the characteristics of an observational method;
- appreciate which observational strategies suit which kinds of research questions;
- be able to select an appropriate observational strategy based on your specific research question;
- identify the varying roles the researcher may play in observational research and their implications for research outcomes;
- understand how observational study reports may be organised to help communicate research findings in a clear and coherent way.

Introduction

We collect all our data by observing the facts that we can see. Strictly speaking then, all research can be classified as observational in nature. What separates this approach from others covered within this book are the series of primary assumptions that govern how it is conducted and the generalisations developed as a consequence. Solely involving the researcher making observations, the use of this strategy in sport is extremely valuable. Through systematic inquiry into the nature and qualities of observable group behaviours the researcher can learn what it means to be a member of a group and how those being observed interact with others to form social connections.

The value of observational research to sport

Directly observing is a fundamental part of learning and an important part of the discovery process for us as researchers. Whether we observe sport performers before, during and after competition, coaches delivering individual or group sessions, sport-related practitioners in their own workplace, gym users during their workouts, children during formal PE sessions or participants in a biomechanics research study, we are able to establish meaning from how people behave in a range of situations. Providing us with unique insights into complex social structures and interconnected behaviours, the application of the observational research approach to sport can offer the researcher a Pandora's box of opportunities. Understanding groups in their natural sporting or workplace environments, away from control and manipulation, provides the researcher with an extremely valuable opportunity to play a number of roles within the research setting and use a range of research methods to collect data.

 Reflection point 7.1

Observational research refers to a non-experimental approach, which involves the direct observation and measurement of behaviour that may occur in a range of settings. Data collection methods can be broadly categorised as primarily quantitative or qualitative based on the nature of the research question. Qualitative observation research emphasises collecting in-depth information on a small number of individuals or within a very limited setting; quantitative observation research emphasises data collection on specific behaviours within larger groups that can be easily quantified.

Although the observational strategy may appear very simple, a great deal of thought is required to ensure the researcher is able to make accurate and meaningful observations. We can all stand on the sidelines of a pitch and make a few notes about how players respond to the referee's decision or watch a runner and comment on her technique as she changes pace. To explore the behaviour we are observing fully, however, whether that be the social interactions, identities and interconnected relationships on that pitch or movement sequencing, timing and rhythm during the run, we must approach this in a much more systematic way. The reasons for conducting observational research may range from a desire to learn about behaviour to a research attempt to test a specific proposition drawn from a theory of human movement.

Learning activity 7.1

Observing behaviour and recording it accurately are key goals when applying this approach. The purpose, therefore, of this activity is to help you become more aware of the different observational skills required when we look at someone's behaviour. It should also allow you to recognise the systematic and selective nature of observation and how your own feelings and knowledge may influence what you notice.

Observe a person who is sat in front of you for 3 minutes. Write down ten statements describing the person and his or her behaviour. Once you have finished, answer the following:

1.   Which statements describe the person as a person (physical characteristics, etc.)?

2.   Which statements describe the person's behaviour?

Now observe a sport performer in action for 3 minutes (the internet may provide you with a good video clip) and again write down ten statements that describe the performer and his or her behaviour. Once you have finished, answer the following:

1.   Which statements describe the sport performer as a person (physical characteristics, etc.)?

2.   Which statements describe the sport performer's behaviour?

Now you've had the chance to observe people from passive to active, try to compare and see what observational skills were required for each. The following questions may help you:

•   Which observation was easiest to do? Why?

•   Which observation provided the most raw materials for description? Why?

•   Consider the order of your statements for both observations. What does this tell you about what is most important or apparent to you?

•   Try to compare your observations with those of another student. What differences or similarities do you notice? How do you explain these? How can you use this information to assist you with your own observational project?

As with other research approaches that occur in natural settings (e.g. case study and ethnographic), away from controlled conditions, the observational research strategy attempts to gain a holistic or whole perspective of the study group. Conducting the research in a natural environment attempts to ensure that freely occurring behaviour is maximised and not contrived or artificial. For example, observing the behaviours of sports centre staff to a sudden influx of members may provide a valuable insight into management processes, staff capabilities and physical resource provision. If you were to construct this situation artificially by asking a group to appear suddenly all at once and then observing the staff's response, you would remove unanticipated behaviours you might want to observe and record. Observing over a period of time allows for a more natural take on the staff, their interactions with members and each other, and their collective behaviours during busy times.

Through freely occurring behaviour across a less manipulated approach, the researcher can then begin to offer solutions to problems that really exist.

Unlike the experimental research strategy, the observational approach is not concerned with having straightforward, right or wrong answers. Furthermore, changing the study direction is quite common because there may be more than one question and new ones may appear as the research process progresses. For this very reason, such naturalistic approaches to research are often avoided by students and their tutors. The very thought that the research direction and question are unknown means that this is not a viable and valid research approach for many.

Such a conclusion is drawn more because of a lack of insight rather than the robustness of the approach. When we accept that change is inevitable with all dynamic systems, the observational strategy is fundamental if we are to know more about sporting behaviours.

 Student case study 7.1

As part of Thomas's MSc Sport Coaching programme he undertook a module entitled 'Developing Expertise in Sport'. This required him to develop an understanding of how coaches develop and maintain expertise, appraising their own coaching practice in the context of current approaches to skill development. To gain an insight into varying levels of coaching practice, Thomas chose to observe behaviours exhibited by coaches of different expertise levels across a range of sports. He hoped this would provide him with an initial framework he could use to inform his practice and his literature gathering.

Thomas selected a systematic approach to his qualitative observational approach, whereby he attended ten coaching sessions across a range of sports and observed behaviours at critical points throughout. Each session ran between 60 and 90 minutes, so coaches' interactions with players and assistants were observed for selected time periods (i.e. 15 minutes each) at the start, mid- and end points of each session. By applying this event sampling design, he took an observer-as-participant role, which allowed some slight involvement with the session (setting up and handing out/collecting in equipment) while he recorded coaching behaviours. Thomas had previously worked alongside his tutor to create a pre-defined data collection template. This ensured that he entered into each observation with an objective recording tool, noting down all linguistic, extra-linguistic, non-verbal and spatial behaviour throughout each designated time period. Furthermore, Thomas created categories that enabled him to record the tone (pitch, strength, depth), volume (high, mid, low) and direction (positive, negative or neutral) of verbal commentary made by the coach.

After he had completed all ten sessions Thomas collated observation templates and made detailed notes of his findings. He was able to identify several common themes that related to coach expertise. These were based around coaches' specialised knowledge of their sport, their organizational skills throughout the session, clarity and continuous reinforcement of session aims and objectives, positive relationships with players and the ability to problem solve quickly and develop a number of solutions. Thomas shared his observations with his tutor and module group, using his findings as the basis of a literature review.

Characteristics of observation research

In many ways the observational approach is unique to other strategies encountered within this book. Although we have already discussed that all research uses observation in one way or another, the nature of this particular research approach provides the researcher with unique challenges that are not always encountered with other approaches. The very nature of observational research requires researchers to take on a specific role with the intention of observing and then capturing social behaviour as accurately as possible. In considering their involvement with any selected participants, therefore, they must consider how the degree of personal contact and insight into the participant's world may influence the validity of the findings; that is, how researchers interact with participants and how their involvement may alter their behaviour.

Take the example of a researcher who, wishing to understand players' behaviour when given a red card, wanted to offer more advice to officials in order to help them defuse aggressive behaviour. If the researcher, as participant in the football game, knowingly intimidated and provoked other players, thereby creating an unnatural response, the observable behaviour would not necessarily represent what is normally displayed when issuing a red card for an offence. If another player, however, not knowing about the ongoing research (i.e. unobtrusive), had instigated provocation then any response would represent behaviour within a more naturally set social context.

It is important, therefore, that researchers understand the role they play in the research and how this can impact on the research setting. They must ensure their role is *empathically neutral* and that they do not project their own beliefs, views, goals, experiences, values or research biases on to the research participants. They have a moral and ethical responsibility as researchers and must consider their important position and how it can impact on the research and the generalisability of findings. Be aware that when the presence of the researchers alters the naturalistic behaviours and social interactions observed, this impacts on the very purpose of why they are there in the first place.

 Research focus 7.1

In a study by Nicholls and Worsfold (2016), an observational research strategy was applied to investigate the observational capabilities of experienced elite coaches whilst they were focusing on soccer-specific actions and playing positions with elite youth players.

Applying a direct observational approach that required continuous monitoring of performance variables, six coaches viewed post-match performance from video evidence in order to make objective assessments of performance. As a comparison, an analytical software package was used as a measure of the 'true' performance outcome, given the increase in accuracy made possible with pausing and rewinding. The identified variables were successful and unsuccessful tackling, short passing, long passing, shooting, dribbling and heading.

A total of 1730 (1165 successful and 565 unsuccessful) actions were recorded when performance was observed by the coaches when compared to the 4463 (3415 successful and 1048 unsuccessful) collected

(Continued)

(Continued)

from the software analytics. Findings revealed that effective observational analysis (coaching recollection) accounted for only 34.1% and 53.9% of successful and unsuccessful actions, respectively.

The authors concluded that poorer observational coach accuracy may have significant implications for talent identification devoid of post-performance analysis. These conclusions reinforced the importance of comprehensive augmented feedback for coaches when assessing performance outcomes with youth players.

A further factor to consider when applying this strategy to answer a particular research question relates to the focus of approach. Observations can, broadly speaking, be split into two categories: macro and micro. *Macro* refers to the observational activity that encompasses a broad focus, viewing the group as a whole and observing all activity; for example, observing a cricket team during their entire innings, or a swimming squad throughout a training session. Focus at a *micro* level, on the other hand, uses small and highly specific behaviours as the unit of observation. The researcher may wish to observe the cricket team only when they're in a huddle after a wicket or the swimming squad between exercise drills. It is important to recognise, however, that these two broad categories are not mutually exclusive. For example, researchers may use the macro approach at the start of a project and change to the micro as their familiarity with this approach increases, and an understanding of the participants and their environment grows.

One of the unique factors of observation is the length of time the researcher spends in the field. Typically, the amount of time depends on the research question and the role assumed by the researcher, as some roles (covered later on in the chapter) require the researcher to gain a degree of rapport with people within a given situation and setting. What will also dictate the time allocated to this is the defined period the researcher has been allotted to complete a project. When considering how long is needed with the selected participants, the time taken to plan needs to be factored in. If you are realistic about what can and cannot be achieved in that time, you will not make unnecessary decisions. Prolonged time in the research setting needs very careful planning and therefore careful consideration when designing a study is essential.

What is often neglected in the planning, and is the distinguishing characteristic of this approach, is the process of entering and leaving the field of study. Again, it is very likely that the research question will dictate this and it will be a relatively straightforward process. There may be projects, however, that require a much more calculated entrance and exit strategy, particularly if the researcher has created strong bonds with the group being researched.

Types of sporting behaviour

One of the most important questions that should be asked during an observational study concerns the behaviours that should be observed. The very nature of this question lies at the heart of any research project and knowing the types of behaviours that are desired will allow for not only focus within the research question, but also selection of the most appropriate research methods. The spin-off is that researchers will be more productive during data collection and able to articulate their findings more accurately.

If you think for a moment about a sporting event you recently watched or took part in, you could probably outline a long list of the behaviours you observed. Before moving on, just stop for 60 seconds and consider all the behaviours you witnessed at that event. Make a mental note of them all now. Once you've done that try and group them based on similar characteristics, e.g. were the behaviours observed in speech or were they displayed in a physical form?

Behaviours we observe with our senses provide us with a window into the complex world of how people function, feel and interact when playing or engaging in sport and exercise. Remember, the social world is multi-dimensional and as researchers our primary goal is to be aware of others – watching, listening and recording what we observe. Hopefully, during the brief exercise above, you would have noticed that behaviours can easily be categorised based on key characteristics. These will range from emotional constructs such as sadness, surprise, anger or fear to more physical manifestations such as pushing, pulling, kicking, hitting or throwing. What you may not have recalled were behaviours linked to linguistic or verbal communication. The type of speech, such as the words used to express thoughts and feelings, the loudness or quietness of voices, the pace of speech and possibly the emphasis placed on certain words or phrases can tell us a great deal about behaviour. The way the father speaks angrily to his son after the football match, the softness of voice used to console a performer who has just lost out on a medal or the emphasis or intonation in positive affirmations used by the coach during a half-time talk can all provide us with a real insight to what participants may have been thinking, based on the outward behaviour they were exhibiting.

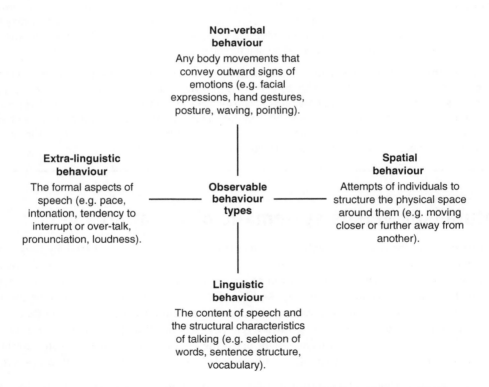

Figure 7.1   Four types of behaviour that may be observed by the researcher.

Having a clear idea about the type of behaviours that may need to be observed within the field allows us to construct appropriate operational definitions ahead of data collection. As illustrated in Figure 7.1, four main behavioural types exist, each likely to be encountered during observational research. Recognising each and knowing how participants may exhibit them are vital to effective data collection.

Key point 7.1

Observational research is a form of non-experimental research (field-based) which is naturalistic. It can take the form of cohort, cross-sectional and case-controlled studies and is often referred to as observational as the research merely observes the behaviour of others.

Reflection point 7.2

The next time you tune into the sports report on television, try and watch out for these four types of behaviour exhibited by the newsreader. Is there one that is more predominant than the others? How many behaviours have you noticed and how often do these occur? Do you find one type of behaviour harder to recognise than the others? What techniques could you use to improve this? Does the newsreader have particular idiosyncrasies, that is, specific behaviours that may be unique to that person? Do the behaviours tend to follow a pattern – a scratch of the arm after a pause in speech, for example? If so, what meanings could we make of this?

Now construct a data collection form. Think about all the information you want to collect while you are observing the newsreader and try to build that into your form. Leave plenty of space so you can write comments and timings. Now repeat the exercise and see whether you are able to capture more of the behaviours exhibited. Has this approach made a difference? What differences have you noticed? How could you adapt such an approach for your project? Can you identify the limitations of this approach? What solutions could you develop to resolve any difficulties?

Naturalistic versus systematic observation

The first decision for researchers will be to select the type of observational strategy they wish to implement. Broadly speaking, these fall into two main categories. The first is known as a *naturalistic* observation that views the observation as an uncontrolled process, in which researchers do not structure the observation in any way. Rather the researchers approach the observation in an unstructured manner, recording behaviour as it happens in a natural setting – whatever that may be! For example, researcher A may wish to observe referee behaviour throughout a game. He starts the observation at the beginning and records right up to the final whistle. He does not stop for breaks, pauses in play or periods of inactivity; he simply records everything he observes with his senses.

The other category is more of a controlled approach and is known as *systematic* observation. These are more careful observations, and are more specific and less global than the naturalistic approach.

The systematic observation is structured with more purpose – whether that is specific events, incidents, types of behaviour or specific time periods. Researcher B may choose to observe the referee only when in a particular area of the pitch, at specific time intervals throughout the game, during times when the referee is booking a player, during specific pauses in play or when giving instruction/feedback to the players. In this way, researcher B is not observing continuously; rather she is basing her observations on critical or pre-defined periods or events.

Observation research design

The broad differences presented above have an impact on the data collected and the findings generated. The selection of the most suitable approach, therefore, provides a key starting point in the development of the research design. If the researchers work through the decision chart shown in Figure 7.2, they will be able to determine which design structure will be best suited to the type of research question they wish to answer.

Consider the three research scenarios listed below. Each one will require reflection back through the chapter and reference to the decision chart (Figure 7.2) in order to find the most appropriate research design. Note that more than one approach could be deployed in order to answer these research questions. The important point, therefore, is the ability to justify why a particular design has been selected over another and what its implications are for the research scenarios.

Try and answer this question as you go along: why do you consider your selected design better than the other approaches?

1. As organiser of an annual football tournament held in a local park, you were aware that an increased amount of litter was left behind following the event last year. Hoping to reduce the amount this year, you place litterbins and notices around the area. You want to find out if people use the bins, where in the park the largest amount of littering occurs, and what exactly is being littered? Which observational strategy could you use to evaluate the successfulness of your 'reduce the litter' campaign?

2. As a basketball coach, you have noticed that, irrespective of the player, when in a specific position on the court, aggressive behaviour is displayed. Not wanting to alter the players' behaviour, you ask a friend to make observations secretly each time the undesired behaviour occurs. You want to know what situations occur just prior to the incidences and what form of aggressive behaviour the player exhibits. Exactly where on the court do these incidences occur, and are other players also involved? Which observational strategy could you use to establish the possible cause of the behaviour?

3. You've just designed a brand new innovative running shoe and want to gauge people's initial thoughts and behaviours when they see it for the first time. Will they be surprised, excited, curious, critical or nonchalant? And what will their body language suggest? Will they be engaged or not really that bothered? Because of the shoe's uniqueness, you are very confident that no one will have seen anything like this before, so capturing their initial responses will be really important. Having organised a focus group and fully briefed all volunteers beforehand, you intend to record their verbal responses and an associate will observe their behaviour. Based on this approach, which observational strategy would your associate use to establish the non-verbal behaviours of the group?

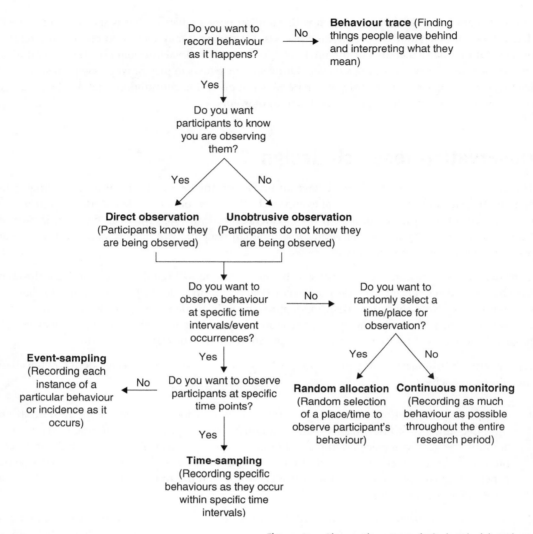

Figure 7.2 Observation research design decision chart.

Now that you have read the three scenarios you should be able to recognise which design matches each problem. Let us start by reviewing research scenario 1. The most appropriate approach would be to conduct a behaviour trace design and observe the evidence either periodically throughout the event or when the event has finished. You are not particularly interested in observing the act of throwing litter away, rather where the litter has ended up. You'll need to know where litter is being placed so tracing evidence throughout the event may allow you to change the locations of the bins and notices. Subsequent observations (i.e. longitudinal design) would then provide you with confirmation of the success of your bin and notice placement. From these findings you can evaluate the success of your campaign and make recommendations to other organisers.

Research scenario 2 requires the use of an unobtrusive event sampling design. Selecting an unobtrusive observational approach eliminates any worry that the players will react differently if they know that they are being observed. Known as the Hawthorne effect, participants can react to the attention they receive from an observer and in turn behave differently. However, not informing the participants that you are collecting data might be considered unethical, so consideration must be given to protecting the participants' rights.

Finally, the research associate in scenario 3 opted for a direct continuous monitoring design that allowed for observation of behavioural responses to the new running shoe throughout the entire focus group session. Selecting this approach ensures that behaviour can be monitored throughout and not at specified time intervals or as a result of events or incidences. Such an approach requires the researcher's full attention and a varied range of data capture tools would need to be used. With large data generation this strategy can provide really valuable insight into the behaviours exhibited by the group, but careful pre-observation planning is essential.

 Learning activity 7.2

The purpose of this activity is to help you focus on the first steps of planning a *direct time-sampling* observational strategy, defining terms and determining whether or not the selected behaviours occur frequently enough to be measured by this approach.

Try and find a coaching session you could go along to where you can observe two players. These may be fellow students during a formal practical lesson, a university or college coaching session or a local team's weekly training meet. Start by choosing six behaviours you expect to see in the course of the session. Ahead of your observation your first task is to write down the six and define them operationally. Remember, the purpose is to define your terms clearly so others can operate from the same basis of understanding.

Behaviour 1

_____

_____

Behaviour 2

_____

_____

Behaviour 3

_____

_____

Behaviour 4

_____

_____

(Continued)

(Continued)

Behaviour 5

_____

_____

Behaviour 6

_____

_____

Now on a separate sheet create a grid for each player, as shown below. Making sure the boxes are large enough to scribe sufficient detail into, write the headings along the first row. Next, in the first column, write in your selected time intervals. If you are observing a 30-minute session, for example, you could break down the time into 5-minute blocks.

Example grid for one player based on 7×7 matrix

Time (minute)	Behaviour 1	Behaviour 2	Behaviour 3	Behaviour 4	Behaviour 5	Behaviour 6
0-5						
5-10						
10-15						
15-20						
20-25						
25-30						

Once you have planned your observation sheet, you can go and observe the two players in action. You are trying to observe firstly whether the players are exhibiting the selected behaviours and secondly the frequency of their occurrence. Using a tally mark system you can quickly know how many times these occur within the given time interval (i.e. if a player shows aggressive behaviour three times in 5 minutes, mark it with /// tally marks in the time interval). If possible, try and note down the events/incidence/activities linked to the behaviour.

After doing the data collection firstly re-examine your operational definitions. Identify any changes you feel would make the tally task easier and more precise. Next, consider what the data are revealing. Are there patterns in behaviour? Are the players showing certain behaviours at particular times? Are there any similarities or differences? What could have influenced these behaviours? Are they linked to types of events/activities within the session or other incidences you've noticed?

Also consider how you could make this activity more advanced. What was the exact duration of the behaviour? And was there an observable effect as a consequence? Comparing behaviours exhibited by different teams, sports or age groups may also provide interesting findings. What about observing behaviours on and off task (e.g. when the player has the football and when the player does not)? Are there differences and what could contribute to these? Do these happen at different times? What could the cause of this be?

Role of the researcher

Determining the researcher's role during observational research data collection is an important aspect and must be selected on the basis of a number of key considerations. Remember, the purpose of the observation is to provide a narrative that informs on a group's complex social structures and interconnected behaviours. Recording what is observed allows the researcher to tag meanings to recorded behaviours and make sense of social interactions. The way the researcher may, or may not, interact with the participants can therefore have significant implications for the value of the data and project conclusions. To understand the importance of the role researchers must consider the problem they wish to solve, the participants' willingness to be studied, the researchers' prior knowledge of or involvement in the participants' environment, and finally their selected observational strategy.

Putting these points into a realistic context, let us consider the following scenario:

> *While watching a school teacher deliver PE lessons to a particular class, we notice the children's behaviour seems to alter depending on the session activities. When indoor gym sessions are conducted the group tends to be more apathetic and disengaged, while when quick cricket is selected more engagement and enjoyment are noticed.*

To understand this problem further and attempt to establish why this may be the case, a student researcher decided to apply an observational approach. She selected a continuous monitoring approach observing the class throughout their two sessions in order to collect as much data as possible. She also observed a second class in the same year group doing the same sessions with the same teacher; in this way she would be able to determine whether it is the session activity that causes the behaviour change or some other factor. Unlike the first class, the second class were unfamiliar to the student researcher and she had to consider that the children's behaviour might change in her presence. She therefore selected to observe both classes without their knowledge. Unobtrusively, she positioned herself in an upper gallery of the sports hall out of sight of the children. Based on this research approach, her role in the project was as a non-participant observer.

Based on the research question, the selected strategy, the group the researcher intends to observe, the environment in which the observation will take place and the influence the researcher's presence may have on the group's behaviour, a role that best suits our research approach must be selected. It is important to recognise that the researcher's role is not set in stone during the research process. Because of the dynamic nature of this research strategy, the role of the researcher throughout the data collection period may change. What is important is that the researcher, as investigator, is able to recognise when this happens, why it happens and how it may impact on the outcome of the research; that is, will the researcher still be able to answer the research question? The role needs to be fluid throughout this process and being adaptable will aid in collecting meaningful observations.

Table 7.1 provides a clear description of the range of roles the researcher could take during the data collection period. Each role will have an impact on the observed behaviours so it is important to build role involvement into the research plan.

Table 7.1   The role of the researcher in observational studies

Role	Description	Benefits/drawbacks	Sporting example
Non-participation	There is no level of involvement with participants and the researcher is either not present at the scene of data collection or out of sight of the group	✓ No influence on participants ✗ May miss observations due to detachment	Watching football fans at a match via a closed-circuit camera system from a location several miles away from the football stadium
Complete observer	There is still no level of involvement, but the researcher is present at the scene. There is no level of interaction or participation with the group	✓ No/limited influence on participants ✗ May miss observations due to detachment	Observing a hockey match while stood on the sidelines
Observer as participant	Mostly involved with observing the participants with only slight involvement with the group	✓ Participants more willing to talk and 'open up' ✗ Brief involvement may lead to misinterpretation and bias	Observing a coaching session, with occasional conversation and physical involvement with the group
Moderate/peripheral member	Balance is maintained between researcher and participants, between participation and observation	✓ Able to view participants from both researcher and participant perspective ✗ Involvement with participants may be difficult to manage	Acting as a classroom assistant, supporting PE delivery by taking parts of the session, while observing the group
Participant as observer	Researcher becomes more involved with the participants' central activities, but does not commit to the group's values or goals	✓ Strong bonds can be achieved that unravel deeper behaviours ✗ Involvement may impact on objectivity of research	Observing a field sport first-hand while on a hunt, but not sharing the same values about animal hunting
Complete participation	The researcher goes native and studies the group in which she/he is already a member. The investigator is seen very much as a member and not a researcher so does not unnaturally alter the flow of interaction	✓ The flow of interaction between researcher and participant allows for a true insider's perspective ✗ Researcher may jeopardise role through over-involvement	Embracing all the rituals of cyclists, that is, shaving legs and using specific jargon in order to find out how they interact and behave as a sporting subculture

| Complete membership | In this ultimate role the researcher and participant relate to each other equally in respect of their shared experiences, feelings and goals. In this role, researchers may never return from the field | ✓ Shared experiences allow for full data-gathering opportunities through a sharing of information
✗ Researcher can be 'contaminated' by the insider's status, beliefs and values, which can bias objectivity | Living with a tribal group in order to observe the role exercise plays in their day-to-day functioning. The need to share experiences and values is required in order to gain acceptance and access to group members. Does not return from the group |

Observation research setting

It is important to remember that, when observing behaviour, the setting in which behaviours are framed can have an influential effect on the group and on how the researcher perceives them. Children dancing in a hall may change their behaviour depending on their familiarity with the surroundings, those who are present and the type of activities others are doing. Sport performers' behaviour may alter if they are playing at home or away, or a crowd's behaviour may be different if they are standing or sitting in football terraces. The skill of describing the setting, prior to observation, will help the researcher make more sense of the actual behaviours. It will also have an important impact on the type of data collection techniques that may be selected as well as the role the researcher plays within the field. If this is defined during the planning stage, the researcher's awareness of its potential influence on behaviours can be realised.

 Learning activity 7.3

Try and observe the two environments outlined below.

Sports hall   Physiology laboratory

If you are unable to observe directly, remember the last time you were in these spaces. For each, list environmental cues that provide you with clues as to the kind of behaviour you might expect or is permitted within each space. Your description should include the physical boundaries of the setting and the arrangement of objects within the setting, i.e. map of setting, layout of equipment, signs, space. You may also wish to consider temperature, other nearby environments that could influence behaviour, the time of day the observations took place, duration of the observation and the date.

Once you have made two detailed lists consider the following points:

1. What features of each environment give the strongest cues as to what kind of behaviour is expected and allowed?

(Continued)

(Continued)

2. Think about those cues that have certain meanings based on social expectations and those that are purely physical.

3. Place an asterisk (*) in front of each statement listed that is an environmental cue linked to specific social expectations.

4. What are the expected social expectations linked to these?

5. What does this tell you about how behaviour in settings is defined?

6. How does the setting influence behaviour? And how may the setting be rearranged to alter behaviour?

Development of data collection techniques

The purpose of the observation is to describe, not judge, and therefore the data collection process and the associated techniques of data recording must ensure the reporting of accurate descriptions that are factual and thorough. As researchers observe, their own experiences and biases can easily impact on their interpretations and therefore they must develop sound techniques that allow for objective recording. If the researchers record the setting that was observed, the activities that took place in that setting and the people who participated in those activities, they should be able to generate an accurate account of the behaviours exhibited within the field of study. In attempting to achieve this, they must make sure that the approach taken to record behaviours is directly linked to the research question and the selected strategy.

How data are recorded can take many forms. The most common in observation research is the use of a diary, journal or reporting template that can act as a scribble pad and/or prompt capturing what the researcher is witnessing. As events, incidences or critical moments occur in the field, the researcher must attentively respond to these, accurately reporting without bias or evaluation. The need for clear written articulation cannot be underestimated if behaviours are to be truly captured.

Using diaries and journals, recording occurrences as and when they happen provides an unstructured approach that requires a high level of experience and ability to articulate observations clearly and accurately. Not bound within a tight framework of pre-determined questions or prompts, rather set within a looser collection of themes, the use of a diary or journal can be extremely valuable as it offers more flexibility. Remember, though, that this research strategy is dynamic, in that the approach and role may change while in the field. The ability to adapt quickly and record the unexpected will offer a more vivid and vibrant description of the interconnectedness of the participants within their natural setting.

 **Key point 7.2**

Consider what can be observed when planning your research data collection approach, and how your data capture tools need to reflect the nature of the behaviours.

• Physical actions linked to movement patterns (fine and gross) may best be captured through video recording.

- Verbal communication between players, or coach and athlete, may require the use of audio-recording devices.

- Expressive behaviour may be captured using a paper-based recording diagram that details body or facial areas.

- Spatial relations and locations within a defined space may be recorded using a motion-tracking system.

- Pictorial records may need to be captured using a camera.

 Research focus 7.2

In a study by McIver and colleagues (2016), an observational research strategy was applied to describe the development and piloting of an Observational System for Recording Physical Activity-Elementary School (OSRAC-E). This system was developed to make direct observations of the levels and types of physical activity and the physical and social dimensions of physical activity with elementary (primary) school children. The categories developed within the observational template included the physical settings, instructional settings and contexts, and all data were recorded (inputted) into a handheld device.

Eight schools participated in the study. Children from each grade were randomly selected from the entire school population, with a final sample of 71 taking part in the observations. Within each school recording took place over the course of a single week. Each child within the sample population was observed for four 20-minute periods. By applying a time-sampling procedure with a 5-second observation window and a 25-second recording period, a total of 40 observation intervals were made by two observers within the 20-minute window.

Overall, there were 11,360 available observation intervals (i.e. 71 children × 20 minutes × 4 periods × 2 = 11,360). This was reduced to 11,076 as some observation periods did not possess any physical activity, or activity was deemed insufficient to be classified as physical in nature. Drawing comparisons between observers, the authors concluded that the OSRAC-E tool provides a reliable and useful direct observation measure of a child's physical activity (type and level) performed within a school context.

The development of observation templates before entering the field allows for pre-defined operational definitions to be embedded in the recording instrument. These will act as reminders, set questions as prompts, timing periods as guidelines and procedural checks as observation progresses. Developing such templates based on the research question and strategy selection allows for the opportunity to think ahead and plan the time in the field wisely. Maximising data collection is paramount, particularly during short-term undergraduate project work, so thinking about what needs to be collected during the observation will create focus and attentiveness.

It may help to answer the following questions:

- Am I interested in knowing at what time particular occurrences happened?

- Do I want to report the number of times a particular behaviour occurred?

- Do I wish to write more detailed accounts as and when incidences occur?

- Do I want to draw pictures that indicate where events took place within the space?

Whether it is one or all of these, the creation of a data-recording template or diary during the planning stage will ensure comprehensive capture of data, without missing or misinterpreting the behaviour observed. Take at look at the observation template shown in Table 7.2. In this example a very structured approach was taken to ensure the researcher reported behaviour in a clear

Table 7.2 Sample observational template used to evaluate coaching performance during group delivery

Outcome	Evidence	Notes
Preparation Did the coach: • welcome players, outline objectives for the activity and communicate ground rules for acceptable behaviour? • check players' equipment, ability and readiness to participate?		
Safety, organisation and group management Did the coach: • identify potential risks within the coaching area? • set up the coaching area and equipment required for the coaching activity safely, reporting any problems to a responsible person? • identify health, safety and emergency issues and procedures related to the coaching environment? • conduct the activity in a safe manner? • ensure the practice area and equipment are suitable for future use?		
Coaching delivery Did the coach: • motivate, encourage and reward players, using effective communication methods? • use language and terminology appropriate for the age and skill level of the group? • adapt the activity to the needs of the individual and the group? • use questions to check for players' understanding of the coaching activity? • use a range of coaching styles to promote learning? • deliver the activities in an appropriate sequence and allow enough time for them to be attempted? • provide clear and accurate explanations and demonstrations that support the appropriate technical model? • observe and correct basic faults? • reinforce the key coaching points at appropriate times? • ensure that all players are actively involved in appropriate activities to develop their performance? • provide and encourage opportunities for appropriate feedback? • conclude the activity summarising players' strengths, achievements and progress?		
Evidence – Session plan (P), observation (Ob), questioning (Q), other (Oth)		

framework. Created to record coach behaviour throughout a group session, the outcomes detailed down the left-hand column provide the researcher with very clear statements that focus the observation during the set period. Prompts, guides and reminders to the researcher ensures that important aspects are not missed during the session.

As mentioned earlier, the selection of the data-recording technique is dictated in many ways by the specific nature of the research question and the observational strategy selected. To illustrate this, let's assume a researcher is applying the observation approach to solve the problem of why, during a high-handicap player's golf swing, her right leg straightens, causing her to lose rotational torque in the backswing. At this point, the researcher could go to the observational strategy decision chart (Figure 7.2) and work his way through until he reaches an approach that would best suit the problem. Based on a decision and the technique he intends to use, he would be unwise to select a time-sampling approach if he were observing the action in real time. With the speed of the movement, it would be extremely likely that he would be unable to see all aspects of her movement and determine the reasons for the unwanted movement. If the researcher was able to use a camera, however, to video the movement and then slow it right down to 100 Hz/s, he could then apply the time-sampling strategy by selecting designated time periods throughout the movement. The option of a video capture technique enables the reseacher to select an approach to assess the player best and resolve her problem.

 Research focus 7.3

The internet is a great place to find a variety of observational templates from a range of research disciplines. Spend some time reviewing the different approaches researchers have taken in reporting what they observe. To get you started, have a look at this template developed to record observations made on PE teachers: https://goo.gl/s4gKx7.

Once you have selected a few templates, think about how they compare and any differences you notice. Try and determine what type of behaviours they are focused on, and consider how you might report such findings if you were to use similar templates during your research project.

Consider another research example that illustrates how the research question and related strategy have a very important impact on the choice of recording technique(s). A student researcher wished to observe movement patterns throughout an entire 60-minute PE session in the hope of determining how much hall space is actually utilised by the children. She opted for a naturalistic continuous monitoring approach, and next had to decide which recording technique(s) to use. Her first thought was a video camera. With lots happening during the session, the ability to record the mass of activity on to video tape and then watch it back later initially seemed appealing. In this instance, however, the use of a camera may be inappropriate, as firstly there may be ethical implications, and secondly the student may be unable to obtain coverage of the entire space all of the time. She therefore concluded that this approach might lead to missing data. Likewise, being a lone observer might not allow her to watch all of the class all of the time and again she may miss times when the children occupy areas out of sight. Instead, the student came up with an alternative plan that allowed her to have eyes on every member of the class while watching all spaces in the area.

To achieve this, additional support was needed. Developing an observational template that divided the larger space up into smaller zones, she allocated one zone to each observer. Remembering to provide each with a very clear brief outlining the procedures to ensure consistency, the researcher was able to monitor all the area all the time. Having six zones and six observers meant that each was able not only to record the amount of time spent in each zone, but also the children who were more/less active, the number of children going into each zone at any one time and the type of activity that took place in each zone.

Collection and presentation of observations

Whichever data collection approach is selected, the ability to note down observations accurately, either during or after field engagement, will impact on the quality of the conclusions. Taking field notes is a skill that needs development and any pilot study preparation should include some element of note taking. A useful exercise is to team up with someone more experienced and independently observe the same activity for a short space of time. Immediately afterwards compare notes and discuss each other's observations. Consider how they may be different and why that might be the case. Think about how each has described what was observed and try and develop a wider repertoire of verbs to help describe behaviours more accurately.

Merely reporting that *the player looked bored* firstly demonstrates a judgement and secondly offers little insight into the player's behaviour. Reporting instead that *the player was looking down at the ground, head tilted to one side, with her hands on her hips and a stooped posture* reflects what can actually be seen. Making an assumption during the observation only prevents researchers from recording what they really see. Describing behaviour through the use of words requires practice so do not underestimate the time needed to develop these skills.

If camera or audio-recording techniques are being applied during the observation, the opportunity to review the footage later allows for more time to go through the tapes. Do not leave this too long after being in the field though, as the more time that passes, the harder it becomes to recollect information. Evidently, making notes during the observation, supported by recorded data, does provide the best solution when and where possible. However, clear articulation through written work is still paramount for effective communication of findings.

An important aspect of observation research is the ability to cut up field notes so that they can reveal the themes that have emerged. Sticking them back together can then provide the narrative and meaning behind the observations. Either before or during the initial stages of data collection, researchers should have established categories of behaviour linked to their research question. These categories, based on the characteristics of the people being observed and events that occur, allow conclusions to be drawn based on the initial research question.

Consider Student case study 7.1. Thomas, in his module work, categorised coaches' verbal communication to evaluate the nature and impact of their voices. For the verbal instruction category, for example, observations were classified by the volume of instruction: high, medium and low, with the message delivered having a positive, negative or neutral response. This level of detail allowed Thomas to develop tentative themes and narratives.

Once finished in the field, the researcher must begin to unpick or cut up the notes and link in observations to themes that have emerged. The researcher can begin to identify certain regularities or patterns in the data by asking: what type of behaviour was it? How frequently did it occur? What were its causes or antecedents? What were its consequences? Who did it impact upon? What were their responses? By attempting to categorise all of the data collected into a formal account so that such patterns, trends, similarities or differences can be identified, the researcher will then be able to start the task of explaining the meaning behind the observations.

The final written report will be a culmination of the observational approach taken. This will begin with an opening literature-supported rationale for the problem and a clear statement of the research question. Followed by a thorough account of the selected strategy, this section will include an overview of the nature of the participants studied, the field setting(s) used, the role(s) the researcher played, the observation type and design selected and the data collection methods deployed. By providing a detailed analysis and interpretation of the data, the researcher will then conclude the report by exploring what the findings mean in terms of further analysis and contextual relevance.

Reflection point 7.3

When you deploy the observational research strategy in your project, you will be developing key employability skills that will have direct relevance to work-based employment situations. Try and reflect on this chapter and your own practical experiences when using this approach and make a list of all the employability skills you are able to demonstrate.

Once you have made a list, try and link these skills to particular aspects of your project work. So, for example, if you feel you have developed an 'awareness of cultural differences' through your project work, signpost when and where during your project this happened – maybe during your field-based observation period when you observed junior sports performers from a range of cultural backgrounds. Following this, attempt to link forward to a range of potential employment situations; choose a career or job you are particularly interested in and think about the role and responsibilities involved. When may you need to deploy these skills and in what situations might this occur? Showing you are able to recognise which employability skills you are developing and being able to apply them to a variety of employment scenarios illustrates an applied vocational awareness.

Chapter review

Throughout this chapter we have explored a non-experimental approach to research. When and how to apply the observational research strategy will depend on the nature of the research question, and is bound by the desire to understand more about our sporting behaviours and how they impact on our social interactions. Selecting an approach that allows the researcher the

(Continued)

(Continued)

opportunity to get closer to the sample enhances the value of observation research in understanding more about sport and exercise in a social context. By recognising the differences between quantitative and qualitative positions, naturalistic and systematic approaches and the impact the researcher's role may play on data collection, you should now be able to:

☑ describe the basic concept of observation research and know how this approach is different from other research strategies;

☑ describe a naturalistic observation approach to research and discuss how this differs from systematic observations;

☑ list and define the four types of observable behaviours and link to appropriate research methods;

☑ appreciate how the observational strategy decision chart can be applied to help select the most appropriate research design.

▬▬ Further reading ▬▬

Finding additional reading in the area of observation research in sport is difficult and only a few texts make any reference to the observational approach. Listed below are several sources outside the area of sport that may be of value to those wishing to advance their knowledge in this area. The only true way to understand this approach, however, is to have a go and experience it for yourself!

Frankfort-Nachmias, C and Nachmias, D (2015) *Research Methods in the Social Sciences*. 8th ed. New York: Worth Publishers, Macmillan Education Company. Chapter 9.

A general research methods text for social science studies. Chapter 9 (Part 3) provides a gentle introduction to the realms of observational research methods, although no reference is made to sport. The rest of the textbook offers a sound grounding in qualitative research and, if this is a field you wish to pursue, then it is well worth the read.

Hackshaw, A (2015) *A Concise Guide to Observational Studies in Healthcare*. Oxford: John Wiley.

Lofland, J, Snow, DA, Anderson, L and Lofland, LH (2006) *Analyzing Social Settings: A Guide to Qualitative Observation and Analysis*. 4th ed. Belmont, CA: Wadsworth Cengage Learning.

Packed full of practical examples, these textbooks will help you with gathering, focusing and analysing your observational data. Set out in a step-by-step fashion, their contents can be easily applied to the study of sport and exercise.

Lee, RM (2000) *Unobtrusive Methods in Social Research*. Buckingham: Open University Press.

An excellent text for those wishing to conduct unobtrusive research. It is logically set out with clear definitions, useful examples and recommended reading following each chapter. The glossary is particularly useful in clarifying understanding of key terms frequently used.

8

Case study research strategy

 Learning objectives

By identifying research situations in which a case study research strategy would be applied, this chapter is designed to help you:

- review the characteristics of a case study research strategy;
- identify the key phases of the case study approach;
- understand how case study protocols may be prepared;
- appreciate how case study reports may be organised to communicate research findings in a clear and coherent way.

Introduction

Studying single or multiple cases in depth provides the researcher with an enriched perspective of an individual, group, programme, organisation or community. By exploring how a case study approach to research can be applied effectively to sport, this chapter provides a guide to the characteristics of the case study strategy. Examining the various types of approach that may be taken, by the end of this chapter you should be able to comprehend the concept of a case study approach to research, identify which approach would be best suited to your specific research question and know when and how to conduct this method to capture your case holistically.

As outlined in Chapter 1, the study of sport has traditionally had a strong emphasis on the quantitative perspective, stressing generalisability, probability, prediction and falsifiability. Several chapters have already explored some of these more traditional research strategies that are deductive in nature. Integral within our study of sport, however, are inductive approaches with a strong emphasis on qualitative elements. Allowing us to ask the 'why' and 'how' questions provides us with a much deeper level of understanding about our case that would otherwise be unachievable through more strictly controlled research strategies.

The value of case study research in sport

In some respect, all research can be considered 'case study' in nature as there is always some case or unit under inquiry. Whether attempting to identify the coach–athlete relationship in swimming, the impact of funding on a local sports club, imagery strategies used by a junior golfer or the force generation patterns throughout a sprint-start sequence, the researcher collects evidence from a research case. The term case study, however, is usually employed to denote a specific form of research inquiry. What really distinguishes a case study from other research strategies is the amount of detailed information or evidence obtained from a case and how the researcher goes about generalising the findings.

 **Key point 8.1**

Case study research is a strategic approach that involves the detailed and intensive analysis of a single case. The term can be extended to include multiple-case research, where two or more cases are compared.

The case's perspective is central to the research process and therefore the researcher must apply systemically a strategy that allows for the description and explanation of phenomena in the natural setting of the case (i.e. naturalistic). Searching for evidence in a natural context, the researcher is able to look at specific meanings, both of processes that may have led to particular outcomes and/or changes that may have occurred over time or between aspects within the case. Investigating a case away from precise manipulation and control, seen as a characteristic of the experimental strategy, the researcher is able to see how a selected case operates and behaviours, events and incidences are shaped.

Rachel, in her final year of a Sport and Physical Education degree, undertook an independent research study to explore the impact of the Sport Premium funding on a local primary academy. Reviewing the different research strategies on offer, Rachel decided that to gain an in-depth picture of how the funding had an impact on the academy, its members, the way it functions and the curriculum she would opt for a case study research strategy.

She understood that any findings made as a result of the case study might be difficult to generalise to other academies, and she would have to be cautious in her conclusions. While recognising the limitations of this research approach, Rachel accepted that, in order to gain a level of evidence that would allow her to assess fully the impact of the Sport Premium funding within the academy, she would have to accept that it was an inherent part of the research strategy.

Prior to the commencement of data collection, Rachel identified the scope and boundaries of the case. She decided to include only teaching and support staff and not involve any external agents allied to the academy. She also decided to focus her study on both formal academy time and any extra-curricular involvement. Having created her case study protocol and a series of case questions to focus on, Rachel decided she would spend a total of 5 days in the school in order to collect as much relevant evidence as possible.

While at the academy, Rachel was able to collect sufficient data to draw several flow diagrams that showed how the Sport Premium funding was being used to support academy sport delivery. In addition, by reviewing archival records and selected documents, she was able to create a detailed list of all those within the academy who had directly benefited from the additional financial support. Based on this list, she was then able to arrange individual interviews with all the individuals and collect interview data about the effectiveness of the funding at the academy. Finally, Rachel was allowed to observe several class-time PE lessons, lunchtime activity workshops and extra-curricular sessions and undertake focus groups with some of the children and their parents in order to get their view of the additional support and how they felt it impacted on their own personal development.

Throughout her case study research, Rachel gathered a varied range of evidence that highlighted the effective use of the Sport Premium funding for a local primary academy. She was able to make several key recommendations to the headteacher and governing body, thereby enhancing the impact. She was also able to create a valuable resource pack that was disseminated amongst the academy for future use.

Generalisability of case study research

Attempting to generalise or transfer findings of human behaviour or occurrences observed from natural settings to others has led to contentious debate among researchers. Questions have arisen centred on the true value of the case study approach in enabling generalisability and whether the results are widely applicable. Unlike experiments, where a high degree of confidence in a causal relationship between phenomena can be achieved, it may be extremely problematic to draw conclusions from a case study and assume all similar cases will behave in the same way. Because of the subjective, naturalistic nature of the case study approach, generalisability of findings should be viewed as a way of approximating future expectations, rather than predicting occurrences and behaviours. The strength of the case study strategy is its ability to create a harmonious relationship between the reader's own personal experiences and the case study itself, facilitating a greater under-standing of the phenomenon within its context. In this way, any generalisations can be viewed as naturalistic and not predictive. Without such precision and control within this research strategy, how the researcher generalises the findings from a research case to other people, groups or institutions requires a sharpened ability to communicate findings in as vivid and vibrant manner as possible. Therefore, it will only be through accurate interpretation and clear presentation of results that any generalisation from case study research is possible.

 Research focus 8.1

In a study by Loturco et al. (2017), a case study research strategy was applied to describe the changes in physical and physiological performance of a two-time world karate champion athlete immediately prior to and after a bout simulation. Through such examination, the researchers hoped to provide a unique perspective of a top-level athlete whilst understanding better the key performance components that contribute to excellence in karate.

By applying a quantitative cross-sectional case study design, the case (i.e. the participating athlete) was described as a 63-kg, 168-cm, 28-year-old male who had twice won the World Championship (in 2010 and 2014). He undertook: (1) squat and countermovement jumps, jump squat and bench throw and maximal isometric force tests (half-squat and bench press, pre- and post-match); and (2) one simulated karate match. The karate-specific test involved a number of attack movements typical to that found within a competitive bout. Each movement was completed in a required time of 3 seconds and the sequence of moves continued, with progressively less recovery between each. The test was complete when the performer had reached volitional exhaustion.

Results were presented in a number of data formats (i.e. tables, graphs) and revealed that the athlete improved 1.1% and 2.9% for the squat jump and countermovement jumps, respectively, after the combat simulation. For jump squat, his power production increased by 6.8% following the bout. Conversely, for the bench throw a reduction in power was detected after the match (7.8%). The maximal isometric force increased for the half-squat (10.5%) and bench press exercises (1.6%). The authors concluded that a world-class performer displays quite different physiological, metabolic and neurological responses when compared to similar highly trained peers, and that coaches should be made aware of the importance of lower-limb muscular power and metabolic responses in outstanding performers.

Characteristics of case study research

Case study research is somewhat unique and distinguishes itself from other strategies discussed in this book. As already alluded to so far, this approach brings with it a range of specific characteristics that can open up opportunities for the researcher to investigate naturally occurring social situations within a sporting context.

By investigating the holistic and meaningful characteristics of real-life cases, such as an individual, managerial processes, organisations, maturation of systems/policies, a class, a family, a school, a club, a team, a town or even a profession, the research itself is integrated into the practical 'natural' experiences and activities of the selected case. Four key applications of the case study approach that attempt to establish the importance of this research strategy have been documented by Yin (2013). These are:

1. the explanation of complex links in real-life settings;

2. the description of real-life contexts in which events occur;

3. the description of events;

4. the exploration of situations in which events create no clear outcomes or consequences.

Through the application of case study findings the researcher is able to seek out patterns and themes within the case. This can then lead to further analysis through cross-comparison with other cases.

Case study framework

The characteristics of this approach can be broken down into three key phases that form a framework for case study research (Table 8.1). It is important to recognise that this framework is flexible and should be moulded to suit the specific requirements of a research study. Applied in the correct order, the application of such a framework can be an indispensable tool to the researcher. Each phase follows a logical order of planning, doing and reviewing. Phase one enables researchers to chart out their case study approach, defining the population, case and data collection procedures. Phase two prepares the researcher for field entry and describes the stages necessary to conduct successful data recording and analysis. The final phase details the interpretation and implementation of findings.

Designing a case study

The design of the case study provides the blueprint or plan according to which the research will be conducted. Setting up a series of guidelines that the researcher follows ensures that the implementation of the research methods maintains momentum, rather than developing into a collection of unrelated components. Case study research design can be comparative (i.e. comparing two or more cases), cross-sectional (i.e. assessing one case at a single point in time) or longitudinal (i.e. assessing the same case multiple times) and therefore the researcher must consider which approach would most suitably link to the research objectives (refer back to Chapter 2).

If a comparative research design is to be selected, researchers must decide whether their previous experience and skills, and specific research timeframe, permit successful completion of the research. When time is a factor, which is often the case with undergraduate research, the *single-case* cross-sectional research design is the best option. This provides a purposeful amount of evidence that allows a thorough understanding of the case, exposes behaviours, events and/or incidences and attempts to explain their occurrences. In contrast, a *multiple-case* approach (i.e. comparative design) allows for comparisons across cases and may allow the researcher to uncover much deeper meaning

Table 8.1   A case study framework (adapted from Eisenhardt, 1989)

Phase	Stage	Activity	Purpose
Phase one	Getting started	• Define and refine the research question(s) • Begin construction of the case study protocol	• Focuses efforts • Creates guidelines and procedures for the course of the project
	Selecting the case(s)	• Specify population/ organisation and set boundaries of case • List what you are specifically looking for in your case	• Sharpens external validity of study • Allows for flexible theoretical development • Strengthens a triangulated approach
	Crafting instruments and protocols	• Decide on the data collection methods • Quantitative and/or qualitative	• Maximises evidence capture • Speeds analysis • Facilitates emergent themes
Phase two	Entering the field	• Data collection and analysis • Flexible opportunistic data collection	• Speeds analysis • Facilitates emerging themes
	Analysing the data	• Within-case description • Multiple-case comparison	• Gains familiarity with data and preliminary theory generation
	Shaping propositions/ hypothesis	• Tabulation of data for each theme • Search for causes (why) behind relationships	• Confirms, extends and sharpens theories • Builds internal validity
Phase three	Enfolding the literature	• Comparison with literature (conflicting and similar) • Build discussion around collected evidence and emerging themes	• Builds internal validity, raises theoretical level and sharpens definitions
	Reaching a conclusion	• Summary through naturalistic generalisation/approximated future expectations	• Ends project with final recommendations, reflection and tentative generalisations

about the relationship between each case, their similarities, differences and the impact these may have. Similarly, a longitudinal design covering a time span of 2–5 years may not be achievable given the timescale and financial resources of most research projects.

If you investigate a case more than once or increase the number of cases within any one study, the complexity of the research, both in research design and evaluation and interpretation of the evidence, will increase. It is therefore recommended that comparative and/or longitudinal case designs are for those who not only have access to sufficient resources and time, but who have also completed a small-scale single-case project and/or appropriate exploratory pilot study work.

Key point 8.2

When developing the research design for a case study project, it is important to be familiar with the different types.

- Cross-sectional case design: a single case is studied at a single point in time.

- Comparative case design: more than one case is studied at a single point in time.

- Longitudinal case design: a single case is studied twice or more across a period.

Preparing the case study protocol

What really makes an effective case study is the preparatory work ahead of the evidence collection. To be successful requires the development of a *case study protocol* that allows continued reminders about the study purpose, any anticipated problems, mechanisms by which the findings will be collected and interpreted and explanations of how the case study will be formatted and presented.

To start with, the case study protocol should include an overview of the project. This should contain the project aims and objectives and any relevant case study issues. Factors such as case study boundaries that define the extent of the case need to be included. Evaluating key players, situations and evidence streams helps researchers to ensure they focus inside the case and concentrate the research question appropriately. It will also help to describe critical incidences within a tighter framework, that otherwise may be difficult to interpret.

Reflection point 8.1

When planning the case study protocol remember to consider the following:

- The aims and objectives of the study: what is the project purpose and what exactly will be done to achieve this?

- Case study boundaries: try to consider the edges of the case. How far will they go? If a school is the case, will the boundaries go as far as parents? governors? education authorities? or just those working within the school (e.g. teachers, pupils and support staff)?

- What will be included and excluded? Consider all sources of information, from people to documents.

- The key players: who are the participants in the case that need to be accessed? These may be *gatekeepers* that open access to others (e.g. a coach of a team).

Background information relating to the case can further help shape the case study protocol and more focused research objectives. Such information may assist in developing a rationale for site/case selection, propositions or hypotheses that can be tested, and maybe the broader theoretical or policy relevance to the inquiry. This again provides researchers with a continued point of reference during the data collection phase and prevents them 'losing their way' while collecting the evidence.

By its very nature the case study approach is a field procedure, so obtaining permission to access the case and study site is vital. The researcher may need to produce documents in advance of any formal entry into the case, so it is important to make sure these are prepared. It would be likely that at the very least the researcher has to present an outline of the case study protocol, along with ethical approval documents. Further material may be required in the form of a supervisor notification letter, data collection templates and informed-consent forms.

Having sufficient resources in place ahead of any data collection in the field is paramount. Access to portable personal computers, writing instruments, paper, dictaphones, video recorders and quiet places to write private notes at the site are all important considerations for effective evidence capture and need to be mentioned in the protocol. Remember, incidences and opportunities may arise sporadically throughout the researcher's time with the case, so being prepared could make a real difference to the quality and quantity of evidence. Where and when possible, making a clear schedule of the data collection activities that are expected to be completed within specified periods of time can help the researcher to plan ahead and organise both physical time and resources wisely. The case study protocol, therefore, is an indispensable item that all researchers must construct.

 Reflection point 8.2

The case study protocol is a set of guidelines that can be used to structure and govern case study research. It outlines the procedures and rules before, during and after the case research project. Case study protocols also ensure uniformity in research projects where data collection is performed in multiple locations and/or if more than one researcher is involved in the data collection process. Using the section heading and contents shown in Table 8.2, the researcher can construct a protocol that provides a suitable project framework. By including more detail at an early planning stage of the project, researchers can ensure they are prepared ahead of field entry.

Table 8.2 Constructing a protocol that provides a suitable project framework

Section	Contents	Purpose
Preamble	Confidentiality issues Documentation layout Presentation/formatting style Layout of protocol	Contains information about the purpose of the protocol, guidelines for data and document storage and final document layout and presentation

General	Overview of research project	Provides brief overview of the research project and the method employed
	Description of the characteristics of the case study method	
Procedures	Initial approach to case(s):	Detailed description of the procedures for conducting each case. These procedures should be utilised to ensure uniformity in the data collection process and allow for within- and between-case comparisons if required
	Selection of case(s)	
	Number of cases	
	Establishing contact	
	Scheduling of visits/contacts	
	Lengths of sessions	
	Equipment and stationery	
Research instruments(s)	Qualitative – interview guides/question templates (open and closed questions)/ recording sheets	To ensure appropriate consideration and instrument structure to facilitate uniformity of data collection
	Quantitative – survey questionnaires/data-recording collection sheets	
Data analysis guidelines	Overview of data analysis processes:	Detailed outline of the procedures of analysis prior to data collection allows for more focused analytical processes and meaningful data interpretation
	How data processing will occur	
	Description of within-case analysis process (descriptive/explanatory/individual case report)	
	Description of any cross-case analysis process	
	Data schema (i.e. themes/topics)	
	Summary of primary types, sources and purpose	
	Summary of secondary types, sources and purpose	
	Description of data display types that will be used in analysis and reporting	
Appendix	Participation request letter	Template letter sent to potential participants inviting them to participate. Adherence to institutional ethical regulations
	University/college ethics approval form	
	Overview of study to non-academic community	

Preparation of questions for the case

When developing the case study protocol, it can be extremely valuable if, in advance of field entry, researchers are able to construct a series of case questions that act to remind them of particular points or incidences they wish to explore. By linking each question with a list of probable sources of evidence ahead of engaging with the case, the potential locations of evidence in advance of data collection can be identified. Reducing unnecessary disruption to the case and ensuring the researcher retains the study focus means that any evidence collected should be more purposefully linked to the research questions.

Take, for example, a student researcher who was interested in evaluating the efficacy of a county Gifted and Talented Junior Sport Development programme. Say she wanted to find out how the programme was organised and how it was delivered. Who was employed by it, when and how were decisions made, and who makes them? Who are the end users and what are their perceptions? By linking these desired research questions with particular sources of evidence, such as the programme director, the director's immediate supervisor, assistants, organisational charts/frameworks/ processes, job descriptions, participants and parents/volunteers and/or coaches, the researcher can begin to create a series of case questions and possible sources of evidence ahead of case engagement. Constructing a table or list that specifies the questions and the potential evidence streams helps the researcher to be prepared. This has a knock-on effect, as the researcher will have time to reflect on her actions, discuss potential problems with her supervisor and, if required, develop alternative plans ahead of data collection.

Learning activity 8.1

Imagine that a researcher is planning to undertake case study research to explore the performance-related experiences (i.e. during training and competition) of the GB track cycling team. In advance of his entry into the field, which will involve a 3-week period at the velodrome and a 4-week period abroad at competitions, list all the different sources of evidence that may be available to the researcher. Attempt to identify where these may come from. What data collection techniques may need to be used to obtain this evidence?

Sources of case study evidence

As part of the case study protocol framework, a series of case questions will have already been constructed. Linked to this, possible locations of evidence will also have been established. Consider that there are five main sources of evidence that the researcher is likely to obtain during this data collection phase:

1. documents and archival records (e.g. plans, policies, data records, minutes of meetings, contracts);

2. surveys (e.g. structured/semi-structured interviews, self-completion questionnaires, focus groups);

3. observations (e.g. linguistic, non-verbal, spatial behaviours);

4. physical artefacts (e.g. pictures, prints, trophies, awards, memorabilia);

5. clinical/non-clinical physical measurement (e.g. cardiorespiratory measures, physical activity levels).

Depending on the case in question, that is, whether it is a single individual or a much larger organisation, the amount and source of evidence are likely to be different. In addition to these five sources of evidence, the researcher could also be collecting important data by capturing video footage, watching films, taking and reviewing photographs, collecting and reading life histories and/or undertaking psychological assessments on participants. In accessing the varied range of evidence streams, the researcher will require a wide range of practical skills to access, collect and process the data.

Entering the case

The researchers' role is to find and evidence as much data about the case as possible. This doesn't mean however that they need to go steamrolling in without any plan. Data collection has to be calculated when and where possible to avoid upsetting the very people who hold the key to the data that are required.

What is important to recognise throughout this stage is that data collection procedures may not always be systematic, as in other research strategies such as experiment or survey approaches. These research strategies are more prescriptive in their logical order or events in collecting data. In the case study approach, the process of collection is much more demanding due to the inherent real-world nature of the case. The need to take advantage of any unexpected opportunities is therefore extremely important in order to capture enriched data about the case. It is during these moments that researchers are very likely to witness the exact issues they wish to investigate or expose incidences that they seek to understand.

Throughout the collection of data, there are a number of important points that need considering. The researcher will be confronted with new situations that should be seen as opportunities for data collection. If you continually have a firm grasp of the issues you wish to study, all encounters can be viewed as possible sources of evidence. Such a grasp focuses the relevant events and information to be arranged into manageable proportions. Reflecting on these events in a personal diary or log will ensure that, during the evidence-processing stage, the researcher is able to recall these moments with clarity.

It is often difficult for a new researcher to remain unbiased during the research process. We all have our own values and beliefs that shape us. Encountering new people in a variety of new situations, as in case study research, can lead to such beliefs influencing how the case is viewed. Such a biased approach affects the researcher's outlook on the case and can have an unwanted impact on the data collection methods. Furthermore, researchers may allow such biases to cloud their judgement when they come to interpret and report the findings. Having an unbiased view away from any preconceived notions or ideas will allow for a more open-minded, non-judgemental, sensitive and responsive approach to people and situations as and when they're encountered.

Research focus 8.2

In a study by Fletcher and Streeter (2016), a case study research strategy was adopted to explore the high-performance environment (HPE) of an elite swimming team. An HPE model, according to the authors, provides a holistic perspective enabling a better understanding of the relationship between the organisational and environmental influences on performance and facilitates a more co-ordinated approach to developing HPEs in elite sport.

Using a purposive sampling technique, this single case was a swimming team with over 15 years of prolonged success in national and international competition. The team consisted of 88 swimmers, organised into five squads. Furthermore, a snowball sampling technique was used to capture additional participants who would add value to the study. A final sample population of 14 was selected (from the target population) and underwent face-to-face interviews based on the HPE model. All interviews were digitally recorded, and full transcriptions were used to construct four core categories based on leadership, performance enablers, people and organizational culture.

The authors concluded that observations made throughout this case study strengthen the value and application of the HPE model. In developing a number of subcomponents that focus upon leadership (vision, support, challenge), performance enablers (information, instruments, incentives), people (attitudes, behaviours, capacity) and organisational culture (achievement, well-being, innovation, internal processes), practitioners attempting to intervene effectively at an environmental level need to be able to influence leaders, facilitate performance enablers, engage people and shape cultural change.

Presentation of case study research

Bringing together all of the evidence collected during case fieldwork is a formidable but rewarding component of the whole case study project. It is here that the researcher can really begin to unravel the narrative of the case and develop the emerging stories about the experiences recorded. Writing up a case study project is often demanding, due to the wide range of evidence collected. Developing a structure, therefore, as we would when writing up a more deductive study, isn't so straightforward. When planning the discussion and analysis, you should seek guidance from a supervisor who has constructed the marking criteria. He or she will be able to provide a detailed picture of where the emphasis should be placed and particular aspects s/he may be looking for.

Typically, the discussion will be made up of a chronology. An outline of the order in which things happened during the field exposure provides a framework. This in turns allows for events to unfold more naturally in the text, with critical incidences linked in as they happened. This approach also offers the researcher an opportunity to make links between incidences and past/future events.

A further aspect that will bring strength to the report will be the logical coherence of the discussion. A chronological account on its own may not highlight all the emerging themes and issues, so the need to emphasise key aspects through cross-referencing will be vital.

Reiterating the research aim and objectives of the project will also allow for a more coherent structure. An attempt should be made to address these and answer emerging questions that developed from the case. Can any kind of generalisations be made or are the findings merely exploratory? Try and think how the end-user, whether a hockey team, yoga club, individual athlete, swimming coach or local authority, may benefit from the findings. The application of the project is what will give it real value. Finally, can any potential theories be inductively generated from the study? And could this be applied to other similar cases or tested through future deductive research?

By thinking about the outline, format and audience for the case study report, effective delivery of the findings can be achieved. Remember that the research will lead to large amounts of documentary evidence, in the form of published reports, publications, memos and other documents collected from the case, so make sure the report is well planned in advance.

 Reflection point 8.3

What to do during case study research	What not to do during case study research
Begin by setting a structure Always begin by setting out your protocol. Without this you will get lost in the process	*Misunderstand your question or answer the wrong question* This needs focus at the very beginning so you understand what you are attempting to do
Stay organised When exploring a specific issue, remember what it is and where it fits into the overall problem. Setting out initial questions will help you stay on track	*Proceed in a haphazard fashion* For example, not identifying the major issues that need to be examined or jumping from one issue to another without outlining your overall approach
Step back periodically Summarise what you have learnt at key times throughout the project and what the implications appear to be. Use a diary to log your progress: it will be invaluable later on in the project	*Ask for a barrage of evidence without explaining to the participants why you need the information* Remember, clear explanation will ensure you receive the data that you really need
Ask for additional information when you need it But make sure that the participants in the case know why you need the information	*Fail to synthesise a point of view* Even if you don't have time to explore all the key issues, be sure to synthesise the point based on where you ended up
Relax and enjoy the process Think of the project as an exploration, journey and problem-solving process. Always focus on actionable recommendations, even though sometimes they may not be the most elegant solution to the problem	*Not asking for help* Whether it is a misunderstanding related to the overall problem, or whether you are struggling with a specific analysis, be sure to ask for help when you need it

Learning activity 8.2

When you undertake case study research you can develop and enhance a wide range of employability skills. Attempt to list the skills you think are needed in order to complete a case study project successfully. Once you have done this, explain where these skills are needed in the following employment roles:

- postgraduate researcher;
- secondary school PE teacher;
- county sports development officer;
- personal trainer;
- physical training officer in the RAF;
- elite athlete;
- exercise referral officer.

Chapter review

Throughout this chapter we have investigated the value and application of case study research to the sporting world. When studying sport the researcher is confronted with a wide range of instances that require a more detailed, enriched account of an individual or group of cases. Not wishing to establish a causal link between variables in a controlled manner, the researcher can select this strategy to capture a case in operation, recording real-world events and incidences. Formulating a well-defined and pre-planned case study protocol, building a range of case designs and utilising varied data collection methods, this approach can lead the investigator down many exciting avenues within sports research. By using a range of sport-related research examples you should now be able to:

☑ describe the basic concept of this approach and identify how case study research differs from other research strategies;

☑ create a logically structured case study research plan that identifies and defines three clear phases of development;

☑ appreciate how the construction of an effective case study protocol can help guide you through the research design process;

☑ consider the skills required to undertake case study research and how these can be applied to a range of employment roles.

━━━ **Further reading** ━━━━━━━━━━━━━━━━━━━━

Sport England. (n.d.) *Case Studies*. London: Sport England. Available online at: https://www.sporteng
land.org/facilities-planning/case-studies/ (accessed May 2017).

A valuable resource for students and lecturers alike. Packed full of sport-related case studies, this site
can be used very effectively as a basis for seminar-based learning activities on the case study method.

Thomas, G (2016) *How to Do Your Case Study*. 2nd ed. Thousand Oaks, CA: SAGE Publications.

This extremely useful textbook provides a strong emphasis on collecting evidence from the case. It
provides plenty of examples and practical advice that can be applied to research in sport and exercise.

Yin, RK (2013) *Case Study Research: Design and Methods*. Thousand Oaks, CA: SAGE Publications.

One of the best-selling books when it comes to the case study method. It is more suited to those wishing to further their understanding of this research strategy; it is full of examples, although not from
a sporting context. Thorough in content and explanation, a must-read if your final-year independent
project is a case study.

9

Ethnographic research strategy

Learning objectives

By demystifying ethnographic research and demonstrating its accessibility to students, this chapter is designed to help you:

- understand the nature of ethnography and identify the key characteristics of this research strategy;

- describe the ethnographic research process and establish the researcher's role in ethnographic fieldwork;

- apply an understanding of ethnography to sport-related research examples;

- identify the range of research methods that can be implemented in ethnography;

- understand and appreciate a 'cut it up and stick it together again' approach to data analysis and interpretation.

Introduction

As a research strategy, ethnography is ideally suited to investigating dynamic and complex activities that we constantly encounter within difference sporting cultures. From aerobics to windsurfing, sport provides us with a broad array of cultural experiences that offer a real insight into how we, as people, act out our day-to-day lives through sport. With the wide acceptance of qualitative research in the field of sport, such methodological diversity allows for a rich range of research to be conducted. To this end, ethnography extends and enhances our understanding as a way towards examining sporting cultures and the people who form them. Only occasionally are students studying sports courses exposed to the practice of ethnography, and regrettably, when this does occur it is often late in their studies.

What is ethnography?

Ethnography is a way of doing research into what is going on in our social world; that is, why people do the things they do. By attempting to understand parts of the world (i.e. the sporting world) more or less as they are experienced and understood in the everyday lives of people 'who live them out', the ethnographic research strategy enables the researcher to find out how people's lives are meaningful to them on their terms.

At the heart of ethnographic research is the ability to observe and listen to people as they go about their everyday lives. This can help us to understand how they behave or think about their lives and the societal structures and customs they function to and within. Ethnographers are, therefore, concerned with studying people in their natural environment rather than in situations that have been artificially created, as with experimental research. This means that ethnography fits into the traditions of constructivism and is typically inductive in nature.

However, in some instances positivist ethnography may be conducted. This may be the case when measurement is necessary, such as the development of codes, diagrams or categories that map the insider's cultural world as a series of inter-related variables. This approach attempts to capture and objectify social meaning rather than interpretively 'telling it like it is'.

 Reflection point 9.1

Brewer (2008, p6) defines ethnography as *the study of people in naturally occurring settings or 'fields' by methods of data collection which capture their social meanings and ordinary activities, involving the researcher participating directly in the setting, if not also the activities, in order to collect data in a systematic manner but without meaning being imposed on them externally.*

Ethnography in sport

Consider why we follow different football clubs – wearing team shirts, spending money to attend matches and travelling around to different stadiums. And why is it that, when in those stands, we respond in particular ways to behaviours we see acted out on the pitch – what do we see as acceptable and unacceptable behaviours? And does this change depending on the group we are with or situation we are in? Our acceptance, for example, may be different when we are with a bunch of like-minded supporters than with our family. Both of these illustrations, one more obvious than the other, are governed by rules, which we have learned and seem natural to us. Ethnography allows us to look more closely at these rules that make our lives meaningful. By centralising the importance of the meanings and cultural practices of people from within the everyday settings in which they take place, we can create a vivid picture of the way that social life, and the impact sport has on it, is assembled and how it influences the way we live our lives.

Ethnography may be particularly appealing for sport research as it can be used to evaluate applied sport interventions, problem solving in sport or enhancing multicultural understanding. Let's not forget that sport has its own culture and, within that larger culture, each type of sport (e.g. tennis vs. horse-riding vs. golf), as well as each individual sport team, has a unique culture. To this end, ethnography is well suited for investigating sporting cultures acted out on real-life settings. As wonderfully illustrated by Krane (2005) and Molnar and Purdy (2017), understanding the lived experiences of athletes and exercisers, through greater understanding of sport culture, can provide an insight into the behaviours, values, emotions and mental states that sport creates in our wider culture.

'Hanging out' with a group of football supporters, for example, will allow the ethnographic researcher an opportunity to see how they go about their day-to-day business and how this may impact on their sporting practices. How may this impact on their commitment to a particular team or acceptance of behaviours that at any other time would be deemed as socially or culturally unacceptable? The researcher must become finely tuned to the patterns and processes that make up the social sporting world as well as the 'bigger' picture, remembering that sport does not occur in a vacuum. By unravelling socially constructed standards, rules and meanings, the researcher takes an unbiased view of people's behaviour as being determined largely by the culture in which they live.

 Research focus 9.1

In a study by Guell and co-workers (2016), the objective was to describe and explore perceptions, practices and motivations for active living in later life. Using an ethnographic research approach that combined interviews with participant observation, the authors purposively sampled 27 participants (aged between 65 and 80 years) from a large rural county in the UK. Interviews focused on life history, articulations and motivations for active living, whilst observations aimed to explore social interactions within the participants' own environmental context.

Data collection was performed by two experienced ethnographers who conducted 72 interviews, lasting between 20 and 60 minutes. Undertaken within the participants' own home, all interviews were recorded, and transcribed verbatim. The interview set discussion themes focusing on the experiences of active and sedentary living, the social context of active and sedentary living (opportunities and choices) and attitudes towards active and sedentary health and well-being. All participant observations lasted between 1 and 3 hours, and included among other things structured yoga classes, active home activities, dog walking, bus rides, gardening, visits to the work place and organised group walks. The emphasis during all observations was placed on the social and physical context and environment and not on the quantity and intensity of the activity.

Data were analysed iteratively and thematic codes were devised from the information gathered. Results revealed that participants regarded a positive attitude as important for healthy ageing; this included staying active, both physically and mentally through sedentary activities. An awareness of adapting to the physical limitations of others (i.e. partners and friends) may influence intensity and frequency of shared activities. Furthermore, the social context plays an important role, forming both a barrier and a catalyst to active healthy living. In summary, the authors concluded that promoting active lifestyles within older groups requires sustained attention to their social context, encouraging broader habits rather than discrete activities.

Characteristics of ethnographic research

Doing ethnography usually means that the researcher has spent some time with usually a small number of people, studied in the place where these people live and function. The data collected will contain accounts of behaviour and speech that occurred in that place. This approach is taken as the researcher recognises that to understand why individuals do something they need to be studied in the context of their life as a whole.

Ethnographic research is characterised by three fundamental tasks: (1) observing people's behaviour; (2) studying what people say they do, believe and think; and (3) interpreting what people actually believe and think. The key characteristics of ethnographic research reveal that there is:

- a focus on a discrete location, event or setting;

- a concern with the full range of social behaviour within the location, event or setting;

- a range of different research methods applied that may combine qualitative and quantitative approaches but with an emphasis on understanding social behaviour and meanings from inside the group;

- an emphasis on analysis that moves from description to the identification of concepts and theories;

- an approach that is unstructured, in that it does not involve following a detailed protocol. This does not mean that the research is unsystematic – simply, the information is collected in a raw form as it happens.

The ethnographic research process

Unlike other research strategies, it is somewhat difficult to break the ethnographic research process down into discrete stages. Because of the flexible, rather organic nature of this approach, a continual process of planning, doing and reviewing occurs. This research process is merely a series of actions that produce the end results. Although the actions are co-ordinated and planned they do not fit into a tight protocol, but rather blend together in an adaptable way. With the unexpected twists and turns that research in a natural environment presents, the ethnographic researcher must adapt and adopt when necessary.

Structuring an ethnographic study

For the researcher undertaking ethnography for the first time, constructing a plan that documents the research strategy will provide an initial framework. Such a strategic plan sets out the broad structure of the research. With ethnographic research, it is not unusual to have last-minute flexible amendments or unanticipated changes to the plan, so careful consideration beforehand can ensure that any changes are smoothly implemented at any time in the process. The overall structure should contain the following considerations (Brewer, 2008, p58):

- outline of the topics addressed by the research with inclusion of the research aims(s) and objectives(s);

- the choice of research setting or field and the forms of sampling employed to select the site/ field and people;

- resources available to the researcher, as well as the time availability. The effects the resources are likely to have on the research should be mentioned;

- the sampling of the time and the events to be experienced in the field;

- method(s) of data collection;

- negotiating to enter the field (to include details of 'gatekeepers' – those who will allow access to people/settings);

- the nature of the researcher's role that will be adopted when in the field and when interacting with people;

- the form of analysis to be used, particularly if any statistical data analysis methods are to be applied;

- details relating to the process of withdrawal from the field;

- ethical considerations.

 Research focus 9.2

In a study by Choi et al. (2006), the purpose was to investigate what an average spectator at a sporting event visually records in a 2-hour span. One of the primary questions was whether the sponsored activities at a sporting venue, such as logo placement, product demonstrations and hospitality centres, matched with the interests of spectators. The study utilised a visual ethnographic inquiry, specifically in the forms of photojournalling and interviewing, to examine the interests of the participants at the event.

By comparing the actual data (the topic of pictures that the participants took) with the activities that the sponsor offered at the venue, the study hoped to indicate which of the sponsored activities, if any, caught the eyes of the sampled spectators. Such findings would allow the effectiveness of sponsorship activation to be evaluated against the sponsor's objectives.

Seventeen adult spectators were recruited; each took photos over a 2-hour period at an action sports championship. They were asked to photograph the 'most interesting or meaningful scenes', limited to a maximum of ten photos each. Following data collection, they shared the photos with the researchers in one-on-one interviews. After all data were gathered, categories and themes from the data were constructed. Categories were determined by reviewing the entire set of photos and were grouped based on repetition and relevance to the purpose of the study. Themes that emerged were: cool signs and graffiti; athletes; friends and family; freebies; music; and self-identity.

The findings revealed that most activities that had sponsor placement at the event indeed matched the interests of spectators. An example was that all participants took at least one photo of an athlete in competition. Within each photo the sponsor's details could be seen. With sponsorship placement located on or near athletes, visibility of logo was clear. This is the primary reason that sport marketers are so enamoured with the concept of 'more logo visibility' at sporting venues, with the photos providing enough evidence that logo placement at this event was tactically solid and in tune with the interest of the spectators. In contrast, the authors found that, for three separate participants, several pictures captured images that portrayed a sense of 'me' or 'self'. Of special interest was a stone with the inscription of someone's name and a picture of a shadow created by two friends. Although trivial to many, several found meaning from such abstraction. These photos reaffirmed to the authors that the brands that excel in their sport marketing programmes are the ones that know how to connect emotionally and culturally with people.

The authors concluded by noting that successful marketing is all about people – how to move them emotionally and how to connect with them. The study shed light on some new consumer insights that may eventually guide sponsors to pursue unconventional yet meaningful sponsorship programmes.

The ethnographer's role

The researcher has a choice of various roles when in the field, often using different ones for different locations or groups, depending on the number of fields being studied, the level of role development and the nature of the data being collected. The roles we develop and the skills we use are implicit to what we know by the term research methods. We must see ourselves as one of those valuable research tools we have in our toolkit, ready to be used when we need it. Just like when we pilot and refine our questionnaires, interviews and diagnostic tests, we must also be prepared to refine and pilot ourselves. Because ethnographic research requires the researcher to participate and engage with a group, we cannot hide behind a piece of paper, laboratory equipment or computer screen; rather the quality of our data will be directly related to the quality of ourselves. There are essentially two levels of participation. As already mentioned in Chapter 6, the researcher can become a:

- complete participant, thereby becoming a member of the group and concealing the research;
- participant as observer, researching the field while becoming fully involved in it.

The first involves being covert: that is, hiding the true intent of the research from the group. The second is overt and relates to being open with the group about the research role and nature. It is rarely the case in practice, though, that such distinction occurs and the degree of covert and overt practice very much depends on how open the researcher wishes to be and how the role develops among the group.

 Learning activity 9.1

Start by making a list of all the research skills you think are important in being an ethnographic researcher. Consider what ethnography is, its characteristics and the type of activities you may be undertaking. Once you have done this, rank them based on their importance to you. Choosing the top ten, assign a mark out of ten next to each that represents how you would rate yourself at this point in time. So, for example, you may have listed 'note taking' within your top ten and rated yourself 3/10 on your note-taking skills at the moment. Be honest with yourself! Now that you have rated yourself for all ten, convert each score into a percentage (i.e. $(3 \div 10) \times 100 = 30\%$). Look down the list and pull out three that have the lowest percentage. These are the ones you would need to improve straight away before you embark on any ethnographic research.

Speak to your tutor or supervisor about how best you could develop these skills and remember to look online and in the library for support. Once you have improved these, have a look at three with the next lowest scores and make these your focus. Try and identify times within your studies when you are using or have used these skills and try and put into practice what you have learned. Before long you will not only have developed the key skills needed to be an effective ethnographer, but also enhanced your employability chances.

It is important for the researcher to consider four main points before embarking on ethnographic fieldwork. These are: ethics (as detailed in Chapter 1); role building and trust; data recording; and field withdrawal. As the researcher you will be the outsider to start with, hoping to become an insider quickly. How well you build this role and how that is viewed by others can make or break the relationship with the group from the very start.

Role building and trust

Think about trust for a moment. Trust between you and your fellow team mates, between you and your coach, between you and your fellow students. How important is trust to you? When you have trust in others and they have trust in you, how readily do they open up and give you information? Developing trust in ethnographic research will allow researchers to develop a role to such an extent that the group will really open up and provide them with the rich life tapestry that the researcher seeks. Trust is based on honesty, communication, friendliness, openness and confidence building, and growing trust ensures that, over time, the group you are working with begin to accept you as a researcher. This acceptance will enter the researcher into their group (i.e. become an 'insider') and allow the researcher to gain a deeper understanding of the group's rules, expectations, social processes and standards – in effect, do what ethnography is all about! Without such trust, the group would be closed and unwilling to accept the researcher.

Learning activity 9.2

Building trust with a group is a process that needs to be continually worked at, negotiated, renegotiated, affirmed and repeatedly reaffirmed. The first stage of the process is in recognising the actions - verbal and non-verbal - that build trust.

Think of a time when you entered a new situation: maybe when you started your course, became a new member of a sports team or club, attended your first freshers training camp or sports trials, started a new exercise class or joined a gym. You will have met new people, whether that be lecturers, gym staff, instructors, coaches, students in higher years or students just like you. At what point did you begin to trust them, in what they were telling you? Why did you trust them? Were there any points when you lost trust? What was the cause? At what point did you feel that people started to trust you? What actions and behaviours that you exhibited may have led to this?

The speed with which the researcher's role develops can be enhanced by a number of factors. By learning the 'native' language of the group, the researcher can show the group a level of understanding, acceptance and commonality. Take cycling, for example. A number of terms are commonly used in cycling, but not in day-to-day language. Terms such as 'through-and-off', 'bonk' and 'bit-and-bit' seem strange to the non-cycling community, but are used when talking about cycling and when out cycling in a group. Knowing language related to training, bikes, diet and racing can ensure you build trust and acceptance quickly. If you think about your own sport, you can probably list several terms or words that may be unique to the activity, or even to your group. Think how accepting of an outsider you would be if s/he had no idea about your sporting 'native' language.

Research focus 9.3

Dashper and St John (2016) explored how formal equestrian competition dress in the course of regular sporting activities contributes to sporting identity; trust within the study group was established quickly. One of the authors, referred to as a participant observer, was a long-term rider who had engaged in practices and conversations regarding equestrian dress code and etiquette for some years. The other author was a master tailor, designer and creative director for international sports and fashion brands. This positioned them in a way that empowered respect in the study group. Trust and openness had been developed by the researchers and the participants, and because they all shared a common focus and interest, the researchers were accepted by the equestrian community.

In a study by Wood and Danylchuk (2011), a much longer time period was needed firstly to develop trust with the participants, and secondly to collect the field data. With the aim of exploring how social interactions may enable continuation of golf participation in females, the researchers firstly engaged in initial meetings, with participant observation continuing over a period of 2 months. This took two main forms: observer

(Continued)

(Continued)

researcher and observer participator. The first involved walking the course with the golfers while they were playing golf every week. The latter, which happened later during the data collection period, involved one of the authors, a novice golfer, being invited by the group to play a round of golf with them. Over time, the researchers gained the trust and respect from the participant group and were accepted by them. Trust with the participants developed gradually, allowing the researchers to establish a more informed 'insider' perspective of the group.

Do some homework on the history of the sport you are studying. So, for example, find out about cycling from a 'big-picture' perspective: who's Chris Froome and what's his story? And who won last year's Tour de France? A visit to the BBC Sport website would fill you in. What about from a local perspective: what's the local cycling scene like? Have there been any races recently? And how many clubs exist locally? Also find out about the basic structure and function of the culture. What do cyclists do when they go training? Do they have any special rituals distinct from other sports? What about their bikes? Most cyclists are obsessed with them, so finding out about all of the components, their functions, different wheels and frames would give you a heads-up as to what standards they would expect from their machines.

Data recording

Planning for effective data recording in the field is a key priority for any researcher. As the ethnographer often accesses a wide variety of data through a range of research methods, preparation will ensure that vital opportunities to record data are not missed. The ability to record data effectively during the researcher's time in the field comes down to a number of key factors. It is likely that researchers will use a number of different data collection approaches to collect and process the data, so having appropriate time to consider what data collection methods they are likely to use will save time later. Being able to write field notes effectively, conduct focus groups, operate video and audio systems and make detailed observations requires a degree of patience and practice.

 Learning activity 9.3

To help plan the data-recording process effectively prior to field entry, it helps to make a list of all the possible data collection methods. All of the different ways in which the data could be recorded can then be established. By identifying the strengths and weaknesses of each data-recording technique linked to each data collection method, the researcher can then begin to justify inclusion or exclusion criteria.

Consider the amount of time it may take a researcher to implement data collection methods. This may include set-up and familiarisation time, and the amount of time it could take to document the data afterwards; what about the analysis required? Consider access to resources and any additional training the researcher may need.

Withdrawing from the field

This sounds slightly strange, considering how the researcher will exit the field before you've entered it, but integrating withdrawal into your research plan is important. The reason is that it starts you thinking about an appropriate timescale of exposure with the group, the nature and extent of data collection and what processes you plan to implement to ensure a smooth withdrawal. As this is an important part of the research design, consideration must be given to your physical removal from the field as well as any emotional disengagement from the relationships established. For most short-term research projects (i.e. 2–5 months' exposure time) within the field, the complexities of withdrawal are relatively minimal, and in some cases, the researcher continues to work with the group long after the research has finished. What is important in this instance is that the researcher and the participants are clear when the researcher activity has ceased and further support continues. This will prevent any misunderstanding and ensure relationships are maintained.

Very few published ethnographic studies document withdrawal procedures within the methods sections and natural removal seems to occur in most once a certain degree of data has been collected. Ensure that the process and mechanics of withdrawal are documented within any report. Providing details and justifying the point of withdrawal demonstrate an ethically and morally responsible researcher who has considered the impact that removal may have on the group.

Effective data collection techniques

A central feature of any research strategy is the formulation of data collection methods. To access social meanings, observe behaviour and work closely with participants, the correct choice of relevant collection approaches will allow for effective data gathering in the field. As can be seen in Table 9.1, research methods, such as participant observation, interviews, focus groups, video and audio recordings and document analysis, provide the researcher with a wide range of techniques and instruments that will enable a full and in-depth understanding of the group's social behaviours.

Analysis and interpretation of ethnographic data

Data can take many forms for the ethnographic researcher – numerical lists, extracts from field notes, long quotations from interviews, entries from diaries, examples from observations, transcripts from conversations, graphic evidence from photographs, or sound bites from audio recordings. Bringing the data together in some kind of order requires a systematic and logical process for analysis and interpretation.

When you bring order to the data, organising into categories, themes and units, you may discover patterns and associations. Any analysis should be seen as a process as well as a research method in its own right. As with most research strategies analysis typically occurs following data collection. With ethnography, data analysis should be seen as an iterative process and one that occurs simultaneously with data collection. This approach allows for ideas or frameworks to be tested, refined and qualified in the field.

Table 9.1   A range of field-based data collection methods can be applied within ethnographic research

Field collection approaches	Description
Participant observation	This field method is most closely linked to ethnographic research: observation occurs alone or by both observing and participating. Participant observation always takes place in community settings, in locations believed to have some relevance to the research questions. The method is distinctive because the researcher approaches participants in their own environment rather than having the participants come to the researcher
Interviewing	To the ethnographer, interviewing is a primary means of grasping the context and content of people's everyday social, cultural, political and economic lives. The interview can range from a highly structured one-to-one approach to broader group focus meetings. Surveys or questionnaires are further forms of interviewing that can be implemented
Diaries	The use of diaries as a form of data collection provides the researcher with time-bound detailed personal reflections and perspectives from group members. Typically being factual in focus, centring on events and activities, diaries are guided by the researcher to ensure that their content informs the research question
Photographic evidence	Photography can be used to great success in ethnographic research, providing a different perspective from the oral or written account of reality. This medium of data collection seeks to represent what is seen without interpretation or mediation via words or impressions from the researcher. This approach emphasises the importance of the 'here and now', capturing precise moments in time. Taken by the researcher or participants, spontaneous photography can offer a different view of reality sometimes missed by more formal data collection techniques
Web forums and chat rooms	Virtual environments comprising forums, chat rooms or open-access discussion boards can be a valuable location for data collection. Observing from a distance or participating in virtual communication can help in understanding cultural rituals, standards and rules. The researcher ensures that appropriate data-recording techniques are applied to capture text for future analysis. Virtual environments can provide a rich source of cultural practice where anonymity can reveal the most interesting of findings

'Cut it up and stick it back together'

An easy way to conceptualise ethnographic data analysis is to view it as a 'cut it up and stick it back together again' exercise. In this way, the task of ploughing through reams of data files in order to find the metaphorical needle becomes less daunting. The three basic steps are:

1. reduction (cut up the data into smaller units, themes or categories – these may be loosely determined prior to field entry, established during simultaneous data analysis or created following field withdrawal);

2. display (stick the data back together into a format that starts to tell a story, unite commonality or highlight differences – during this stage the researcher should have the research question firmly at the centre of thought);

3. draw conclusions (make sense and meaning from the findings).

Key point 9.1

Managing ethnographic data can be a daunting task for the novice researcher. Fortunately, a number of computer software packages exist to help you handle the large amounts of data likely to be collected during ethnographic research. Packages such as NUD*IST or NVivo may provide a way in which inputted data can be more easily categorised, linked and interpreted. It is worth asking your supervisor or seeking assistance from your library support services as to whether you have access to these types of qualitative data packages. Alternatively, you may be able to download demo versions from online sites that give you sufficient time and functionality so that you can undertake data analysis for your project.

Molnar and Purdy (2017) recognise data analysis for the researcher as a series of processes, which can begin both during and after data collection. These steps can be seen as:

- data management (organising the data into manageable chunks);

- coding (indexing the data into categories, themes or units);

- content analysis of any collected documents relating to the field and/or group;

- qualitative description (identifying the key events, people, behaviour, etc.);

- establishing patterns in the data (looking for recurring themes, association between the data);

- examining cases that do not fit within the categories or themes, or are unexpected in the context of the field and/or group.

Interpretation of ethnographic data is no easy feat, even for the most accomplished researcher and seeking support from your supervisor is recommended. Your ability to understand the stories behind the data will to a large extent come down to your own coverage and understanding of the research literature, as well as your prior experiences of data collection, analysis and interpretation. Practising these before you commence your research would be of extreme value. It is worth considering a number of key points when it comes to interpretation.

- What goes with what? Try to consider what patterns or clusters you are looking for in the data. Are you attempting to identify patterns or clusters in the data that relate to 'self-identity', 'signs of self-deprecation' or 'negative thoughts', etc., that may reveal an insight into your sporting group?

- What is there? Try counting particular phrases, metaphors, occurrences or signs. Identifying frequencies may give you an insight into the cultural individualities present in sport.

- What does it mean? Making contrasts and comparisons, subdividing themes further and making links can reveal associations between topics otherwise considered unrelated.

- Where do we go from here? Building a logical chain of evidence and developing theoretical/conceptual understanding can lead to coherent and meaningful conclusions that unravel complex social and cultural meanings to behaviours recorded.

Research focus 9.4

In a study by Burke et al. (2008), the aim was to examine ethnographically how a group of high-altitude climbers drew on a range of cognitive principles to interpret their experiences during an attempt to scale Mount Everest.

By becoming 'insiders' with six mountaineers during their preparation, early climbing exposure and following the attempt, the researchers were able to collect data in the form of in-depth interviews captured on videotape and detailed observations recorded as field notes. The generated data were subjected to content analysis, in which the researchers sifted through the data several times to immerse themselves and understand, interpret and report the participants' experiences from an empathetic position.

The first step for the researchers involved reading the interview transcripts and field diary with a view to identifying where, when and under what circumstances the phenomenon of research interest (i.e. cognitive dissonance) was alluded to in the participants' experiences. Thematic issues that the researchers identified were:

- situations in which participants became aware of falling short of their expectations of being capable climbers;

- enduring a great deal of physical discomfort without the reward of reaching the summit;

- spending large amounts of money to endure a great deal of physical discomfort;

- placing the personal goal of climbing the mountain before their family.

Next, similarities in the data were identified to examine the ways in which the participants experienced cognitive dissonance and how this related to their sense of self and the situations they found themselves in. Connections across the data were explored to identify patterns as they emerged in the participants' accounts of their experiences on the mountain. Emerging themes and categories were noted and analytic memos were used to make preliminary and tentative connections to various processes that had been identified within the participants. These were interpreted and presented with the aim of making sense of the climbers' cognitive dissonance experiences during such physical and psychological extremes.

 Learning activity 9.4

Consider your own hectic day-to-day life for a moment. Let's take yesterday. Just stop and reflect on yesterday. From the point your eyes opened to the point they closed. Think about all the activities you got up to, the places you went to, the people you met, the things you talked about, the behaviours you exhibited and the rituals you performed. Based on these, your life can quite simply be broken down into categories or themes and then subdivided even further. Take the category of 'social contact', for example. This could be subdivided into friends, family, acquaintances and strangers. This could be divided further, so for acquaintances there may be subordinates, peers and superiors.

If we were to observe, record and interview you we could start to identify, based on our categories, some of the cultural behaviours, standards, rules and rituals within your life. How many times did you mention friends and in what context: positive, negative or neutral? Did you repeatedly talk about practical activities that indicate particular behaviours or social customs? Did we observe a particular eating or drinking pattern that may indicate something about you and your cultural standards?

Now your life may not be that interesting, but apply the same principles to a group of snowboarders, windsurfers, female bodybuilders, elderly yoga practitioners, junior coaches or aerobics instructors, and we may find that their lived experiences as athletes, exercisers or coaches offer us a greater understanding of sport culture by providing a real insight into their unique cultural behaviours, values, emotions and mental states.

Writing and presenting ethnographies

The writing of our ethnographies brings together many hours of research planning, field involvement, data collection and analysis. It is unfortunate that this is often the part that receives the least attention, but is probably the most significant (particularly in terms of your grade). You will have already written much, in the form of field notes, transcriptions, observation letters and e-mails, so drawing all the findings together can seem an uphill battle.

It is worth noting at the start of this process that writing ethnographic research centres on the 'truthfulness' of our interpretations and accounts. By undertaking a process of reflection that takes into account credibility of data (i.e. an authentic representation of what actually occurred), transferability of the material (i.e. making what actually occurred intelligible to the reader), dependability of the interpretation (i.e. that an illogical, biased position is not presented) and confirmability of the study (i.e. sound methodology that is auditable through the written report), the validation of truth in our research can be upheld.

As with all presented research, sections should relate to the aims and objectives, background to the problem, research strategy, findings and discussion. Details covering the choice of research setting or field, sampling techniques, resources used, field-based data collection approaches, nature of the researcher's role, form of analysis, details relating to the process of withdrawal and ethical considerations should all be included within the research strategy section.

One of the most straightforward approaches to writing ethnographies is to focus on the emerging categories or themes that have been identified throughout the analysis process. In the study by Choi et al. (2006) (Research focus 9.2), for example, the emerging themes of: cool signs and graffiti; athletes; friends and family; freebies; music; and self-identity were identified and discussed separately with a final conclusion to make wider social and cultural sense of the data. Through narrative, associations between such themes and their wider cultural meanings can start to be explored. In effect, this approach requires you to go through the categories or themes, summarising, quoting passages, and making sense by sticking the bits back together in an attempt to understand the bigger picture.

As outlined by Mills and Morton (2013), writing and presenting ethnographic research should contain most, if not all, of the following features:

- a depiction of what the 'story' is about (does the report clearly explain themes, categories and associations?);

- a sense of context, whether that be social, political, economic and/or educational;

- an ability to trace and track the history and the progress of the research (will the reader know when and why the researcher made key decisions and what effect these may have had on data collection and analysis?);

- an illustration of how and why key insights and concepts emerged (this will be more than a list of methods);

- data that are clearly presented through a range of textual accounts, quotations, data displays and photographs;

- conclusions that show connections between themes, categories and concepts in a systematic and organised way allowing for theory development.

Chapter review

In this chapter we have considered the importance of the ethnographic research strategy to sport and identified that the ethnographer is not merely a conduit for data collection in social life, but an active participant in the construction of social accounts. Ethnography is a unique research approach that offers a wide range of opportunities to those interested in learning more about sporting cultures. By demystifying the research process, providing sport-related research examples and describing methods of data collection, analysis and interpretation, application of this research strategy can result in meaningful research projects as well as the development of important employability skills. By using a range of sport-related research examples throughout this chapter you should now be able to:

☑ define ethnography in the context of sport research and identify how and why this research strategy is distinct from others;

☑ describe the stages of the ethnographic research process;

☑ define the role of the researcher and appraise the factors that will improve data collection;

☑ appreciate the range of field-based data collection approaches and describe the relevance to ethnographic research;

☑ understand a 'cut it up and stick it back together again' approach to data analysis and interpretation.

Further reading

Brewer, JD (2008) *Ethnography*. Maidenhead: Open University Press.

LeCompte, MD and Schensul, JJ (2010) *Designing and Conducting Ethnographic Research (Ethnographer's Toolkit)*. Lanham, MD: Rowman Altamira.

For those serious about ethnographic research, these books consolidate early chapter content by further examining the meaning of ethnography and placing it in a methodological framework.

Crang, M and Cook, I (2007) *Doing Ethnographies*. London: SAGE Publications.

This is an excellent research book focusing primarily on the wide range of ethnographic field methods the researcher can use. Building on the data collection approaches outlined in this chapter, the authors present clear examples to assist understanding and application.

Mills, D and Morton, M (2013) *Ethnography in Education*. London: SAGE Publications.

Don't be put off by the educational emphasis! The authors have informatively presented an engaging book that offers the reader a real insight into the whole approach to ethnographic research. The three sections on analysing, use and writing about ethnography are highly recommended to anyone wanting to undertake ethnographic research.

Molnar, G and Purdy, L (2017) *Ethnographies in Sport and Exercise Research*. London: Routledge.

Sands, R (2002) *Sport Ethnography*. Champaign, IL: Human Kinetics.

These books are solely dedicated to sport ethnography, so are a must-read for those interested in this research approach. Both are packed full of excellent sporting examples, real-life case studies and a clear description of the ethnographic research process.

10

A mixed-research approach to sport

Learning objectives

By linking your understanding of sport in practice to sport-related research examples, this chapter is designed to help you:

- explain how a mixed-research strategy can be an effective approach to sport research;
- describe uses of the mixed-research approach to sport and show how different research methods can be used in combination;
- appreciate the associated strengths and weaknesses of a mixed approach to research.

Introduction

Research into sport offers a multitude of opportunities that are diverse in topic and broad in approach. As has been covered so far in this book, a number of research strategies and associated research methods exist that allow for the exploration and explanation of sporting behaviour from a range of perspectives. These could be observational if we were interested in coaching behaviour, ethnographical if we wished to examine the sociocultural functioning of a sports team or experimental if our questions centred on performance enhancement. Each research strategy can be selected based on the nature of the inquiry and questions that need answering. As in all research, the selection of an appropriate research strategy from a clearly stated research question creates the link between aims and research methods.

Sometimes, however, single or 'mono' strategies alone may limit the researcher's ability to explore the topic fully and explain the meanings of the findings. When we use multiple approaches to sport research, we can capitalise on the strengths of each single approach and offset their different weaknesses. It could also provide more comprehensive answers to our research questions, going beyond the limitations of a single research approach. Such *mixed-research* strategy is most appropriate when we have a specific issue or problem that is best understood through both exploration and explanation.

 Student case study 10.1

As part of a project team that consisted of an MSc sports performance postgraduate researcher (Robin) and two final-year Sport and Exercise Science degree students, Caroline and Rebecca (the undergraduate students) were tasked with exploring why so many elderly residents who had previously been diagnosed with type 2 diabetes had failed to complete a physical-wellness exercise programme (two sessions a week for 4 weeks) at their local leisure centre. In addition, Robin (the postgraduate researcher) wished to find out how participation could be increased and maintained. As the exercise programme was repeated in six different local venues, the students had access to a reasonably large target population (n = 120). The sessions were provided free of charge, at times that were deemed amenable to all. At first, more than 20 exercisers completed the first three sessions at each location. By the fifth session, however, attendance had dropped for all by up to 75%.

The students' approach was to obtain both quantitative and qualitative data to understand more about the frequency of attendance, intensity of physical activity during sessions, social relationships among the session members and the instructor, reasons for participation and 'outside of session' daily functioning. The students decided to break the project into two distinct parts, with phase one taking place at the exercise sessions and the second outside of session time in a more informal venue. The first phase was quantitative in nature and involved two components: (1) a 5-point Likert scale physical activity questionnaire; and (2) session-based observation. Following data collection, basic statistical analyses were performed on the data and a number of themes emerged.

The second phase of the research was qualitative and involved a survey strategy approach in which a number of informal focus groups took place with attending and non-attending elderly residents. The students used the themes that had emerged from phase one to develop a guide for their questions for the groups. In addition, they undertook semi-structured interviews with the programme instructors.

Using a mixed-research approach in a sequential manner (i.e. one phase following the next), the students were able to build on exploratory findings determined in phase one to explain the reasons for poor retention.

(Continued)

(Continued)

They were also able to recommend strategies to enhance and maintain attendance. Based on their findings, reasons for the drop-off in attendance throughout the programme were attributed to: exercises being perceived as too demanding with intensity being too high; instructors having little or no interaction with the group before or after sessions; and no additional advice or support being given on healthy lifestyles for home-based implementation. Feedback from all those interviewed revealed that involvement in the programme could be increased through more effective travel arrangements, a home-based support system that helps the elderly integrate the exercises into their everyday life and more empathetic and friendly instructors.

Combining methodologies: can paradigms be mixed?

We all know how rich in detail sport can be, and with the interconnected disciplines of the natural and social sciences encountered through our study, it seems logical to assume that many research questions will require the researcher to bring together a range of research approaches. Researchers wishing to understand the link between exercise and quality of life, group dynamics, leadership and performance achievement, or coaching strategies and player improvement, for example, may need to go beyond a single research approach to explore and explain fully behaviour and meaning. For the researcher interested in understanding more about sporting behaviour and its meanings, combining quantitative and qualitative research and the associated research methods sounds like a good idea and one that may allow for deeper learning and understanding.

To answer questions about sport and exercise through the implementation of research, understanding of appropriate sources of knowledge (e.g. interviews, observations, experiments), data analytic strategies (e.g. quantitative and/or qualitative), underlying philosophies of various research methodologies and the development of alternative paradigms need to occur. While several of these have influenced the field of sport research, there is still the need to develop and accept alternative ways of examining human behaviour within sport. Researchers who adopt a mixture of approaches, concepts, tools and methods can extend their current practices and discover how sport impacts on our life from a physical and social perspective.

 **Key point 10.1**

A paradigm is a term that is used to describe a cluster of beliefs and dictates for scientists in a particular discipline what should be studied, how research should be done, and how research should be interpreted.

(Bryman, 2015, pp629-30)

Bryman (2015) recognises two positions that are linked to the debate on whether approaches should be mixed by combining quantitative and qualitative research. The first is an epistemological view, namely that each paradigm is unique and therefore incompatible. Because of the contrasting ontological and epistemological assumptions (see Chapter 1), the nature of mixing research would be considered not possible. The second position is the technical one, where the focus is on the strengths of data collection and data analysis techniques rather than the philosophical assumptions governing each. As can be seen throughout the book and particularly in Table 2.1 in Chapter 2, research methods should not be seen as being bound to each paradigm (i.e. quantitative versus qualitative), but rather 'free agents' that can operate across boundaries. If researchers take a technical position, they adopt a more pragmatic or practical approach to their research, opening the gateway to mixed-research approaches.

 **Research focus 10.1**

In a study by Crowther and colleagues (2017), a sequential mixed-research approach was selected to investigate the variety of recovery strategies used by athletes. Specifically, researchers were interested in understanding the perceptions and usage of recovery at different competition levels across a wide range of team sport athletes. Both data collection phases applied the survey research strategy, with each adopting different methodological paradigms.

The first phase of the research was numerical in nature and focused on gaining insight into the demographics of the 331 athletes included in the study. Scores were recorded in a structured questionnaire: 14 team sports were represented. Athletes who competed in local competition were most represented (53%), followed by national (20%), regional (14%), county (9%) and international (2%). Among the sports, basketball was the most represented (22%), followed by rugby league (20%) and rugby union (20%). Across all sports and levels of competition athletes competed in 0–7 games per week, equating to 0–600 minutes of competition per week, and trained for 0–30 hours or more per week.

The second phase of the research was qualitative and involved open-ended questions. This was designed to explore the recovery patterns and habits of the athletes. Each participant was asked initially to answer 'yes' or 'no' to a series of questions, that then prompted free-text responses. Findings revealed that 95% of athletes performed a recovery strategy following competition, with 55% after pre-season training and 57% after in-season training. In order of popularity, stretching, food and fluid intake and land-based activity were recovery strategies selected by athletes following performance. Free-text responses highlighted the value of recovery as a way of 'recharging' mentally and physically after performance.

Using a mixed-method approach Crowther and co-workers demonstrated that athletes may not always be aware of recovery strategies that may assist them with both physical and mental recovery following performance. By collecting numeral data a deeper perspective of their study demographic was established. This was followed by more qualitative insight that explored approaches taken by athletes. The authors stated the importance of contextual information about different recovery strategies for coach and athlete practice.

A multi- versus mixed approach to research

As can be seen from the preceding chapters, a wide range of research studies have been described that use different research methods of data collection and analysis within a single research paradigm. For example, Choi et al. (2006; see Research focus 9.2) conducted an ethnographic qualitative study in which they collected photographic evidence from participants as well as conducting unstructured interviews. In the quantitative study conducted by Larsen et al. (2016; see Research focus 4.2), a range of physiological and performance measures were recorded during a performance assessment, while afterwards the performers completed a cognitive qualitative assessment. As is evident from the approach taken in each of these two studies, the application of selected research methods is broadly compatible with either the qualitative or quantitative paradigm. This can be known as a multi-approach to research and is the most typical form of research encountered.

 **Learning activity 10.1**

Select two research articles from the same topic area but with contrasting research perspectives (i.e. qualitative and quantitative). For example, they may be two articles about anxiety and sporting performance in football, cardiovascular benefits of exercise in the elderly or gifted and talented in youth sport. Focus only on the research strategy (i.e. research design and methods) for each. Make a list of the research method(s) used: try and think about the nature of the data collected, how the data were collected and the type of analysis performed.

Next, consider whether combining these studies would have improved our understanding of the topic. Would a mixture of the perspectives be of any benefit? Try and consider why. How might they have been combined? Could one be viewed as exploratory and the other explanatory? Do their findings complement each other? What may limit the combination of the two research strategies? What problems do you see if they were combined?

An alternative is mixed-approach studies that attempt to bring together methods from different paradigms. In a mixed-approach study the researcher may choose to conduct a series of semi-structured interviews with a small number of performers, combined with a large-scale survey. This kind of integration of qualitative with quantitative approaches is also referred to as a mixed-research strategy.

What is a mixed-research strategy?

A mixed-research strategy is one where the researcher mixes or combines quantitative and qualitative research approaches, concepts, techniques and methods into a single study. As indicated above, the term mixed research could be viewed as synonymous with the popularised term 'mixed methods'. The label 'mixed research', however, in this context is broader, more inclusive and clearly paradigmatic. A mixed-research strategy is more than just a mixture of methods; rather it is a mixture of ontological and epistemological positions that do not compete, but complement each other. Philosophically, mixed research makes use of the pragmatic paradigm and system of philosophy. Its logic of inquiry includes the use of induction (or discovery of patterns), deduction (testing of theories and hypotheses) and abduction (uncovering and relying on the best of a set of explanations for understanding results).

 **Key point 10.2**

A *mixed-research strategy* combines quantitative and qualitative research approaches, concepts, techniques and methods into a single study.

Purposes of mixed research in sport

There are four key reasons why a mixed-research approach to sport is of value. These are expansion, triangulation, complementarity and development. *Expansion* refers to the growth of knowledge by applying different research approaches to assess sporting phenomena to expand the scope and range of research studies. *Triangulation* relates to how the researcher applies different research strategies to measure the same sporting phenomenon, thereby increasing confidence in the conclusions. *Complementarity* relates to strategies which are used to investigate different aspects or dimensions of the same sporting phenomenon to deepen and broaden the interpretations and conclusions from a study. Finally, *development* refers to how results from one research approach can be used to inform the development of the other (e.g. instrument development).

In areas of applied sport and exercise psychology, coaching science, education in sport, sport management and business and long-term athlete development, to name but a few, research excellence has led us to understand much about how we act, perform, respond and develop as individuals and groups through our sporting endeavours. There is still much we do not know about social interactions, behaviours and their deeper meanings acted out through sport. By mixing strategies through the implementation of different research approaches, researchers position themselves well to develop new instruments and techniques, evaluate method compatibility and suitability and expand research studies through the growth of new questions that may reveal new and exciting knowledge about our social and personal functioning within sport.

Developing a pragmatic approach to mixed research in sport

The application of a mixed-research strategy to sport attempts to legitimise the use of multiple approaches in answering research questions, rather than restricting or constraining researchers' choices. Sport is after all a complex milieu of natural and social phenomena. In appreciating this, the mixed-research approach to sport should be inclusive and complementary, accepting that a wide-ranging approach to research strategy and method selection can provide a vehicle for broader sporting inquiry. As has been a common theme throughout this book, the most fundamental aspect for research success is question formulation: research strategies should follow research questions in a way that offers the best chance of obtaining useful answers. Many research questions emerging in sport are therefore best and most fully answered through mixed-research solutions.

Put simply, the pragmatic researcher opts for strategies and associated methods that are more useful within specific sporting contexts (e.g. answers to practical problems), not those that necessarily are tied into single paradigmatic positions. As has been emphasised throughout this book, the researcher's quest for knowledge and the evolvement of research questions should lead to the most appropriate research strategies, rather than to a dogmatic view of research and its associated assumptions.

Reflection point 10.1

Try to think of a research problem that could be tackled using a mixed-research approach. Consider the advantages this strategy would have over a single-strategy perspective and the type of research methods you might implement to obtain the required data.

Characteristics of mixed research

In order to mix research in an effective manner, the researcher first needs to consider all of the relevant characteristics of quantitative and qualitative research. For example, the major characteristics of traditional quantitative research are a focus on deduction, confirmation, theory/hypothesis testing, explanation, prediction, standardised data collection and statistical analysis (see Table 1.2 in Chapter 1). The major characteristics of traditional qualitative research are induction, discovery, exploration, theory/hypothesis generation, the researcher as the primary instrument of data collection and qualitative analysis (see Table 1.3 in Chapter 1).

Research focus 10.2

In a study by Giacobbi et al. (2008), the purpose was to examine links between physical activity and quality of life experienced by individuals with physical disabilities recruited from a wheelchair users' basketball tournament. This mixed-research approach involved an integrated survey and ethnographic research strategy, combining quantitative and qualitative methodologies. Such an approach was deemed necessary to evaluate the frequency and intensity of physical activity behaviours, social relationships and daily functioning in a manner consistent with quality-of-life literature previously reviewed by the authors.

Through a parallel mixed-research approach, which involved the collection of quantitative and qualitative data simultaneously, adapted physical activity questionnaires were administered alongside semi-structured interviews to a range of physically impaired performers. The physical activity scale questionnaire, specifically designed for individuals with physical disabilities (Physical Activity Scale for Individuals with Physical Disabilities: PASIPD), consisted of five subscales: home repair/lawn and garden work; housework; vigorous sport and recreation; moderate sport and recreation; and occupational activities. The instrument scoring system produced a mathematically maximum score and an estimated metabolic equivalent value (e.g. energy expenditure) for each of the five factors and a total score. These numerical data were then subjected to statistical analysis methods. The interviews were semi-structured and based on a pre-determined guide of questions focusing on the: (1) nature of the participants' disabilities; (2) occupational or school-related activities of daily living; (3) perceived benefits of physical activity; (4) motives that sustain involvement in physical activity; and (5) evaluations about the individual's life.

With the purpose of this mixed-research study being to explore the role that physical activity plays in the quality of life for individuals with physical disabilities, the researcher's findings revealed that descriptions of the physical activity experiences, perceived benefits and motives for participation highlighted several themes of importance: psychological benefits; physical health benefits; social opportunities; social influences; and increased overall quality of life.

Gaining an understanding of the strengths and weaknesses of quantitative and qualitative research puts a researcher in the position of mixing or combining strategies and collecting multiple data using different strategies, approaches and methods in such a way that the resulting combination is likely to result in complementary strengths and non-overlapping weaknesses. As shown in Table 10.1, combining quantitative and qualitative research approaches has both strengths and weaknesses that researchers must be aware of before embarking on a mixed-research study.

Table 10.1   Strengths and weaknesses of a mixed-research approach (extracts from Johnson and Onwuegbuzie, 2004)

Strengths
• Words, pictures and narrative can be used to add meaning to numbers
• Numbers can be used to add precision to words, pictures and narrative
• Can provide quantitative and qualitative research strengths (see strengths listed in Tables 1.2 and 1.3 in Chapter 1)
• Researcher can generate and test a developed theory
• Can answer a broader and more complete range of research questions because the researcher is not confined to a single method or approach
• The specific mixed *research designs* discussed in this chapter have strengths and weaknesses that should be considered (e.g. in a two-phase sequential design, the results from phase one can be used to develop and inform the purpose and design of the phase two component)
• A researcher can use the strengths of an additional method to overcome the weaknesses in another method by using both in a research study
• Can provide stronger evidence for a conclusion through convergence and corroboration of findings
• Can add insights and understanding that might be missed when only a single method is used
• Can be used to increase the generalisability of the results
• Qualitative and quantitative research used together produces more complete knowledge, necessary to inform theory and practice
Weaknesses
• Can be difficult for a single researcher to carry out both qualitative and quantitative research, especially if two or more approaches are expected to be used concurrently; it may require a research team
• Researcher has to learn about multiple methods and approaches and understand how to mix them appropriately
• Methodological purists contend that one should always work within either a qualitative or a quantitative paradigm
• More expensive
• More time consuming
• Some of the details of mixed research remain to be worked out fully by research methodologists (e.g. problems of paradigm mixing, how to analyse qualitatively quantitative data, how to interpret conflicting results)

Effective use of this approach is a major source of justification for mixed research because the end result can be superior to studies where a single methodology is followed. For example, adding qualitative interviews to experiments as a manipulation check and perhaps as a way to discuss directly the issues under investigation and tap into participants' perspectives can enrich the study and provide more meaningful answers.

 Learning activity 10.2

Try and summarise the key strengths and weaknesses of a mixed-research strategy. If you want to use this approach then it is important you are able to justify its value over a single-strategy study.

Design of mixed-research study

The design of a mixed-research study can be loosely based on three key decisions (Creswell, 2014).

1. What order does the researcher want the quantitative and qualitative research methods to appear in the study?

2. What priority will the researcher give to the quantitative and qualitative data collection and analysis procedures?

3. At what stage will the researcher want the quantitative and qualitative findings to be combined?

Each of these should be dictated by the nature of the research question and not familiarity with and confidence in using particular research approaches. The decision about the order, priority and integration of data collection and analysis should be explicitly stated in any research plan or protocol before the collection phases begin. Integrated into the overall design plan, the researcher's decisions should be carefully considered to ensure that data collection and analysis are relevant and implemented at the right time.

Mixed-research designs can occur in one of two ways. The first is known as a parallel design and relates to the mixing of qualitative and quantitative approaches within the same stage of the research process (i.e. one phase). For example, take researchers who want to evaluate the effectiveness of a new physical training aid during dance performance. Implementing a parallel design, they could collect physiological and movement data, in addition to simultaneously recording participants' verbal description of effort or their subjective likes and dislikes about the aid. In this instance, the researcher is able to collect both quantitative and qualitative data at the same time in the study and the implementation is simultaneous.

The alternative approach is known as a sequential design: qualitative and quantitative approaches occur in a sequence, with one phase of collection happening before the next. If a researcher wished to explore professional coaches' opinions on the value of volunteer coaching, the first phase (qualitative) might involve several small-scale focus groups to explore the topic and develop emerging themes. The second phase (quantitative) might then involve the development and deployment of a closed-question survey to a much larger number of coaches who were typically representative of the professional coaching community.

Most sequentially designed mixed-research studies consist of two phases. The order in which these phases occur (i.e. quantitative and qualitative) will depend on the nature of the question. Two key questions the researcher may wish to ask are: (1) what information needs to be emphasised/established first in the study: quantitative or qualitative? and (2) will theory be built, tested and explained (induction > deduction > abduction) or tested and deconstructed and then explained (deduction > induction > abduction)? In addition to the order in which quantitative and qualitative approaches occur, there is the question of the dominance of each. Will each approach be of equal weighting in the study or will one be considered a major approach and the other a minor?

Associated with each design approach is how the collected data will be combined for analysis. For the researcher, the term 'combined' simply refers to the stage of the research process where quantitative and qualitative data will be mixed, analysed and then interpreted. Take, for example, the parallel-design study illustrated above. Because the data were collected simultaneously during a single phase, the combination of data will occur during the interpretation stage of research. For the sequential-design example provided, combining data collected from professional coaches may occur during data collection, analysis, interpretation or a combination of all three. For phase one of the study, qualitative data recorded in the focus groups could be transformed into numerical codes during analysis. For phase two, the survey administered to the coaches may be a combination of open and closed questions, therefore eliciting qualitative and quantitative data.

 Learning activity 10.3

By applying the description above to the three published research studies found within this chapter (see Research focus 10.1 and 10.2, and 10.3, below), try to answer the following questions:

- Is the study a parallel or sequential design?
- In what order do the quantitative and qualitative approaches appear?
- Are the approaches of equal weighting or is one more dominant than the other?
- At what point are the findings combined?

Data analysis in mixed research

The researcher can implement a number of approaches when it comes to data analysis within mixed research. As reviewed in Table 10.2, a broad range of approaches to data analysis can be implemented within a mixed-research strategy. If different collection instruments and procedures are administered within the mixed-research strategy (e.g. focus groups, interviews, observations,

Table 10.2   *Five broad approaches to data analysis in a mixed-research strategy (adapted from Creswell, 2014)*

Data analysis approach	Design type	Description and example
Data transformation	Parallel design	This approach involves transforming qualitative into quantitative data or vice versa (e.g. unstructured interviews with several fitness centre managers resulted in the theme 'recession' being mentioned 17 times)
Multiple-level examination	Parallel design	This approach involves collecting quantitative data at one level (e.g. survey with a sports team) while at the same time collecting qualitative data at another level (e.g. interview data with individual players to explore the role of players within that team)
Outlier exploration	Sequential design	In this approach, phase one quantitative analysis could highlight outliers that phase two qualitative research could investigate (e.g. tachycardia recorded in a participant could lead to follow-up interview)
Instrument development	Sequential design	This approach can allow for the development of categories or themes from qualitative data collection that can be used to create quantitative surveys (e.g. a focus group with children could lead to the development of a PE observation sheet)
Data separation	Both	This approach involves qualitative and quantitative data being analysed separately where one does not inform or influence the other (e.g. isokinetic data of lower-limb bilateral strength and interview data examining training history)

clinical measurements, diagnostic tests, questionnaires, photography and content analysis), data analysis will occur by way of quantitative (descriptive and inferential numeric analysis) and qualitative (description and thematic text or image analysis) techniques. The relationship between each analysis technique can be broadly categorised into five approaches: data transformation; multiple-level examination; outlier exploration; instrument development; and data separation. The approach selected will be governed by both the research design and the research question.

 Learning activity 10.4 ━━━━━━━━━━

Key questions that the researcher may wish to ask when designing a mixed-research study:

- Has a definition of mixed research been clearly stated?
- Has the selection of a mixed-research approach been justified?
- Are the criteria for selecting a mixed-research strategy identified?

- Are both quantitative and qualitative research methods stated and justified?

- Are sampling strategies for both quantitative and qualitative data collection mentioned?

- Is an explanation given of how these relate to the mixed-research strategy?

- Are specific data analysis procedures indicated?

- Are procedures for validating both quantitative and qualitative data discussed?

 Research focus 10.3

In a study by Watson et al. (2016), the purpose was to explore the implementation of a dance mat scheme and offer insight into its uptake as a physical activity intervention. The scheme was a regional initiative that provided opportunities to participate in exercise classes using exergame dance mat systems (computer-based interactive dance mats). Introduced into all secondary schools within two local districts ($n = 22$), the study centred on five intervention schools (purposively sampled from the target population). A total of 120 pupils (sampled based on convenience) and 20 teachers (purposively sampled) were involved in data collection.

The authors selected a sequential mixed-research approach, with quantitative findings from previous observations (Azevedo et al., 2014) informing the qualitative direction of this current study. This mixed-methodological strategy firstly involved examining the effect of introducing the dance mat exergaming systems on physical activity and health-related outcomes in 11–13-year-old students using a non-randomised controlled experimental research strategy (the 2014 study). Outcomes revealed that dance mat exergaming was associated with improvements in body composition measurements and parameters of health-related quality of life, but outcomes were insignificant as regarding increases in physical activity.

The second phase of the research (the 2016 study by Watson et al.) adopted a qualitative survey strategy and involved both individualised teacher interviews and focus groups with pupils. Interviews lasted between 10 and 30 minutes and were semi-structured, directed through a thematic topic guide. The focus group consisted of 3–6 pupils with themes exploring their experiences and expectations of the dance mats. All interviews and focus groups were audio-recorded and transcribed verbatim. NVivo was used to develop a thematic framework that mapped the core and subcategories emerging from that qualitative data. Key findings highlighted different expectations between teachers and pupils, with the mats not being used routinely as a means of increasing physical activity. This was based on contextual issues (school routines/environmental constraints), technological failures and expectations on how and where they could be used.

Combining two research strategies in a linked mixed-methods approach, the authors were able to conclude that, within the sample population, exergames may not be an effective way of increasing physical activity levels (study one), and dance mats were not used routinely enough to show a significant effect on physical activity (study two). These combined studies demonstrate the benefit of using mixed methods to evaluate complex physical activity interventions.

Chapter review

In this chapter we have examined the benefits and limitations of the mixed-research approach to sport. Mixed research can be seen as a combination of quantitative and qualitative methodologies for the purpose of gaining a greater understanding of sport behaviour and its associated meanings. By developing research designs combining research methods in a number of ways, we can start to implement a mixed-research strategy to examine a much wider perspective of sport. Through the use of sport-related research examples you should now be able to:

☑ describe how a mixed-research strategy can be of benefit to sport research;

☑ list a wide range of strengths and weaknesses associated with the mixed-research approach and justify its use in sport research;

☑ design a mixed-research study that considers order, priority and combination of findings;

☑ recognise sport-related research that has implemented a mixed-research approach.

Further reading

Bryman, A (2015) *Social Research Methods*. 5th ed. Oxford: Oxford University Press.

Creswell, JW (2013) *Research Design: Qualitative, Quantitative, and Mixed Methods Approaches*. 4th ed. Thousand Oaks, CA: SAGE Publications.

Creswell, JW (2014) *A Concise Introduction to Mixed Methods Research*. Los Angeles, CA: SAGE Publications.

These three books will provide extended notes on the combining paradigms debate – quantitative versus qualitative – as well as a detailed perspective on mixed-research design. Although not linked particularly well to sport and exercise examples, concepts are clearly stated and easily transferable to sport.

Clark, VLP and Ivankova, NV (2015) *Mixed Methods Research: A Guide to the Field* (Vol. 3). Thousand Oaks, CA: SAGE Publications.

Tashakkori, A and Teddlie, C (2010) *SAGE Handbook of Mixed Methods in Social and Behavioral Research*. Thousand Oaks, CA: SAGE Publications.

Further supporting key concepts and practical aspects of this chapter, these handbooks offer the reader an extended coverage of mixed research within social sciences. They also expand on design types and analysis processes, which may be of value when planning a mixed-research study.

Sparkes, AC (2015) Developing mixed methods research in sport and exercise psychology: critical reflections on five points of controversy. *Psychology of Sport and Exercise*, 16: 49–59.

For the interested reader, this excellent article provides a well-resourced guide to the application of pragmatism to the area of sport psychology. It argues the case for a mixed-research paradigm within sport research, and you should read it once you have a firm grip of the key concepts covered in Chapter 1.

Glossary

Action research   An approach that attempts to improve the social situation under investigation whilst at the same point generating knowledge about it.

Association   Any relationship between two measured variables that renders them statistically dependent.

Attributes   Properties possessed by one or more persons or objects. By measuring and comparing attributes the researcher can establish patterns within or between groups.

Attrition   The tendency for participants in the study to drop out through illness, injury or refusal to continue to be involved.

Between-group design   An experimental approach where two or more different groups of participants are subject to different experiences or treatments.

Case   An individual unit being studied. A case could be a person, team, school, club or organisation.

Case study research   A research strategy that involves the detailed and intensive analysis of a single case. The term can be extended to include multiple-case research whereby two or more cases are compared.

Causation   A concern with establishing causal connections between variables, rather than mere relationships between them.

Closed questions   A question employed within a survey that presents the respondent with a set of possible answers to choose from (as opposed to *open-ended questions*).

Cluster sampling   A procedure in which at an initial stage the researcher stages areas (i.e. clusters) and then samples units from those clusters, usually using a *probability sampling* technique.

Cohort   A group of persons sharing a particular statistical or demographic characteristic (e.g. all the participants live in the same postcode area).

Comparative design   A research design that involves identifying differences and similarities between two or more cases in order to establish theoretical insights.

Confounding variable   A variable that is not controlled in an experiment and may affect the dependent variable.

Constant   An attribute that does not change or vary throughout the course of a study.

Constructivism   An ontological position that asserts that social phenomena and their meanings are constructed and do not necessarily reflect external realities. From this perspective, knowledge is dependent on social experience, human perception and social conventions.

Content analysis   A method by which textual and visual documents are analysed and categorised in a systematic and reliable manner in order to produce quantitative data. The term can also be applied to qualitative content analysis.

Control group   Used to try to establish whether any effect found in the intervention group is due to the intervention or would have occurred anyway.

Convenience sampling   A procedure that selects a sample based on their availability to the researcher.

Correlation co-efficient   A measure of the strength and direction of the relationship between two variables. This approach is applied when the two variables are both measured at the interval or ratio level of measurement.

Correlational research   A research strategy that involves the analysis of relationships between variables.

Counterbalancing   A process of controlling for order effects in a repeated measures design by either including all order of treatment presentation or randomly determining the order for each participant.

Covert research   An approach by which those who are being researched are not aware, or not fully aware, of the researcher's identity and/or role.

Cross-sectional design   A research design that involves collecting data from a sample at one point in time.

Curvilinear relationship   A relationship between two or more variables, which is depicted graphically (i.e. scatter plot) by anything other than a straight line.

Data   Material that is either numerical or textual, which is generated and collected in the research process for the purpose of analysis. Data are the product of the research and determined by the research process.

Data analysis   A process of gathering, organising and synthesising data with the goal being to highlight useful information.

Data collection   The period within the research process that involves preparing for and collecting data by engaging with a target sample or population.

Deduction   An approach to research by which a conclusion is reached from previously known premises. For example, a conclusion may be reached by deduction from the combination of a theory and some facts about a specific case (as opposed to *induction*).

Dependent variable   A variable that is causally influenced by another variable (the *independent variable*).

Descriptive statistics   An approach that is used to describe or summarise the characteristics of a sample.

Ecological validity   The degree to which behaviours that are observed and recorded in a study reflect the behaviours that occur in a natural setting.

Empiricism   An approach that uses observations to answer questions about the nature of behaviour.

Epistemology   The branch of philosophy that concerns the theory of knowledge, that is, what is true and how we come to believe its truth.

Ethics   A theory or system of moral values, such as what is right and wrong.

Ethnographic research   A research strategy that involves the researcher immersing him- or herself in a social setting for an extended period of time, utilising a wide range of research methods.

Exercise science   A discipline that studies the application of scientific principles and techniques with the aim of enhancing or maintaining physical fitness and overall health.

Experimental research   A research strategy that involves the testing of a hypothesis, usually through the manipulation of an independent variable to measure the changes in the dependent variable. Typically involves an intervention and control condition/group.

External validity   The extent to which the research findings can be generalised to the population and different social settings.

Extraneous variable   Any variable other than the dependent and independent variable that may influence the relationship between the two. In true experiments all possible extraneous variables are controlled.

Falsification   The process of trying to disprove a proposition, hypothesis or theory.

Field notes   A description of events observed during field research in a social setting and recorded at observation, or shortly afterwards.

Field research   Research carried out in a naturally occurring setting rather than in a controlled setting such as the physiology or biomechanics laboratory.

Focus group   A form of group interview in which several participants, in addition to a moderator/facilitator, explore a range of topics with the aim of generating a range of opinions.

Gatekeeper   Persons within the research process, whose assistance enables the researcher to access those the researcher wishes to research: for example, a coach of a football team or a manager of a fitness centre.

Generalisability   The extent to which findings from the researcher's sample can be claimed to reflect accurately the characteristics of a wider population than that from which the researcher sampled.

Haphazard sampling   A procedure that involves selecting participants in a haphazard manner, usually based on their availability.

Hypothesis   An informed speculation, which is set up to be tested, about the relationship between two or more variables.

Independent variable   A variable that has a causal impact on another variable (the *dependent variable*).

In-depth interview   A method of data collection that is often open and unstructured in nature that explores a topic in significant detail from the interviewee's perspective.

Induction   An approach to research by which generalisations are generated by seeking commonality in cases. In social research, this approach generates theory from evidence (as opposed to *deduction*).

Inference   The act or process of deriving logical conclusions from premises known or assumed to be true.

Inferential statistics   Statistics that allow the researcher to make inferences on the likelihood of the sample findings being replicated in the population.

Informed consent   A process whereby participants provide consent to become involved in the research, being made fully aware of the implications of their involvement.

Internal validity   The extent to which data collected accurately reflect the reality of beliefs or behaviours of those from whom the data were collected.

Interpretivism   An epistemological position that requires the researcher to grasp subjective meaning of social action (see *qualitative* research).

Intervention group   A group that receives an intervention.

Interview   An approach that requires a face-to-face talk in order to generate data. Interviews may be one-to-one or conducted as *focus groups*.

Interview guide   Relates to a list of themes, topics or categories to be covered during the interview. Often synonymous with the term interview schedule, that provides a framework of linked questions/prompts for the interviewer.

Interviewer effect/bias   The potential for the researcher to distort the behaviour of interviewees based on their own social characteristics, opinions and expectations.

Level of measurement   A term used to describe the varying mathematical scaling of numerical variables that can be recorded by the researcher. These include nominal, ordinal, interval and ratio levels of measurement.

Likert scale   A scale used to gauge a respondent's attitude to a particular question. Involves the construction of a scale (i.e. 1–5) where the respondent scores based on his or her preference (e.g. 1 = strongly disagree, 5 = strongly agree).

Longitudinal design   A research design in which data are collected on a sample on at least two separate occasions.

Mail survey   A self-completion questionnaire that is distributed via a postal service.

Measurement   The process of obtaining the magnitude of a quantity, such as length or mass, relative to a unit of measurement, such as a metre or a kilogram.

Methodology   A position concerned with the logic, potentialities and limitations of research methods.

Mixed research   A research strategy that involves mixing or combining quantitative and qualitative research approaches, concepts, techniques and methods into a single study (also see *triangulation*).

Multi methods   An approach that utilises two or more research methods positioned within the paradigm into a single study (e.g. the use of social observation and focus groups).

Narrative   The construction of process/sequence within the text. Often relates to the tale or story found within the text.

Narrative analysis   The process of deconstructing narrative to identify sequences, patterns and interactions within the text.

Naturalistic   Research that takes place outside of controlled conditions (e.g. within the setting of a school).

Negative relationship   A relationship between two variables whereby one increases and the other decreases.

Neutral relationship   A relationship between two variables whereby change in one variable is not accompanied by change in another variable.

Non-equivalent control group   A quasi-experimental research design in which participants are allocated into an experimental and control group according to naturally occurring features.

Non-experimental research   An approach to research that does not adhere to an experimental strategy that originated from the natural sciences.

Non-probability sampling   A procedure that does not select participants using a random sampling approach (as opposed to *probability sampling*).

Objectivism   An ontological position that asserts that social phenomena and their meanings are not dependent on any features of the particular subject who studies it.

Observation   A form of data collection method that is used to record observable behaviours. These may be both verbal and non-verbal in nature.

Observational research   A non-experimental research strategy that involves the direct observation and measurement of behaviour that may occur in a range of settings.

Ontology   A branch of philosophy concerned with questions of what exists, and how we view reality.

Open-ended question   A question employed within a survey that does not require the respondent to choose between a prescribed set of answers (as opposed to *closed questions*).

Outlier   An extreme value in a distribution, that is either very high or low compared to the average.

Paradigm   A cluster of beliefs that in the context of research dictates what should be studied, how research should be done and how results should be interpreted.

Participant   A person or group of people who participate in the research project.

Participant observation   A research design in which the researcher immerses him- or herself in a social setting for an extended period of time, observing and recording behaviour (see *ethnographic research*).

Pearson's *r*   A measure of association (i.e. strength and direction) used to explore the association between two variables.

Pilot/piloting   A procedure that involves pre-testing of research methods (i.e. instruments and procedures) in order to identify weaknesses in data collection approach.

Population   The universe of units from which a sample is drawn.

Positive relationship   A relationship between two variables, whereby as one variable increases the other also increases.

Positivism   An epistemological position that emphasises the use of natural approaches (i.e. experimental research) to study social reality.

Pragmatic   In a mixed-research approach, a pragmatic view sets aside paradigm or position differences between research methods used, and priority is given to the research question and process.

Prediction   A statement made about a future occurrence that can be tested in a rigorous form (i.e. hypothesis testing).

Probability sampling   A procedure that selects participants using a random sampling approach (as opposed to *non-probability sampling*).

Purposive sampling   A procedure that involves selecting a sample on the basis of particular characteristics or an identified variable (e.g. all those who started swimming at a local pool within the last 3 months).

Qualitative   A methodological position that emphasises words rather than quantification (i.e. numbers) in the collection and analysis of data (as opposed to *quantitative*).

Quantitative   A methodological position that emphasises quantification (i.e. numbers) rather than words in the collection and analysis of data (as opposed to *qualitative*).

Quasi-experiment   A research approach that is close to being an experiment except that participants are not randomly assigned to groups but rather selected based on naturally occurring features.

Questionnaire   A question-based data collection instrument designed to be distributed and filled in by a respondent in the absence of a researcher (i.e. self-completion questionnaire).

Quota sampling   A procedure that involves the non-random allocation of participants into different categories.

Random sampling   A procedure based on the random selection of units from a sampling frame.

Randomisation   The process of controlling for all extraneous variables by ensuring that the variables operate in a manner determined by chance.

Relationship   An association between two variables whereby the variation in one variable coincides with the variation in another variable.

Reliability   The degree to which a measure is considered stable.

Repeated measures design   A research design that involves the same participants being studied at different times or under different conditions.

Representative sample   A sample that reflects the characteristics of the population from which it was drawn.

Research design   The term employed in this book to refer to the logical and systematic structure or plan by which data collection can take place.

Research method   The term employed in this book to refer to the execution of the study (incorporating the implementation of instruments, techniques and procedures used to collect data).

Research objective   The purpose for which the research is being carried out (e.g. to describe, to understand, to explain, to evaluate).

Research question   The overarching question that focuses the topic and defines the scope, scale and conduct of the research study.

Research strategy   The term employed in this book to refer to logic of inquiry (set of ground rules/ principles that shape the decisions we make when selecting and implementing our research design and methods).

Sample   A segment of the population that is selected for the research study. The method of selection is known as *probability* and *non-probability sampling*.

Sample bias   Bias occurs when the sample characteristics are different from that of the population.

Sampling frame   The listing of all units within a population from which a research sample is selected.

Sampling variability   A term used to refer to degree of variation shown in a sample when compared to the population from which it was drawn.

Scatter plot   A graphical representation of the relationship between two measured variables.

Semi-structured interview   A data collection procedure that involves the interviewer developing a series of questions that is in the general form of an *interview guide*. This procedure offers the interviewer some degree of flexibility in the interview structure.

Snowball sampling   A procedure that involves the researcher making initial contact with participants who then use their contacts to establish more research participants (see *non-probability sampling*).

Spearman's rank order correlation   A measure of association (i.e. strength and direction) of the relationship between two ordinal variables.

Sport science   A discipline that studies the application of scientific principles and techniques with the aim of improving sporting performance.

Statistical significance   A concept that allows researchers to estimate, by way of statistical tests, how confident they can be that the results derived from a study based on a randomly selected sample are generalisable to the population from which the sample was drawn.

Stratified sampling   A procedure that involves randomly assigning units to a sample based on categories (i.e. strata).

Structured interview   A data collection procedure that involves the interviewer asking all participants exactly the same questions in order, with the aid of a rigid interview guide.

Survey research   A research strategy that involves describing the characteristics of a population. Whether that is another group, organisation or community, the approach allows the researcher to find out how the population is distributed on one or more variables.

Systematic review research   A research strategy that involves the identification, evaluation and interpretation of all available research (i.e. primary and secondary evidence) relevant to a particular research question, topic area or phenomenon of interest.

Time sampling   A sampling technique that involves using a criterion for deciding when measurement (e.g. observations or interviews) will take place.

Triangulation   The use of more than one research method within a study so that the validity of the findings can be cross-checked.

Unobtrusive research   An approach that does not involve making the participants aware of the research, therefore reducing their reactivity to the project.

Unstructured interview   An informal data collection procedure that involves the interviewer using a list of topics/issues to explore participants' understanding.

Validity   A concept concerned with the integrity of the conclusions generated from research (see *external* and *internal validity*).

Variable   An attribute that stands for a value that may vary (see *dependent* and *independent variable*).

Within-group design   An experiment approach where all participants test (and respond to) all treatment combinations (as opposed to a *between-group design*).

References

Andres, L. (2012) *Designing and Doing Survey Research*. London: SAGE Publications.

Azevedo, LB, Watson, DB, Haighton, C and Adams, J (2014) The effect of dance mat exergaming systems on physical activity and health-related outcomes in secondary schools: results from a natural experiment. *BMC Public Health*, 14 (1): 951–64.

Blaikie, N (2009) *Designing Social Research*. 2nd ed. Cambridge: Polity Press.

Blaxter, L, Hughes, C and Tight, M (2010) *How to Research*. Maidenhead: McGraw-Hill Education.

Bloms, LP, Fitzgerald, JS, Short, MW and Whitehead, JR (2016) The effects of caffeine on vertical jump height and execution in collegiate athletes. *The Journal of Strength and Conditioning Research*, 30 (7): 1855–61.

Boland, A, Cherry, MG and Dickson, R (Eds) (2013) *Doing a Systematic Review: A Student's Guide*. London: SAGE Publications.

Brewer, JD (2008) *Ethnography*. Maidenhead: Open University Press.

Brinkley, A, McDermott, H and Munir, F (2017) What benefits does team sport hold for the workplace? A systematic review. *Journal of Sports Sciences*, 35 (2): 136–48.

Brown, G, Essex, S, Assaker, G and Smith, A (2017) Event satisfaction and behavioural intentions: examining the impact of the London 2012 Olympic Games on participation in sport. *European Sport Management Quarterly*, 17 (3): 331–48.

Bryman, A (2015) *Social Research Methods*. 5th ed. Oxford: Oxford University Press.

Burke, SM, Sparks, AC and Allen-Collinson, J (2008) High altitude climbers as ethnomethodologists making sense of cognitive dissonance: ethnographic insights from an attempt to scale Mt. Everest. *The Sport Psychologist*, 22: 336–55.

Burton, E, Farrier, K, Lewin, G, Pettigrew, S, Hill, AM, Airey, P and Hill, KD (2016) Motivators and barriers for older people participating in resistance training: a systematic review. *Journal of Aging and Physical Activity*, 1–41.

Capostagno, B, Lambert, MI and Lamberts, RP (2016) A systematic review of submaximal cycle tests to predict, monitor, and optimize cycling performance. *International Journal of Sports Physiology and Performance*, 11 (6): 707–14.

Cavallerio, F, Wadey, R and Wagstaff, CR (2016) Understanding overuse injuries in rhythmic gymnastics: a 12-month ethnographic study. *Psychology of Sport and Exercise*, 25: 100–9.

Centre for Reviews and Dissemination (2009) *Systematic Reviews: Guidelines for Undertaking Reviews in Healthcare*. York: York Publishing Services.

Choi, A, Stotlar, DK and Park, SR (2006) Visual ethnography of on-site sport sponsorship activation: LG Action Sports Championship. *Sport Marketing Quarterly*, 15: 71–9.

Christensen, LB, Johnson, B and Turner, LA (2014) *Research Methods, Design, and Analysis*. 11th ed. London: Pearson Education.

Clark, VLP and Ivankova, NV (2015) *Mixed Methods Research: A Guide to the Field* (Vol. 3). Thousand Oaks, CA: SAGE Publications.

Cohen, L, Manion, L and Morrison, K (2017) *Research Methods in Education*. 7th ed. London: Routledge.

Colonetti, T, Grande, AJ, Milton, K, Foster, C, Alexandre, MCM, Uggioni, MLR and Rosa, MID (2017) Effects of whey protein supplement in the elderly submitted to resistance training: systematic review and meta-analysis. *International Journal of Food Sciences and Nutrition*, 68 (3): 257–64.

Cozby, PC and Bates, SC (2012) *Methods in Behavior Research*. 11th ed. New York: McGraw Hill Higher Education.

Crang, M and Cook, I (2007) *Doing Ethnographies*. London: SAGE Publications.

Creswell, JW (2013) *Research Design: Qualitative, Quantitative, and Mixed Methods Approaches*. 4th ed. Thousand Oaks, CA: SAGE Publications.

Creswell, JW (2014) *A Concise Introduction to Mixed Methods Research*. Los Angeles, CA: SAGE Publications.

Crowther, F, Sealey, R, Crowe, M, Edwards, A and Halson, S (2017) Team sport athletes' perceptions and use of recovery strategies: a mixed-methods survey study. *BMC Sports Science, Medicine and Rehabilitation*, 9 (1): 6–16.

Cunningham, I, Mellick, M and Mascarenhas, DR (2012) Decision making and decision communications in elite rugby union referees: an inductive investigation. *Sport and Exercise Psychology Review*, 8 (2): 19–30.

Dashper, K and St John, M (2016) Clothes make the rider? Equestrian competition dress and sporting identity. *Annals of Leisure Research*, 19 (2): 235–50.

Dawes, JJ and Spiteri, T (2016) Relationship between pre-season testing performance and playing time among NCAA DII basketball players. *Sports and Exercise Medicine*, 2 (2): 47–54.

De Vaus, D (2005) *Research Design in Social Research*. Thousand Oaks, CA: SAGE Publications.

De Vaus, D (2013) *Surveys in Social Research*. 6th ed. New York: Routledge.

Eisenhardt, KM (1989) Building theories from case study research. *Academy of Management Review*, 14: 532–50.

Faber, IR, Elferink-Gemser, MT, Oosterveld, FG, Twisk, JW and Nijhuis-Van der Sanden, MW (2017) Can an early perceptuo-motor skills assessment predict future performance in youth table tennis players? An observational study (1998–2013). *Journal of Sports Sciences*, 35 (6): 593–601.

Field, A (2017) *Discovering Statistics Using IBM SPSS*. 4th ed. London: SAGE Publications.

Fink, A (2012) *How to Conduct Surveys: A Step-by-Step Guide*. Thousand Oaks, CA: SAGE Publications.

Fisher, A (2011) *Critical Thinking: An Introduction*. Cambridge: Cambridge University Press.

Fletcher, D and Streeter, A (2016) A case study analysis of a high performance environment in elite swimming. *Journal of Change Management*, 16 (2): 123–41.

Fraenkal, JR, Wallen, NE and Hyun, H (2011) *How to Design and Evaluate Research in Education*. 8th ed. Maidenhead: McGraw-Hill Higher Education.

Frankfort-Nachmias, C and Nachmias, D (2015) *Research Methods in the Social Sciences*. 8th ed. New York: Worth Publishers, Macmillan Education Company.

García-Ramos, A, Padial, P, de la Fuente, B, Argüelles-Cienfuegos, J, Bonitch-Góngora, J and Feriche, B (2016) Relationship between vertical jump height and swimming start performance before and after an altitude training camp. *The Journal of Strength and Conditioning Research*, 30 (6): 1638–45.

Giacobbi, PR, Stancil, M, Hardin, B and Bryant, L (2008) Physical activity and quality of life experienced by highly active individuals with physical disabilities. *Adapted Physical Activity Quarterly*, 25: 189–207.

Gough, D, Oliver, S and Thomas, J (2017) *An Introduction to Systematic Reviews*. 2nd ed. London: SAGE Publications.

Grandjean, BD, Taylor, PA, and Weiner, J (2002) Confidence, concentration, and competitive performance of elite athletes: a natural experiment in Olympic gymnastics. *Journal of Sport and Exercise Psychology*, 24: 320–7.

Grix, J (2002) Introducing students to the generic terminology of social research. *Politics*, 22: 175–86.

Guell, C, Shefer, G, Griffin, S and Ogilvie, D (2016) 'Keeping your body and mind active': an ethnographic study of aspirations for healthy ageing. *British Medical Journal Open*, 6 (1): 1–10.

Gupta, L, Morgan, K and Gilchrist, S (2016) Does elite sport degrade sleep quality? A systematic review. *Sports Medicine*, 1–17.

Hackshaw, A (2015) *A Concise Guide to Observational Studies in Healthcare*. Oxford: John Wiley.

Hitchcock, G and Hughes, D (2003) *Research and the Teacher*. 2nd ed. London: Taylor and Francis.

Imai, A and Kaneoka, K (2016) The relationship between trunk endurance plank tests and athletic performance tests in adolescent soccer players. *International Journal of Sports Physical Therapy*, 11 (5): 718–24.

Jensen, E and Laurie, C (2016) *Doing Real Research: A Practical Guide to Social Research*. London: SAGE Publications.

Johnson, RB and Onwuegbuzie, AJ (2004) Mixed methods research: a research paradigm whose time has come. *Educational Researcher*, 33: 14–26.

Keeble, S (1995) *Experimental Research 1: An Introduction to Experimental Design*. Edinburgh: The Open Learning Foundation, Churchill Livingstone.

Keeble, S (1995) *Experimental Research 2: Conducting and Reporting Experimental Research*. Edinburgh: The Open Learning Foundation, Churchill Livingstone.

Krane, V (2005) Using ethnography in applied sport psychology. *Journal of Applied Sport Psychology*, 17: 87–107.

Lanhers, C, Pereira, B, Naughton, G, Trousselard, M, Lesage, FX and Dutheil, F (2017) Creatine supplementation and upper limb strength performance: a systematic review and meta-analysis. *Sports Medicine*, 47 (1): 163–73.

Larsen, J, Cassel, CL and Knuth, J (2016) A quasi-experiment of exercise modality effects on cognition and fitness in healthy women. *Journal of Sports Science*, 4: 333–40.

LeCompte, MD and Schensul, JJ (2010) *Designing and Conducting Ethnographic Research (Ethnographer's Toolkit)*. Lanham, MD: Rowman Altamira.

Lee, RM (2000) *Unobtrusive Methods in Social Research*. Buckingham: Open University Press.

Lofland, J, Snow, DA, Anderson, L and Lofland, LH (2006) *Analyzing Social Settings: A Guide to Qualitative Observation and Analysis*. 4th ed. Belmont, CA: Wadsworth Cengage Learning.

Loturco, I, Nakamura, FY, Lopes-Silva, JP, Silva-Santos, JF, Pereira, LA and Franchini, E (2017) Physical and physiological traits of a double world karate champion and responses to a simulated kumite bout: a case study. *International Journal of Sports Science and Coaching*, 12 (1): 138–47.

McIver, KL, Brown, WH, Pfeiffer, KA, Dowda, M and Pate, RR (2016) Development and testing of the observational system for recording physical activity in children: elementary school. *Research Quarterly for Exercise and Sport*, 87 (1): 101–9.

McManus, CJ, Murray, KA and Parry, DA (2017) Applied sports nutrition support, dietary intake and body composition changes of a female athlete completing 26 marathons in 26 days: a case study. *Journal of Sports Science and Medicine*, 16 (1): 112–16.

McNeill, E and Meade, MM (2017) Golfer's perspectives: the role of the caddy in facilitating a golfer's psychological performance. *Sport and Exercise Psychology Review*, 13 (1): 39–46.

Mills, D and Morton, M (2013) *Ethnography in Education*. London: SAGE Publications.

Molnar, G and Purdy, L (2017) *Ethnographies in Sport and Exercise Research*. London: Routledge.

Montgomery, DC (2012) *Design and Analysis of Experiments*. 8th ed. New York: John Wiley.

Mulrow, CD (1994) Rationale for systematic reviews. *British Medical Journal*, 309: 597–9.

Nicholls, SB and Worsfold, PR (2016) The observational analysis of elite coaches within youth soccer: the importance of performance analysis. *International Journal of Sports Science and Coaching*, 11 (6): 825–31.

Ntoumanis, N (2001) *A Step-by-Step Guide to SPSS for Sport and Exercise Studies*. London: Routledge.

Okubo, Y, Schoene, D and Lord, SR (2016) Step training improves reaction time, gait and balance and reduces falls in older people: a systematic review and meta-analysis. *British Journal of Sports Medicine*, 51 (7): 586–93.

O'Leary, Z (2017) *The Essential Guide to Doing Your Research Project*. 3rd ed. London: SAGE Publications.

Petticrew, M and Roberts, H (2005) *Systematic Reviews in the Social Sciences: A Practical Guide*. Chichester: Wiley Blackwell.

Rabelo, FN, Pasquarelli, BN, Gonçalves, B, Matzenbacher, F, Campos, FA, Sampaio, J and Nakamura, FY (2016) Monitoring the intended and perceived training load of a professional futsal team over 45 weeks: a case study. *The Journal of Strength and Conditioning Research*, 30 (1): 134–40.

Research Methods Knowledge Base (2006) *Introduction to Validity*. Available online at: http://www.socialresearchmethods.net/kb/introval.php (accessed June 2017).

Rønnestad, BR, Hansen, J and Nygaard, H (2016) 10 weeks of heavy strength training improves performance-related measurements in elite cyclists. *Journal of Sports Sciences*, 1–7.

Sands, R (2002) *Sport Ethnography*. Champaign, IL: Human Kinetics.

Slimani, M, Chamari, K, Miarka, B, Del Vecchio, FB and Chéour, F (2016) Effects of plyometric training on physical fitness in team sport athletes: a systematic review. *Journal of Human Kinetics*, 53 (1): 231–47.

Sparkes, AC (2015) Developing mixed methods research in sport and exercise psychology: critical reflections on five points of controversy. *Psychology of Sport and Exercise*, 16: 49–59.

Sport England. (n.d.) *Case Studies*. London: Sport England. Available online at: https://www.sportengland.org/facilities-planning/case-studies (accessed May 2017).

Stojanović, E, Ristić, V, McMaster, DT and Milanović, Z (2016) Effect of plyometric training on vertical jump performance in female athletes: a systematic review and meta-analysis. *Sports Medicine*, 1–12.

Swann, C, Crust, L, Jackman, P, Vella, SA, Allen, MS, and Keegan, R (2017) Psychological states underlying excellent performance in sport: toward an integrated model of flow and clutch states. *Journal of Applied Sport Psychology*, 1–27.

Tashakkori, A and Teddlie, C (2010) *SAGE Handbook of Mixed Methods in Social and Behavioral Research*. Thousand Oaks, CA: SAGE Publications.

Thomas, G (2016) *How to Do Your Case Study*. 2nd ed. Thousand Oaks, CA: SAGE Publications.

Truelove, S, Vanderloo, LM and Tucker, P (2016) Defining and measuring active play among young children: a systematic review. *Journal of Physical Activity and Health*, 1–32.

Walliman, N (2010) *Research Methods: The Basics*. London: Routledge.

Walliman, N (2011) *Your Research Project: Designing and Planning Your Work*. London: SAGE Publications.

Watson, DB, Adams, J, Azevedo, LB and Haighton, C (2016) Promoting physical activity with a school-based dance mat exergaming intervention: qualitative findings from a natural experiment. *BMC Public Health*, 16 (1): 609–91.

Wellington, BM, Leveritt, MD and Kelly, VG (2017) The effect of caffeine on repeat high intensity effort performance in rugby league players. *International Journal of Sports Physiology and Performance*, 12: 206–10.

William, C and Wragg, C (2004) *Data Analysis and Research for Sport and Exercise Science: A Student Guide*. London: Routledge.

Wood, L and Danylchuk, K (2011) Playing our way: contributions of social groups to women's continued participation in golf. *Leisure Sciences*, 33 (5): 366–81.

Yin, RK (2013) *Case Study Research: Design and Methods*. Thousand Oaks, CA: SAGE Publications.

Index